CONTENTS

To busy people everywhere striving to find work-life balance—working to live, not living to work—those who instinctually know that support teams of trusted advisors create space for family and friends.

LIST OF FIGURES

CHAPTER 5

CHAPTER 6

CAPITAL SISTERS

A human being is born into this world fully equipped not only to take care of him or herself, but also to contribute to enlarging the well-being of the world as a whole. Some get the chance to explore their potential to some degree, but many others never get any opportunity, during their lifetime, to unwrap the wonderful gift they were born with. They die unexplored and the world remains deprived of their creativity and their contribution.

—Dr. Muhammad Yunus, Nobel Lecture, 2006[1]

I HAVE COMMITTED A PERCENTAGE of the profits from this book to Capital Sisters International. Their mission is to connect impoverished women in developing countries who need tiny business loans with investors willing to provide them. Capital Sisters International works to advance the economic empowerment of women through entrepreneurship. They provide household investors with an opportunity to address poverty on a global scale.

As a woman with a platform, I think it is imperative to reach back and give other women a hand, a chance to change their financial destiny. As a pilot flying around the world, I have seen what true poverty looks like, especially in war-torn regions. I am grateful to have been afforded the opportunity to change my situation in life and am glad to support an organization putting words into action.

Capital Sisters targets women because they represent 70% of the world's poorest people—those living on less than two dollars a day. Women are disproportionately poor because of centuries of systemic exclusions and biases that are triggered simply by virtue of their being born female. They suffer from a lack of education, an inability to own or inherit property, exclusion from financial services and job markets, and an absence of social status that makes them powerless in the face of discrimination.

As a new real estate investor, I learned early on about OPM: other people's money. One strategy to start building wealth was to partner my sweat equity with a money lender's cash to make something happen. This reinforced my commitment to creating win-win deals and feeding the team. If you tried to suck all the profit out of a real estate deal, for example, not many people would be willing to work with you a second time.

Studies show that women borrowers are also a good investment. They are creditworthy. They focus on health, invest in the future, and find their voices. Research has shown that women repay their loans at a rate of more than 95% and are willing to pay market interest rates, enabling microfinance institutions to cover their costs, provide critical health and education services, and operate sustainably.

Christine Lagarde, managing director of the International Monetary Fund (IMF) says, "Access to credit is a key link between economic opportunity and economic outcome. By empowering individuals and families to cultivate economic opportunities, financial inclusion can be a powerful agent for strong and inclusive growth."[2] Financially, Capital Sisters has a unique approach because they developed an Impact Investment Fund. Despite the success of the microfinance industry over the past three decades, the industry is not currently meeting the global demand for microloans. Capital Sisters' innovative approach to philanthropy gives traditional donors the opportunity to become investors, and traditional investors an opportunity to become socially responsible investors. Their Sister Bonds Investment Fund provides a vehicle for those who want a portion of their portfolio invested in assets that provide a social benefit in addition to a financial return.

I believe wealth is more than just money. Capital Sisters has found a way to combine money and giving back in a way that makes financial sense for someone who may not be in a position to simply give to a charity. It's a win-win.

INTRODUCTION

Have you ever felt as though you missed out on some crucial knowledge about money, that everyone knows something you don't know?

I was about seven when my family moved to a hippie commune known as "The Farm" in Nashville, Tennessee. I always thought we were poor, but I found a 2007 article in *Vanity Fair* that filled in some holes for me[3], and I learned more from my friend Rena Mundo's documentary, *American Commune.*[4] The founder, Stephen Gaskin, had a master's degree and taught at the college level, and many of the founding members were upper-middle-class English majors. While we lived in poverty, ten nonprofit companies were formed to add value to the community and twenty private businesses supported the things, like medicine, still required by any large group of people trying to live off the grid. "We're out to change the world" was the mantra. Living on The Farm was a choice this community, including my parents, made intentionally.

On The Farm, everyone did household chores interchangeably. We all did our part to add value to the community. Most of us, boys included, had long hair and braids. Traditional gender norms did not exist; some men wore skirts. I don't know too many people my age who grew up without indoor plumbing. That's right, you guessed it, that meant an outhouse; in the winter, we tried to pee before bedtime.

We also didn't have money. No one did. I never went to a store to buy candy as a kid.

Because of my early upbringing, I have a unique way of seeing the world. That's the good part. The challenging part is, I missed out on a lot of life experiences and social norms. As an adult, I had to catch up on understanding how to function in a world whose rules were often different from The Farm's. As a result, a feeling of being left behind followed me through most of my life.

When it came time for me to create my own future, I decided to become a pilot. I attended the Air Force Academy and joined the Air Force. Flying C-130s around the world took me a long way from The Farm. I worked hard, learned all I could, and adapted to life in the military. I purchased a house. I achieved many of the goals I set out to achieve. And yet somehow I felt I had not lived up to my potential, that everyone knew something I didn't know.

That feeling of being left behind came to a head when I learned that two of my fellow squadron members, who had also been my classmates in college, owned multiple rental properties. At the time, I was maxed out learning how to fly the C-130 cargo airplane, execute our airdrop mission, and deploy to the desert. I didn't have time to do anything else. I thought I was doing well to have purchased my own house, but these guys were pilots and landlords, too.

Although I knew there were different scoreboards in life, I didn't want to live paycheck to paycheck or shrink my expectations to match a limited nest egg. I wanted to create a life that allowed me to pursue my passions: riding horses, art, and getting plenty of sleep.

I realized that I needed to get clear about my goals if I wanted a different trajectory for my life. A famous quote that has been misattributed to Albert Einstein is "Insanity is doing the same thing over and over and expecting different results."[5] I was on the path to becoming a moderately successful retired Air Force officer because moving around from specialty to specialty—logistics officer to pilot to professor of biology, in my case—tended to limit career progression. Did I have to accept that financial destiny? Moving away from the secure road I was on—toward retirement with a pension after twenty years of active duty—was scary. But I was also miserable living a life smaller than I felt it should be, so I decided to disrupt my life.

I set out to learn everything I didn't know about money, to find out what "everyone else knew" and finally catch up.

I completed an MBA. I got a job in finance. I got my Series 65, Series 66, and life licenses. And I started my registered investment advisory (RIA).

For that initial job, my training was in selling insurance and setting up individual retirement arrangements (IRAs) for every person who walked in the door. I was not motived to be the best salesperson; I wanted to help people, so I didn't feel fulfilled. More discouraging than that, though, were the faces of the people who came in for guidance. In their eyes, I saw that same confusion I once felt about how the world of money works. Did they also feel left behind? Did they also feel as though they had missed the most important class in school?

After a few months I asked my boss, "When do we get to the part where we start helping people?"

I will never forget the quizzical way he cocked his head to the side. He clearly didn't understand my question.

I wanted to change people's lives, so I started my own business to do just that. I believed the money would follow.

One reason I started my RIA was to help my family. I decided early on that if I did nothing else but take care of them, the investment of starting my business would be worth it. I shifted the financial course of my immediate family with my hard-earned knowledge. We evaluated their current resources and circumstances, along with the challenges and opportunities coming down the road, and made a plan to help each of them achieve their desired lifestyle. Rather than focus on one "right" approach, we shifted their money to different types of investments that would help them meet their financial needs and goals.

As my family's financial health changed for the better and my clients began to grow wealth, I realized that most people had little knowledge of how investments actually work and that myths and their beliefs around investments kept them from gaining that knowledge. Their assumptions held them back—they were being left behind.

Financial insecurity is bigger than my family. In the 1970s, pensions started disappearing with the quiet rise of 401(k)s, shifting the burden of retirement planning onto individuals. A large group of hardworking Americans have focused on taking care of their families, worked hard at their jobs, and are now caught off guard by having learned they should have prepared more diligently for retirement. I think it is fair to say that the collective unconscious—a teaching put forth by Carl Jung about common beliefs[6]—of our country still clings to the idea a pension is to be expected after a lifetime of work.

Baby Boomers' thinking about retirement was shaped by their parents, who grew up in a time when pensions were common. For example, in the 1950s, a typical Sears salesman could retire with a nest egg worth more than a million in today's dollars.[7] Sears phased out its profit-sharing plan beginning in the 1970s. According to the IRS, a profit-sharing plan accepts employer contributions only. If a salary deferral feature is added, it becomes a 401(k) plan.[8] Professor Joseph R. Blasi,[9] who directs Rutgers' Institute for the Study of Employee Ownership and Profit Sharing, has written about how many presidents, beginning with George Washington in 1792, supported the idea of workers sharing in company profits to build a strong country. After the Employee Retiree Income Security Act of 1974 (ERISA), initiated under the Nixon administration, was signed into law by President Gerald R. Ford and passed by Congress with strong bipartisan support, new Federal policies on 401(k) plans had some unintended consequences. [10]You are now responsible for your own retirement.

How can it be that pensions are gone? Why didn't we know we had to save so much for our retirements?

Many of my clients have admitted to feeling stupid when they learn hard truths about retirement. These are educated, intelligent people who did not understand that their 401(k)s are defined contribution plans, not defined benefit plans, meaning that there is no guaranteed stability in their 401(k) accounts. Many of them were very unprepared for retirement before they sought professional guidance. While they were focused on their professions, they assumed they were earning a retirement.

It is highly frustrating when you learn that reality is different from what you always assumed it was. I felt this frustration when I left the hippie commune and entered public school, where I learned that two-seater outhouses were odd and I was the "weird one." I felt it when I transitioned from the military, where I trained to be good at what I did, to running a business that requires sales expertise. The fact is that stable factory, coal mining, and department store jobs with pensions for a solid thirty years of work have all but disappeared. They have been replaced by part-time, minimum wage jobs without benefits and defined contribution plans for knowledge workers. This has crept up on much of our country.

So how are people getting ahead and growing wealth in this new world of money? What is it they know that you don't know? Is it even possible for someone with limited resources to achieve financial security?

Buckminster Fuller said, "You never change things by fighting the existing reality. To change something, build a new model that makes the existing model obsolete."[11] I think there is a place in life where the ideal world you want to foster with your energy meets the world as it is now. To get to that place, you need to understand what wealthy people know and you don't (or haven't until now): Where your money lives is more important than how much you have.

When you make educated choices, changing where your money lives can change how your financial world grows. This works because it takes advantage of existing laws and regulations governing how you pay taxes. Knowing how to leverage your money so that it earns interest while it is in savings, waiting to be used, helps when you are in the process of earning that money. The more money you have, the easier it is to separate your investments from what you need to live on. However, in the years when you are both earning money and trying to build assets, you must understand the best places to grow your money that will still allow you access to it if you need it.

The good news is, it is possible to navigate today's system. You just have to understand that the strategies for building a secure retirement are different than those you may have learned growing up. The process begins with a reallocation of your resources, so your money can achieve a balance between protection and growth.

Years after I made the unconventional decision to walk away from my active-duty Air Force pension, I learned a term that applied to what I had done. In the early 1990s, Harvard Business School professor Clayton Christensen coined the term "disruptive innovation." "Disruptive Innovations… are innovations that make products and services more accessible and affordable, thereby making them available to a larger population."[12] I have taken what I've learned about business and money and created an approach that will help you reach your personal best financial potential.

In this book, I bring strategic thinking from real estate investing, business concepts, and tax and financial advising together in a holistic approach. I have an ability to see how systems work together. This is a hard-earned mental muscle strengthened both by academics and my real-world experience learning to fly three different aircraft systems in the Air Force. I taught biology, and we covered the systems of the human body. I also wrote a book, *Out of the Saddle: 9 Steps to Improve Your Horseback Riding,* that discusses how riding dressage is very much like learning to fly.[13] In it, I distill how to approach riding if you are learning as an adult and do not have a natural instinct for it. I learned in pilot training and in my riding that the "naturals" are not the best teachers. You want to learn from someone who has had to sweat and think and ponder because they can translate the complex into bite-size pieces of information. Because of my unique life experiences, I have the skill of making processes work well and sustainably for the people navigating them.

You don't know me yet, so I'll tell you that I like to be completely transparent. One of my advance readers shared some feedback with me. He was concerned that I wrote this book to sell you on financial advisors. Do I think you should have professional help? Yes. Do you have to have professional help? No. Do you need my help? Maybe. My mission is to ensure that you are introduced to concepts that will help you create an actionable plan for your financial success. I'm not withholding any information; it's all in the pages of this book. *I don't want you to be left behind.* I am sharing everything you can do for yourself to succeed financially—up to the point where decisions necessarily become customizable because you and your situation are unique.

The Air Force has core values I still stand by: "Integrity First, Service Before Self, and Excellence in All We Do." Vishen Lakhiani, thanks to his book *The Buddha and the Badass,* got me thinking about my values as they relate to my business. He shares: "In most cases, anyone can imitate your business. But nobody can imitate your business if it's built based on YOUR STORY. When your values infuse your business, you've given a special life to your creation."[14]

I want you to have the same positive shift in your financial destiny that my family and current clients have enjoyed. Life is hard enough. Building security and predictability for your family should not be a guessing game. You are not as "behind" as you think you are, and I'm about to show you how to catch up.

HOW TO USE THIS BOOK

Do you have friends who read the ending of a book before they commit to reading the entire thing? Are you one of those people? Flip to the last page of almost any current magazine and you will see that the publishers have placed a one-page article or "fun facts to read" item there.

My math teacher in high school talked about how to approach learning a new subject. He said that when we open a book, we should read the table of contents first. Then we should read the summary at the end.

My chemistry teacher at the Air Force Academy said that if you try to hang a coat up on the wall but there are no hooks, the coat will just fall to the floor. Therefore, you should read the "Key Takeaways" section toward the end of each new chapter—before you read the chapter itself—to put hooks in your mind. The questions will prepare your mind to receive new information so that, as you read the chapter, your brain will say, "Pay attention here, we already know this will be important."

Understanding your learning style is key when you are digesting new information. Visual learners prefer pictures. Kinesthetic learners like a more "hands on" approach. Auditory learners like to listen, so audio books may be best for them. And in my experience teaching biology at the Air Force Academy, teaching new copilots how to manage a crew, and teaching horsemanship skills to students at the Shanghai Equestrian Center, the adage "See one, do one, teach one" rings true.

You will notice I use simple, round numbers like \$100,000 or \$1 million in my examples to keep focus on the concepts, not the math. Please add or subtract zeros to adjust examples for your financial reality.

You have preferred ways to process information, and this book is written to serve different learning styles. Each chapter includes stories to help you understand the concepts. For those of you who are super busy, I've put section headers and key takeaways in bold type so you can flip through and see what grabs you. The key takeaways specify what you should know after reading the chapter. If you read a key takeaway and do not get the point, consider going back to reread that section. I have also included an exercise in each chapter that will help you synthesize the information and personalize it for your own life. I encourage you to pick up a pen and do the exercises. The physical act of writing solidifies concepts, even if you don't review your notes later. And for the kinesthetic learners who might say, "I think I'm tracking your point. Show me an example so I can take your concept and see how it would apply to me," I have included a case study at the end of most chapters.

Please note that the case studies reflect the assumptions I've made to illustrate each point. This is why it can be so confusing when you seek financial advice; it can seem like you're getting different answers to the same question. Advisors should be very transparent with their assumptions, and you should feel empowered to ask clarifying questions. It is important to level set terminology and assumptions (in other words, make sure the words I'm using mean the same to you) in a discussion. You will note that I qualify statements throughout this book. I do this because there can be an exception to almost every rule. This book is designed to share good questions to ask, not to be the final word. Remember, because of legislation, our financial reality is fluid. This is why surrounding yourself with a team of financial experts is your best chance to maximize your financial potential.

CHAPTER 1

LOCATION, LOCATION, LOCATION

*"He who has a why to live for can
bear with almost any how."*

—*Friedrich Nietzsche*[15]

- Have you ever felt like you are struggling with competing financial priorities that limit your options?
- Do you feel in control when you talk about money?
- Did you learn about money in school?
- Do you feel like you don't have enough money to invest?
- Do you know where you are in your financial life cycle?
- What are the holes in your financial plan for retirement?

MY IRISH CATHOLIC GRANDFATHER PROVIDED for a family of nine. He was the sole breadwinner, as was expected in his generation. To me, as a kid growing up, Grandpa was the nearly bald guy in glasses, sitting in his recliner in his comfortable house clothes, who would occasionally bark, "What are you kids doing?" He was sometimes funny, sometimes scary.

It shocked me to learn he'd had a life before us. He was a young man once, with a full head of hair! He had been in the war overseas. And he'd had entrepreneurial dreams that were overcome by the need to provide for his ever-growing family. This took a toll on him.

When my mom went to medical school at forty-two, after I'd left for college myself, I asked her why she didn't go right out of high school. She confided that she'd qualified for a state scholarship, but my grandfather had kept it from her. In fact, he told her, "You're not going to college, you're getting married and will be trapped like the rest of us."

My grandfather's generation accepted the fact that you got married, bought a home, raised kids, and worked until you earned a pension, and that was a good enough life. And yet for him and so many, it wasn't "good enough." Far from it.

The frustration of having to subvert passion and inspiration in favor of responsibility and reality can be soul-crushing, and I want to change this for you.

When I was a senior in high school, my mom dragged me to an airshow. Seeing the Thunderbirds fly for the first time sparked something in me. I walked around the static displays and asked a pilot what it was like to fly one of those planes.

She replied, "I don't know. Women aren't allowed to fly on the Thunderbird team."

My spark ignited, and this led to me attending the Air Force Academy. I eventually got to fly. But my C-130 didn't go upside down, and it wasn't on the pointy end of the spear (meaning I was in a support role instead of out in front), so for me it felt like a little reminder of my failure to achieve my goal of flying a fighter aircraft. I did like the missions. Delivering needed people and supplies on dirt-strip landings was cool. But it didn't feel like my dream.

I was eleven years into my Air Force career, on a predictable path to finishing my retirement and earning a coveted pension, when I started to wrestle with big philosophical questions like, "I only get one life. I could get hit by a bus tomorrow. Do I go for what I want or compromise to have a perceived sense of security?"

It is hard to live the life of your dreams and plan for a future when you feel like you are not being paid enough. I usually felt like my daily living expenses and responsibilities were great enough that I could not invest much. Even when I did have some disposable income, I didn't know how to find an advisor I could trust. Further, as someone with a type A personality who likes to be in control, I felt like I should be able to figure out money and do it myself. I only had twenty-four hours in a day, and I had a lot of adventures on my list. Money was something I needed, but it didn't feel inspiring to obsess over it and I didn't know how to change my financial destiny as I saw it.

When I mentally pulled the trigger—admitting out loud that I was not going to be an airline pilot, I was not going to work in a nine-to-five cubicle job, I was going to be an entrepreneur—the ground started shifting under my feet. I studied successful, wealthy business owners to see what they knew about money that I didn't. Many of my life experiences around money came into focus in a very different way. I learned about making money in chunks instead of a monthly paycheck, but I didn't know what to do with those chunks. When I started asking questions, I got confused. My real estate training taught me that the stock market was a waste of time. Some of my finance training taught the "buy term and invest the rest" strategy. Other schools of thought said that fixed annuities were the only way to go. Where was the truth in all this? And which path would help me achieve my goals?

It's no wonder people give up on their passions, their retirement dreams. Finance is a world of mixed messages, outdated methods, myths disguised as truths, and "experts" who, despite their good intentions, do not see the whole picture for their clients.

You want to achieve and retain the lifestyle you desire, but you struggle with competing financial priorities and time limitations. You want mental space available for creative outlets, more time with your family, and the ability to pursue your passions. What you may not realize is that you are also dealing with procrastination, uncertainty, and the feeling that you don't have enough money to invest. You are bombarded by media messaging that tells you that you should be investing, creating an amazing life, and doing it all alone.

This is frustrating not because there is a lack of information, but because there is an overload of information and it is hard to sort through. You have heard tales of loss in the stock market. And you may not even realize how legislation and the tax code have driven the demise of pensions. You now have to create your own retirement, but it was not always like that. Legislation and codes are constantly changing, and I will delve into that in Chapter 8 so you have insight into it as part of your bag of knowledge. For now, I want to share what you *can* control to make a positive impact on your finances.

BAG OF KNOWLEDGE

WHEN I WAS A YOUNG PILOT, MY INSTRUCTOR SAID I WAS ISSUED AN EMPTY BAG OF KNOWLEDGE AND A FULL BAG OF LUCK, AND MY JOB WAS TO FILL UP MY BAG OF KNOWLEDGE BEFORE MY LUCK RAN OUT.

What I discovered in my own journey will help you cut through the noise and misinformation and create a strategy that enables you to follow *your* spark and live a better life—maybe even the life of your dreams. Had I understood this shift in mindset in my twenties instead of my forties, it would have changed my financial future dramatically. This mindset shift is at the core of the work I did with my extended family to help lift them out of financial insecurity. And it's the foundation of the work I do with clients and share with audiences.

Simply put, where your money lives is as important as the amount of money you have.

After I understood that the right money moves could change my financial destiny, I made it my personal mission to help my family, my clients, and now you through this book.

I can't guarantee that you're going to earn $35,000 a month or $10,000 a month. But I can show you how to live as if you do. It comes back to where your money has been growing. For example, if your money has been growing inside of a traditional IRA, about 20-30% of that money belongs to the government in taxes (depending on your personal tax bracket). You may look at your IRA and think you have $100,000 in that account, but you actually have about $70,000. If you need that $100,000 to fulfill a dream, perhaps you need to move the money to a more tax-advantaged account so you can do just that.

Your money should live in a place that will help you get to your goal. For example, if you want to grow money for retirement, putting it into a savings account doesn't make much sense, because a savings account doesn't earn any kind of interest right now. And money for retirement does not need to be liquid. But by the same token, if you need money in case the car breaks down, the washing machine dies, or another of life's little emergencies happens, you don't want to tie your money up inside an IRA because you won't be able to access it without paying penalties. It's very important to understand what job your money has and why you have your money in specific places.

Your money's job should be to help you realize your vision. Based on your risk tolerance, your money should be working in either a safe money account (SMA) or a growth account (GA). I find that most people

VISION

THIS IS YOUR BIG-PICTURE GOAL.
IT IS WHAT YOU WOULD WISH
FOR IF MONEY WERE
NO OBJECT.

do not know where their money lives. I encourage you to think about this for a minute. As an advisor, my goal is to help you move your accounts (either SMA or GA) from taxable to either tax-deferred or tax-free situations. You have multiple options for specific investment vehicles you can use inside these accounts, and I will go into detail about those in Chapter 6. The crucial first step, though, is saying out loud: "My goal is_____!"

SMA: SAFE MONEY ACCOUNTS ARE PLACES TO PUT YOUR MONEY WHERE IT WILL NOT LOSE VALUE ON A DAY-TO-DAY BASIS, LIKE BANK ACCOUNTS, INSURANCE PRODUCTS, OR CDS. YOU WILL SOMETIMES SEE SMAS REFERRED TO AS GREEN MONEY.

GA: GROWTH ACCOUNTS LIKE REAL ESTATE, STOCKS, BONDS, MUTUAL FUNDS, EXCHANGE-TRADED FUNDS (ETFS), AND INVESTMENTS IN BUSINESSES HAVE RISKS ATTACHED. YOU WILL SOMETIMES SEE GAS REFERRED TO AS RED MONEY.

After you understand your goal, you can go back and say, "How do I want to get there? I'm a very conservative person and I don't like any risk." Or maybe you are okay with some risk, in which case you can ask, "Well, how old am I? How long until I plan to retire? Do I like my job and think I'm going to stay awhile?" You can survive a little more risk because your money is doing its thing while you're still working and paying for your food, clothing, and shelter.

In this chapter, I'll share some true stories with you to help you see the power of making the right money moves, no matter how much you have.

You don't have to cross your fingers and hope that retirement will work out for you. You don't have to subvert your passion so you can take care of your family. And you don't have to wait to grow your money until you have "enough" to invest.

> "FINANCIAL WORLD" REFERS TO A HOLISTIC VIEW OF YOUR MONEY, PRESENT AND FUTURE. ARE YOU ABLE TO CREATE SPACE FOR FREEDOM AND CREATIVITY IN YOUR LIFE YET? OR ARE YOU STILL BUSY MEETING YOUR BASIC NEEDS LIKE FOOD, CLOTHING, AND SHELTER?

The bottom line is, if you change where your money lives, you can change how your financial world grows. Now, let's be clear, you could cash out your 401(k), buy a boat, and stop growth in your financial world, but that's not the kind of change I'm talking about. I will show you what can happen if you stop stuffing money under your mattress and put it to work for you. You can start today.

CAN WE RETIRE?

JUDY WANTED TO RETIRE AT sixty-two because all her friends were retiring.

I asked her, "Judy, you worked so hard to earn your doctorate—don't you want to enjoy teaching for a while?"

Judy was certain she wanted to retire. She'd been teaching for about ten years, and she only had $100,000 in her 401(k). She hadn't set up the matching contribution or looked into making it a Roth IRA, and she had no idea of the account's risk level.

"Judy, you've been making $120,000 a year for the past ten years—spending most of it traveling to see your grandkids. And on bailing out some of your kids when they needed money. $100,000 is not going to be enough to get you through one year like you've gotten used to living."

Judy replied, "I've done my calculations. If I take my small pension from my last job and start Social Security right away, we can meet our monthly expenses. Ron has agreed to make the mortgage payment, and he's going to cash out some stock as well."

Both Ron and Judy come from some pretty long-lived gene pools. My goal was to try to get them financially healthy; I did not feel comfortable with the fact that the same children Judy was still supporting on and off were also her number one backup plan. As a pilot, I will tell you that there's nothing better than runway in front of you and altitude below you. Judy and Ron's goal was to retire right away, so I had to help them make the best choices with what they had. Here was my approach.

Step one: Figure out Judy and Ron's immediate food, clothing, and shelter needs—think Abraham Maslow's hierarchy of needs (Figure 1), a motivational theory in psychology that shows humans cannot achieve self-fulfillment before their basic needs are met.[16] I suspected that Judy's calculations did not allow for life's unexpected emergencies. As a planner, I'm most comfortable accounting for worst-case scenarios.

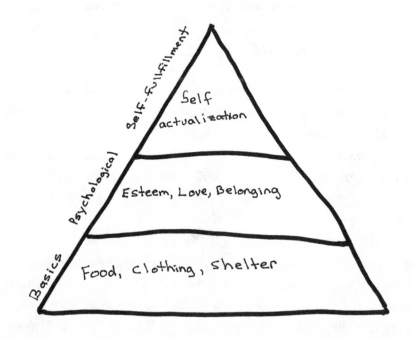

Figure 1: Maslow's Hierarchy of Needs

Step two: Identify the money decisions being made and see if those decisions maximized the value of the couple's dollars. Ron was going to cash out $100,000 of the money he had in stocks and use it to pay off the house. This appealed to them emotionally; however, after I shared an alternate strategy with tax advantages, he stopped that action. When coupled with Judy's Social Security, Ron had enough pension dollars to cover their daily living needs.

I was able to take Judy's $100,000 401(k) and use that to fund some permanent insurance, with an accelerated death benefit to be used to pay for future long-term care for each of them. I explained to Ron that this would protect him if Judy passed first or if either of them needed long-term care, like his parents did.

Because of recent, big stock market drops, Ron agreed to put a significant portion of his $400,000 into an annuity so he would not lose any more money. The Rule of 100 shows that at his age, it made more sense to have balance with some guaranteed investments.

The Rule of 100 says to subtract your age from one hundred to balance the at-risk and guaranteed investments in your portfolio. For example, if you are seventy years old, subtract your age from one hundred and you come up with thirty. As

RULE OF 100

THE RULE OF 100 SAYS TO SUBTRACT YOUR AGE FROM ONE HUNDRED, AND THAT IS HOW YOU SHOULD BALANCE THE AT-RISK (GA) INVESTMENTS AND GUARANTEED (SMA) INVESTMENTS IN YOUR PORTFOLIO. IT IS A GOOD STARTING POINT FOR DISCUSSION ABOUT HOW YOU WANT TO MANAGE YOUR MONEY.

a starting place for asset allocation, 70% of your assets should be safe and no more than 30% of your money should be at risk.

Ron did keep $75,000 of telecommunications stock in a GA because he had a very real and unbreakable emotional attachment to this money. It was tied to his sense of accomplishment and manhood. The good news is that Judy, as I suspected, decided she wanted to continue working after she retired. The college asked her to stay on and teach, so she was able to secure her position. I find that many of my clients get the itch to retire when what they really want is simply a nice break from the daily grind.

Judy had started her Social Security benefit when she thought she was not going to work anymore. We were able to stop her Social Security, which allowed her benefit to continue growing. We had to pay back a few months, but that was no big deal, especially given the significant difference between retiring at sixty-two and seventy: $1,800 per month. Ron had taken his Social Security at sixty-two, before he was even retired, so he was locked in at a reduced amount. He actually had to pay taxes on his Social Security from ages sixty-two to sixty-five because he was still working at the time.

Judy was getting a decent paycheck—in fact, the most money she'd ever made. We funded a new SMA that provided a safe place for her money to grow tax-deferred so she could travel once she really did decide to retire and had some extra money available for long-term care needs.

We moved the $100,000 Ron was going to use to pay off the house into another SMA. I explained that the money was there if he ever wanted to pay off the house—but it would grow, he would not have to pay taxes until he took money out, and he could still take the mortgage tax deduction by keeping the loan in place. A good strategy creates more choices instead of limiting options.

Using the Rule of 100 as a guide to realign their SMAs and GAs, Ron and Judy went from trying to retire on the bare minimum—a situation in which they would be unable to survive a disaster—to bringing in more than $100,000 a year in combined pensions, benefits, market investments, and annuities. Once Judy retires, this will go down, but she's accrued almost $70,000 in savings—in an account that once typically only had a few hundred dollars in it at any given time—in the years since she decided to un-retire and keep working. Ron and Judy have long-term care protection and are using 401(k) money to pay for it. The mortgage is getting paid off with pension income and the $100,000 has grown and is still available to pay off the mortgage if Ron ever wants to do so.

Changing where your money lives is about creating options. You will find that being in the driver's seat, with your money in the passenger seat, instead of your money driving and limiting your decisions about where you go, really feels good. Ron and Judy were heading down the road to using savings to pay off their mortgage, confusing a satisfying emotional feeling with the savviest financial decision. After they understood that there was another strategy available, they got back in control of their money and where it was going to work for them. Instead of having the $100,000 locked up in the house and inaccessible, they kept the option of paying off the mortgage if they choose and still have that money liquid for other unexpected needs. By changing where their money lived, Judy and Ron changed their financial world for the better. Instead of having everything in the market at their age, we created some balance and showed them how their different accounts had different jobs. Now they are in control.

FINDING CONTROL IN LIFE'S TWISTS AND TURNS

MY CLIENT JOE SHARED THIS story from his youth. He invested with a broker in his late thirties, hoping to make a good return on his money. The situation didn't work out and, Joe, a stubborn young engineer, didn't draw the best lesson from the experience. He took all his money away from the broker. Instead of learning the lesson that he needed to find a financial advisor to work with who could actually help him, he just abandoned investing altogether. Joe didn't understand that most brokers do not look at a holistic financial picture; they only focus on the account you have with them.

He started dumping money into his 401(k). In his mind, he had solved the problem: He got rid of the broker who lost his money and put his money into the 401(k). But again, he was going from one extreme to the other. All his "eggs" were still in one basket, just a different basket. He was still unprotected from those gaps in his defensive plan.

Life is not neat and simple like Figure 2, starting from zero and going to retirement. Life is never a straight line; there are ups and downs, zigs and zags, as in Figure 3. There's the market, the economy, your employment, whether you have kids—all these different factors come into play. It's usually not a good idea to have all your money in one place because it works right up until the point when it doesn't.

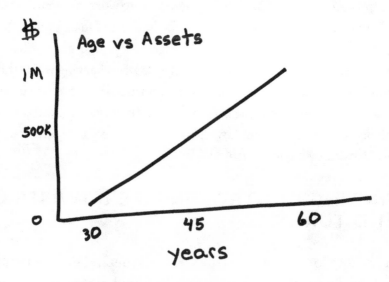

Figure 2: XY Graph of Age vs. Assets, Ideal World

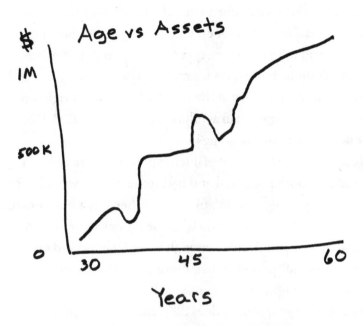

Figure 3: XY Graph of Age vs. Assets, Real World

Joe stuck with the XY ideal-graph life longer than most because he worked with a strong company, had a good job, and was single. He didn't have a family dynamic that would have nudged most other people into taking some different steps. He was by himself. His needs were minimal.

Joe did not really notice what his money was doing because it was just in the market, mostly company stock, and the company was doing well. That worked for quite a while—until 2001 happened, there was a huge drop in the market, and his account dropped by nearly 40%. Then it happened again in 2008. He went from being a very comfortable millionaire to having $400,000 when all was said and done—a huge money change. He thought he was living large and then, suddenly, he didn't have much money left. You can add zeros to this number or subtract them to fit your own reality; the feeling of loss is real at any number if it is *your* number.

After I knew this backstory, I could educate Joe's older self.

I explained, "It's your money, and we're going to show you how to protect it. And if it makes sense, you should do it. If it doesn't make sense, don't do it. But please let me just try to teach you a little bit because your money is just at the mercy of the market right now. And you've gone from more than a million down to $400,000. How much lower do you want to risk going?"

We had to go through a lot of intense personal work to get to a place where he was both protected and had some money working for him in a GA. Just putting all these pieces together was a huge emotional journey that had very little to do with the money itself, but a lot to do with him being open-minded enough to understand and learn a little bit. Money is multidimensional, more than just the ones and zeros controlled by computer programmers. It has more moving parts.

The idea that your money does different jobs for you can be a novel one. Some of your money is in savings for an emergency fund. Some of your money is in insurance to protect against worst-case scenarios. Some of your money is in the market, earning higher rates of return to keep up with inflation. There are all these different places where you can put your money, and you don't want all your money in any one place. You want to understand what your money is doing for you and how is it going to work. You want to be in charge of your money.

MONEY AND YOUNG ADULTS

LET'S GET REAL FOR A minute and talk about needs versus wants. Remember your first apartment after you left home? I remember feeling put upon when I had to use my own money to buy a shower curtain, toilet paper, and underwear. These were all things my mom had taken care of, while my money had been spent on fun things like eating out and movies. Now, in my business, I see a lot of my clients' kids as a courtesy. They struggle, like I did, with the idea they are not going to have the exact same standard of living as they did with Mom and Dad. One nineteen-year-old, Alice, had a twelve-dollar-an-hour job and a twenty-dollar-a-day Starbucks habit.

I asked about it and she was adamant. "I get hungry. What am I supposed to do, starve?"

Starting out in life, you may have a level of financial support from your parents. It may not be what your friends have. You may be thinking, "What? Life's not fair? How come I wasn't told?" The sooner you develop good savings habits, the sooner you will see desired results—just as you do with dietary and exercise habits. In my grandfather's day, credit cards were not an option because they didn't exist yet. Today, just like the candy bars and delicious snacks on display at every checkout line and coffee shop to entice you, you are sent credit card applications well before you understand debt, how it can compound, and how credit can lead you to digging yourself into a hole. You have probably heard about compounding interest in a positive light, but just like the force in *Star Wars*, there is also a dark side.

I DON'T MAKE ENOUGH MONEY YET

TAMMY WAS AN EYE-OPENING CLIENT for me. She had a master's degree and was still only making about $42,000 a year. In the military, I was paid based on my rank, so I never had to deal with being paid less as a woman. Then I started my own business, so I again avoided the situation of being paid less than my male counterparts. Tammy came to me because she knew she needed to do something with her financial world.

I showed Tammy where she could go and opened possibilities for her consideration. We picked a few things she could do. At the beginning, it was important for her to establish the good habits that would help her control her financial world—small steps, like making sure she had an emergency fund for things like car repairs. We did this even though she was carrying some credit card debt. Mathematically, it makes sense to pay off the credit cards first. But I have found that sometimes it's much better to break a bad cycle. We talked about what kind of credit card debt she had.

I asked her, "Are you a shopper? Did you have to pay an unexpected medical bill? Did you say 'screw it' and put a vacation on the card?"

We put a plan in place to get the card paid off. At the same time, we set up an automatic account to build up her emergency fund. This fund was in place to prevent her from putting anything else on her credit card.

We started a small, permanent life insurance policy so she could start growing some tax-deferred money and lock in a good premium rate while her health was good. For Tammy, this insurance cash value would also grow to be another emergency fund in a few years. She had a 401(k) at work and we upped her contribution so she could take advantage of the matching, almost free money.

Time is one of your best friends when it comes to growing money. Like the tortoise, slow and steady definitely helps you win the race. Now Tammy is married and she and her husband are debt-free. It took a few years. Their savings are now growing exponentially. They already have insurance in place if they decide to have kids. Their long-term care solution is also growing now. And they have their 401(k)s in a market growth strategy that is appropriate for their ages.

Because we created a strategy for Tammy to grow into, she has continued to gain positive traction. There is a reason for everything she does, so she is dedicated to her process. She knows her "why." Intentionally putting her money into specific places with specific jobs allows Tammy to feel secure in her financial world.

FINANCIAL MYTHS AND RETIREMENT HOLES

A CLIENT, SAMANTHA, CAME TO one of my Social Security workshops with a few holes in her plan. She is a widow. She was still working, coming up on retirement in about two years, and she was nervous about it. Samantha didn't know if she was going to have enough money to live on in retirement. She was in a very fearful place and trying to cope by keep her life small.

The first thing she told me when we sat down was, "I don't need much. I don't have any kids depending on me and I can live on $30,000 a year."

Unfortunately, that's the place a lot of people come to in their heads. They think, "Well, I don't know if I have enough. Once I retire, I'll have my house paid off. I will live very conservatively, and I won't need that much." My college roommate, June, used to say, "Expect the worst, it's the best you're going get." I find that people protect themselves emotionally by making their worlds small, so they feel like they have enough.

I asked Samantha, "Why don't we take an inventory of what you have right now?"

She gathered her whole financial junk drawer of all things money. It turned out she was an excellent saver with a respectable emergency fund. She had a couple of different 401(k)s because, like most people, she had worked at several different jobs. She didn't know where all her 401(k)s were, so we had to track them down. It turned out that most of the money was in the market and some was in an annuity. She was still paying fees for 401(k)s with her old companies. We had a lot of productive, good work to do cleaning up what she already had before we even started to change anything. You could almost think of this initial step as pulling out a board game and organizing all the cards and pieces so you know what you're playing with.

Now I was ready to get back to this notion of living on $30,000 a year in retirement. Her annual salary was about $120,000.

I said, "Okay, so you think that when you retire and have free time to travel, pursue your hobbies, whatever it is that you like to do, you're going to actually need less money than you do now?"

She told me, "Well, I've heard I'll only need 75% of what I was making when I retire."

I didn't mention that $30,000 was nowhere close to 75% of what she was making.

Instead, I said, "I can just tell you from experience that for most people, what you live on today, right now, is your best estimate of how much you're going to need to live on in retirement. Because the fact is that we're all staying healthy longer, we're living longer, and when we retire, we finally have some time to play. We don't want to plan on having less money."

Since she had come to my Social Security workshop, I started there. "Let's talk about Social Security. Do you want to start it now, at sixty-two? Are you going to take it at sixty-six, your full retirement age? Or will you wait a little longer?"

She exclaimed, "What do you mean? I'm going take it as soon as I can. Everyone knows that!"

"Well, absolutely. That's something that you can do, but would you consider letting me show you why you might not want to start early?"

That was the beginning of our conversation about the holes in her financial plan. Was her money living in the right place to take her where she wanted to be in retirement? It was kind of a long conversation because we kept coming up against these different myths that she believed in.

We all have holes in our financial plans because of the financial myths we believe in, which I will discuss in much greater detail in Chapter 2. Some of the most common myths are: "I will need much less to live on in retirement," "I don't need whole life insurance because I can do better investing on my own," "The stock market will make me rich," and "I won't need long-term care insurance when I'm older."

Samantha told me again, "I need a lot of money and savings, and I need to take my Social Security as soon as I can. And I am going to live on only $30,000 a year."

Many of these deeply hardwired money myths you believe are actually based around fear. You don't want to run out of money. I'm with you on that point. I don't want you to run out of money either.

Samantha didn't really like what she knew about the market. She knew people that had lost a lot of money in 2001 and 2008.

I asked her, "Do you realize you have almost 100% of your money in the market right now?"

She said, "I hadn't really thought about it."

When I asked her about insurance, she said, "I'm a widowed woman. I'm retiring. I don't have any dependents. I don't need insurance."

"Well, okay. But what are you going to do for long-term care? What's your plan for that?"

"Well, I probably won't need that."

"How does it feel to rely on 'probably not getting sick' as a plan for your elder years?" I asked.

The response I got was a severe pursing of her lips and a slow shake of her head.

I went on, "If I can show you how you can have money for long-term care, would you be interested in looking at that together? You would still have access to your money if you needed it, but you'd have some set aside in case you needed health care."

Samantha liked the idea of her money doing more than one thing. She liked having a savings account that was set aside for long-term care. She liked knowing which 401(k) she was going to start spending first to live on and which 401(k) was going to stay in the market a little longer to earn some higher returns.

As we shed some light on different financial myths she was holding onto, she started to see possibilities beyond making her life small enough to live on $30,000 a year. Her shoulders started to relax a little bit, like a visible sigh of relief.

I said, "I know you said you only need $30,000 to live on, but what if we just went ahead and set you up for $45,000 and you can just save the extra?" She was okay with that plan. And I loved it because we got her organized.

However, when we did our first annual review, she came back in a little bit of a tizzy because she was still fearful. I think she was holding her breath, wondering if I had told her the truth, as if our meeting would be the big reveal of how I had been too optimistic. We went back through her planning binder and reviewed everything.

She said, "It's just like you said it would be."

I said, "Yes, we built in some things that are guaranteed, and we identified the things that were going to be risky. That way everything is known; even the unknowns are known." As a former military planner, I always like to plan toward the worst-case scenario because better is always acceptable. Her emergency fund was larger than expected. This became a theme.

"Samantha, why do you have $50,000 in your savings account?" I asked. "We figured out you would keep $10,000 in your emergency fund, which is still about $7,000 more than you need given your must-pays."

We moved the extra $40,000 into her whole life insurance savings plan.

When she came back the next year I asked, "Samantha, why do you have $50,000 in your savings account again?"

This is one example of why I know money is so much more about emotion than math. Samantha and I agreed. We didn't know why, but apparently $50,000 was her safety number. So we left $50,000 in her savings account because that made her happy.

Remember I mentioned holes in financial plans being a problem? One of the things I expected to happen started to happen. Samantha came to me and said, "I'm going to need to get new windows."

I said, "Okay, how much is that going to cost?"

Samantha replied, "It's going to be $25,000."

I couldn't resist. "It's like seems to me like you told me a couple years ago that you were going to be able to live on $30,000 a year. Now you want to spend your entire year's allotment on windows?" .

I got a sheepish shrug in reply.

I said, "We've planned for that. Life is going to continue to happen, and that's why we had to think bigger than $30,000 a year."

The next year, she had some very expensive dental work. (Is there any other kind of dental work?) She was able to also take care of the dentist's bill, but we ran into another myth she was holding onto. Loans are bad. Debt is bad. Period. We had created a whole life savings plan for her as a safe place for her money to grow better than it would in a bank account. An advanced strategy was for her to borrow the money from herself, creating a loan—to herself—and then paying it back at her convenience. While it made sense in theory, when we created the account, the idea of taking out a loan triggered a long-held myth, backed by fear: Debt is bad. We spent time looking at how much interest she would pay if she used a credit card versus taking out a loan from herself. We got back to a good mental space, but it took some time. This kind of success with money requires trust, verification with numbers, and time. Her trust in me allowed her to sit with her fear while I showed her the numbers that backed up the decisions.

Samantha was a perfect case of someone who came to me with holes in her financial plan, myths she believed in, and a lot of fear around running out of money. She was going to take her Social Security early, which would have locked her into a lower amount for the rest of her life. What we were able to do was allow her to hold off on taking her Social Security so she could let it grow. Just giving her some options changed her outcome tremendously and for the better.

THE FINANCIAL LIFE CYCLE

BY THE END OF THIS book, you will know how to plug the holes in your retirement plan and create a financial team to help you. There are three primary parts of your financial life cycle, and I would like you to think about where you are in yours. I like to call them the "Get it," "Got it," and "Give it" phases (Figure 4), which are traditionally referred to as "accumulation of wealth," "distribution of wealth," and "transfer of wealth." Financial systems marketing and advertising focus on the "Get it" phase, encouraging you to save and invest as much as possible. You are driven to specific product solutions, such as "SuperMutualFundX" or "AmazingAnnuityY." Without a holistic plan that looks at your entire life, you can work at climbing the "Get it" hill, arrive at the top in your "Got it" phase, and realize that your plan was all about offense and did not include any defensive strategies to protect your money. I go into more depth around these strategies in Chapter 8.

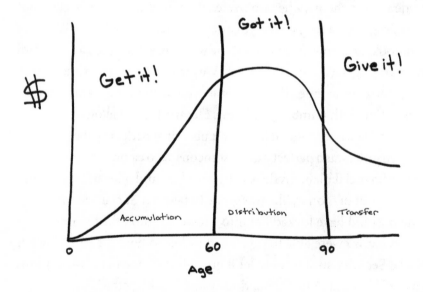

Figure 4: Financial Life Cycle

Many clients I work with come in with the attitude that their kids can fend for themselves. Maybe you feel this way, too. However, once we start looking at strategies that allow you to spend money in your

"Got it" phase without fear of running out and also leave something for your kids, it becomes empowering to be able to do this for your family. It's even more exciting when you realize that charitable giving and taking care of yourself and your family are not mutually exclusive. If you plan well, you can set yourself up with the ability to spend and create a legacy for your church or cause. However, if you tackle the known financial problems in a linear order, like most do—grow a large nest egg, then retire, then realize you need long-term care coverage, then realize you want to protect your spouse, then realize you want to leave something for your family—you miss out on leveraging time to your advantage.

Now that you've seen a few different problems solved, I challenge you to expect more from your money experience. You should expect to do more, experience more, and visualize a bigger life. It's possible once you understand that changing where your money lives can change how your financial world grows.

TO WRAP UP

YOU NOW KNOW IT IS perfectly normal to struggle to balance your creative desires with the realities of supporting yourself. Maslow's hierarchy of needs captures the basic needs we must cover so we can grow into our happiness. Financial success is possible because it's not just about how much money you have, but also understanding how money works that will create a good financial plan for you. You know that your money covers three stages, your "Get it," "Got it," and "Give it" phases, and that a holistic approach will allow you to use compounding interest over time as you grow in your "Get it" phase. Changing where your money lives can change how your financial world grows and plugging holes in your financial plan will set you up to enjoy retirement.

KEY TAKEAWAYS

- Start planning now to give yourself as much time as possible. As a pilot, I say, "There's nothing less useful than altitude above you or runway behind you."
- No matter how much money you have, you can grow your financial world simply by shifting where your money lives.
- Win-win is possible! Charitable giving, creating a legacy, and having enough can coexist.
- By the end of this book, you will know how to plug the holes in your retirement plan and create a financial team to help you.

TAKE ACTION EXERCISE

RULE OF 100[17]

Subtract your age from one hundred. What do you get? _____

(For example, if you are sixty-five years old, subtract your age from one hundred and you come up with thirty-five. As a starting place for asset allocation, 65% of your assets should be safe and no more than 35% of your money should be at risk.)

When it comes to money, you don't know what you don't know. The additional rub is, there is more information available about money than you can possibly process in your spare time. Have you ever taken one of those simple questionnaires when setting up your work retirement account or IRA? You know, the ones that come up with a simple number that tells you your category? The intent of the question "Do you prefer conservative, moderate, or aggressive growth?" is to establish what amount of risk you are comfortable with, but I think this is a faulty question. We are all okay with making money. The real question is, how much money are you willing—or able—to lose? Money in the market is at risk because it goes up and down, even with the conservative accounts. Guaranteed money, in CDs, bank accounts, or life insurance products like cash value insurance or annuities, never goes down. Such accounts may not offer the highest interest rates, but you will not lose money. The Rule of 100 is a starting place for conversation about what is right for you.

CASE STUDY: A HOLISTIC APPROACH

I BELIEVE IN A HOLISTIC approach to money management. What this means is that before I start recommending a client stops buying coffee a few times a week, I like to see if they can streamline what is already being spent in their budget. If, together, we can "find" money in their financial bubble, they can start putting this money to work for them without even changing their current lifestyle. This is a different way to understand money because it looks at your financial world strategically, from a bigger picture.

> # HOLISTIC APPROACH
>
> I BELIEVE THAT YOU ACHIEVE SYNERGY WHEN YOU CONSIDER ALL OF YOUR FINANCIAL DECISIONS AND HOW THEY INTERACT. TRADITIONALLY, IT'S COMMON TO STOVEPIPE THESE DECISIONS.

An analogy I like to use is the difference between the approaches of a doctor of osteopathic medicine (DO) versus a doctor of medicine (MD).[18] A DO is trained to look at a person holistically and focus on preventative care. This requires an almost two hundred additional hours of hands-on schooling beyond MD training. MDs have an allopathic approach that focuses on research-based medicine and often treats symptoms with medications or surgery.

In my financial practice, I come across many people who think their 401(k) will be sufficient for their retirement. When they retire, they like to leave their 401(k) with the same company because it is easy, it feels like a safe decision, and they didn't have to think about it while they were working. This is "symptom" thinking.

Having to spend your nest egg is very different than growing it. I ask these clients simple questions like, "What happens if you get sick and need to use your 401(k) for medical care?" Their financial worlds can quickly go from secure to not having enough money. Good management of an individual's or family's entire financial world uses strategies to plug as many of these kinds of "holes" as possible.

Use the following example to see how you might think about money differently. This is one of the first things I do with my clients to introduce the idea that where their money lives can change how their financial world grows.

I start by asking, "Melody, how much is your car insurance deductible?"

"It's $250."

Next, I ask, "If you are in a fender bender and need to get some repairs that will cost you $875, will you file a claim?"

"Well, no, because then my insurance rate will go up. And it's not worth my time or the hassle to recover $625."

"Here's what I'd like you to do. Go ask your car insurance provider how much your annual insurance premium would be with a $500 and $1,000 deductible and let me know."

Melody reports back. "Okay, here's what I found out. My premium right now with a $250 deductible is $2,000 a year. A $500 deductible would be $1,800 a year and the $1,000 deductible would be $980 a year."

"It looks like there's not much of a difference with a $500 deductible, only $200. But let's look at the $1,000 deductible."

Melody exclaims, "It's $1,000 a year less! Who knew?"

I say, "Let's not get ahead of ourselves. Here's my clarifying question. You said you would not file a claim for an $875 repair job. What would the difference in your financial world be if you had a $1,000 deductible instead of your current $250 deductible?"

Melody replies, "Whoa, I see where you are going with this. I was going to foot the bill for my repairs so my insurance didn't go up. If I had a $1,000 deductible, the situation would be the same, but I would 'find' $1,000 in my budget that could be available for something else."

This is a simple action step anyone can do to take control of their financial world. Melody was paying $2,000 for her car insurance to have a $250 deductible. Does an insurance company give you all your money back if you have a good year and don't get into a wreck? No. Some companies will send you a small refund, but you never get it all back, and certainly not $1,000. If she adjusts her policy to a $1,000 deductible, she frees up $1,000, changing where this same $1,000 lives in her financial world (Figure 5).

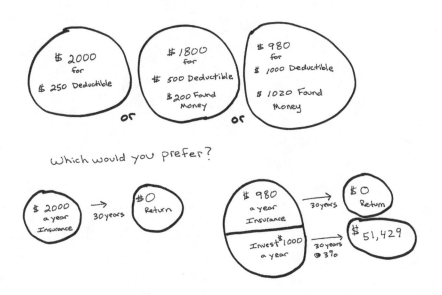

Figure 5: Reallocating Money—Car Insurance Example

Think about the simple concept of compounding interest. If Melody then took this $1,000 and invested it in an account earning 3% interest over thirty years, she would have $51,429. (NOTE: You will see that I use small interest rates in my examples to keep the math simple; this is because I want you to notice that the concept works with small numbers. Higher interest rates only make the situation better.)

To blow your mind one more time: What if you used this $1,000 you were already spending to buy some cash value life insurance that would protect your 401(k) from an unexpected future medical expense? Instead of having your $1,000 live at the car insurance company for a $250 deductible you would not use, you could let this $1,000 live in an insurance policy that would grow tax-deferred, have some protection from lawsuits, have a death benefit for your family if needed, and be available to protect your future 401(k) nest egg. Wealthy people understand: Your money can do more than one thing for you at a time. Now you know this too.

CHAPTER 2

FINANCIAL MYTHS THAT
LIMIT YOUR WEALTH

When the student is ready, the teacher will appear.

—*Chinese proverb*

- Have you ever felt embarrassed or ashamed because you didn't understand something you thought you should?
- Have you ever forgiven someone else for something you don't forgive yourself for?
- Have you ever believed something was true and then learned it was false?
- Are there things you believe in that you know are not true but still feel comforting?

ACCORDING TO DR. BRENÉ BROWN, a research professor at the University of Houston Graduate College of Social Work, shame is an "intensely painful feeling or experience of believing we are flawed and therefor unworthy of love and belonging."[19] Personally, I like to be the "knower" of things and it's embarrassing when I don't know something I feel I should. It's even worse when I find out something I thought was true wasn't! There is so much information available today, and advertising does a great job of making us feel like we should be our own financial gurus even though money management is not taught in most schools. Brown says that shame needs "secrecy, silence and judgement" to grow.[20] I think it's a relief to know that many people do not know about money, and that a good planning process shows you the "why" behind possible choices. I'd like to begin tackling financial myths by sharing a personal memory that turns out okay.

As Air Force Academy cadets going into our third year, we were allowed to have vehicles. Some cadets were lucky enough to have their parents buy them cars. They would say that their parents could use their college funds to pay for the cars; it was like they felt entitled to car ownership. Have you ever had a conversation with someone and realized that they live in a very different financial reality from you? A cool thing for the rest of the cadets was that banks would offer car loans to the senior cadets.

The summer before the bank loans for senior cadets were offered, I found out that there were some dealerships downtown offering this thing called a bridge loan. To me, this meant that I would be able to get transportation and have some newfound freedom. Financially, I had no idea what it meant. I wanted to be able to pick up a set of keys and go wherever I chose instead of having to beg an upperclassman to borrow a car and usually compromise with a group about what we would do. As an introvert, I really needed my alone time and independence.

About six months later, I was talking with a classmate who had also bought a Ford Probe, a much nicer model than mine. He told me that it was a nice little "starter" car for $13,000.

Naïvely, I said, "Wow, that was a great deal. I got a $26,000 bridge loan."

His head snapped back almost involuntarily and the look of pity he gave me was unexpected. I was hit with a wall of shame and embarrassment and I'm sure I flushed red from my neck up to my hairline. I averted my eyes, mumbled an excuse, and walked away.

I had paid $26,000—twice as much—for a more basic version of the same car! How was this possible?! I knew his parents had bought the car for him. I didn't have cash, so I had to get a loan and pay more. His parents had cash on hand and got a better deal. It didn't make sense to me. What?! Rich people have money *and* get better deals on things? That moment planted a seed in my head: I needed to understand more about how the world worked.

This guy was no more capable than me. We'd been through the same training, crawled through the same obstacle courses, hiked through the same woods in survival school, and marched around the Terrazzo every day, and he was heading out into life without a car payment. He was going to have more buying power right off the bat—an ability to save and invest just because of his circumstances, not because of what he had personally accomplished so far. This was a turning point in my psyche. I became a sponge for knowledge. I wanted to know what wealthy people did and what rules they lived by. It was clear that their realities differed from mine, and I wanted in.

I started picking up tips as I went along. My biology professor recommended I try to buy a duplex or fourplex so I could rent out the other spaces. I didn't grasp at the time that he had not recommended I buy a home, but that I buy an investment. I had the nugget of information, but I didn't really understand how to make it all happen. I ended up buying my first home in Florida because I couldn't find an apartment to rent in a safe neighborhood that was also in my price range. But that investment tip was in my head, and I still own that home in Florida. I call it my lieutenant house. I have learned much more about real estate investing since and I'm a little chagrined about some things I've done, but it's all part of the learning process. I made the best decisions I could with the information I had at the time. Luckily, life seems to provide continued opportunities to make better choices as I receive more insights and education.

Like most young officers, I invested with a financial company that got me started with an IRA and some insurance. The planning thought process made sense to me and still does. But I have much better strategies and execution models now than I did then. Two things I learned about the hard way were front-loaded funds and life insurance.

BUY TERM AND INVEST THE REST

THERE IS A SENTIMENT THAT YOU ARE BETTER OFF BUYING TERM INSURANCE INSTEAD OF WHOLE LIFE INSURANCE AND INVESTING THE DIFFERENCE IN PREMIUM IN THE MARKET. AS I DO WITH ALL THESE KINDS OF QUESTIONS, I RUN THE NUMBERS. NO GUESSWORK IS REQUIRED. CLEARLY DEFINED ASSUMPTIONS, SUCH AS YOU WILL SYSTEMATICALLY INVEST IN THE MARKET LIKE YOU WOULD IN A WHOLE LIFE POLICY (NOT STOPPING AND STARTING), AND KNOWING WHAT PROBLEM YOU ARE TRYING TO SOLVE ARE THE IMPORTANT DATA POINTS.

Investing is good, but there are layers of complexity involved in the "how" part of the equation. I wrote off insurance for almost ten years as a money suck, and the "buy term and invest the rest" model made a lot of sense to me. With the knowledge I had at the time, it was a good strategy.

The niggling question at the back of my brain was about what wealthy people were doing. Why were they still using insurance as part of their portfolios? This is when I learned more about taxes and investing rules and trying to grow money with more savvy. Everyone wants savings to grow. Why did some people use a "buy term and invest the rest" strategy while rich people had strategies that approached wealth accumulation through a different lens? Have you ever read "what I wish I'd known then" stories? I went through a phase of feeling frustrated about this. I could have a bigger nest egg right now if I just had some insights sooner!

You must forgive yourself for not knowing a concept or idea until you did. You must forgive yourself if you once made a choice that you now know was not the best. The pain of shame or embarrassment is almost physical. You must give yourself permission to be human, learn as you go, and make better choices when you have more information.

If you are holding the feeling of self-forgiveness, I ask you to consider the following myths, if you have believed them, and, if so, whether they are serving you now. The challenging part about these myths is that they contain grains of truth. One reason they exist is to help you make sense of the world and simplify its complexity. You like to feel in control, and money easily becomes overwhelming. Know that you are not stupid or wrong for believing any of these stories. They may have served you well.

Is the proverb (often erroneously attributed to Lao Tzu) at the beginning of this chapter, "When the student is ready, the teacher will appear," familiar to you? If you're reading this now, you are ready to consider some new ways of taking care of yourself and your family. I will endeavor to show you the grains of truth embedded in these myths, and how different strategies can help you do even better.

MYTH #1: THE STOCK MARKET WILL MAKE YOU RICH

IT'S AN INTERESTING PART OF the American psyche that we believe in hard work and "pulling ourselves up by our bootstraps," but we really do like our Cinderella stories, too. Aristotle talked about truth with a capital "T," meaning that there are some things in life that are true whether you believe them or not.[21] The stock market is one of these complex things in life that you didn't ask for but have nonetheless. Every morning on the news, an announcement of the Dow Jones Industrial Average and the clanging of the bells comes through your speakers. Almost any time I go for coffee or to a restaurant, I hear someone talking about this stock or that mutual fund. It's funny how this sparks a little competitive feeling, like I may be missing out. It's not logical, but it happens, even to me.

You need to remember that the market today is a world for statisticians and mathematicians. Terminology in and around the market is complicated. I am going to break down what you need to know about the concepts.

Merchants in the 1600s needed a way to raise money to grow their businesses beyond what they could put together by themselves. In 1602, the Dutch East India Company issued the first paper shares.[22] The market became a centralized way to fund companies. The simple concept of buying low and selling at a higher price for a profit was immediately obvious.[23]

Fast forward to today. The stock market is complex because there are many companies selling shares, other companies managing the sale of shares, different kinds of funds, and lots of money moving through each day. There is a need to make sense of all this chaos. Market indexes were developed to try to measure how money moves in the market and how to profit from the movement. There are multiple indexes, like the Dow Jones Industrial Average (DJIA), the Standard and Poor's 500 (S&P 500), and the National Association of Securities Dealers Automated Quotations (NASDAQ) composite. Money managers use indexes and other data sources to capture what has happened in the past and make their best predictions of future money movement. The goal remains to buy low and sell high.

As you may remember from school, you can use numbers to prove any point. If you google "market return," you will quickly be lost in a soup of terms like "annualized return," "compound annual growth rate (CAGR)," "actual return," and "annual return," and you can go down a rabbit hole chasing formulas and interpretations. If you love that kind of thing, go for it. If you just want to know how the market can help you gain security for retirement, this is what you need to key in on.

Historically, the average rate of return for a long-term investment in the market is 10%. The Macrotrends website[24] can show more specific data, or you can google your favorite index to verify this number. The point is, earning a 10% rate of return will allow you to keep up with inflation and keep your nest egg viable, but you will not become rich. For example, if you invest $100,000 and earn 10% over thirty years, you will have $1,744,940. If you are in the "Get it" phase of your life cycle, growing your investments, pay attention to the difference between investing $500 a month or $1,000 a month for thirty years.

If you invest $6,000 a year, or $500 per month, earning 10% for thirty years, you will have $1,039,646. If you invest $12,000 a year, or $1,000 per month, earning 10% for thirty years, you will have $2,079,292. Doubling the investment ($500 à $1,000) only doubled the outcome. The market did not make a big difference in the account after thirty years. You accumulate wealth by making money and having good savings habits.

MYTH #2: THE STOCK MARKET IS THE ECONOMY

WHEN YOU LISTEN TO THE news in the morning and hear about the stock market, how does it influence your day? If you don't fully know how the market works, why does it have any emotional hold on you? When I don't fully understand something, I try to weave new information into what I already know. Education is key. J. David Stein has a podcast called *Money for the Rest of Us*, and his episode "The Stock Market Is Not the Economy" is a perfect launching point for this conversation.[25]

Learning that the stock market is not the economy might initially throw you for a loop because we always hear politicians and talking heads say that things are good because the market is doing well. The question you should ask is, "Things are good for whom?" Suppose the price of oil in the stock market has risen by fifty dollars a barrel. Unless you have this investment and are willing to cash out of the market, you will not be able to use this money. Further, if you do have this investment and cash out of the market, you no longer have an investment working for your future security. The stock market doing well is good for investors who already have their food, clothing, and shelter needs covered and are growing their additional assets. The stock market does not impact the average person's day to day life in any tangible way. This will ring true once you think about it.

When the economy is doing poorly, the stock market can flourish. What? Why? The market is where people invest their money, their extra money, their retirement money that won't be touched for years. When the economy is doing poorly—for example, maybe the housing market is slow—then the stock market is a place to invest money. Investing is about getting your money to work for you while you are sleeping, and money will go where there is opportunity for profit. The stock market or stock exchange can be defined as "a market in which securities are bought and sold."[26] The market is a place where you are trying to buy low and sell high to make a profit. Chapter 5 will discuss many of the market risks that exist, including rumors, fears, political upheaval, and so on. The market is more of a prediction of where people think things are going in the future.

Your personal economy is the money you are living on today. The national economy deals more directly with the production and consumption of goods and services.[27] It is grounded in today's reality of jobs and small business success. Think of your day-to-day living.

My goal is to help you create a financial plan that does not cause a tightening in your chest when you turn on the radio and hear that the Dow is down. Filtering advertisements and marketing is challenging because ads are designed to push emotional buttons and make you buy a product.

You may be asking, "Why would I want to invest in the market at all?" The market is a tool that helps you grow your savings more than you could in a bank account. You can sit down with an advisor and run historical models that show how a $1,000 investment will do over different periods of time and see how, over long-time horizons, growth does occur. The market will go up and down. This is called volatility. What makes it frustrating is the timing of the ups and downs. If only Magic 8-Balls were accurate.

What you may not know is that, historically, the market rebounds within six to eighteen months after a decline. Figure 6 shows how the market recovers. You can visit www.macrotrends.net for more detailed data.[28]

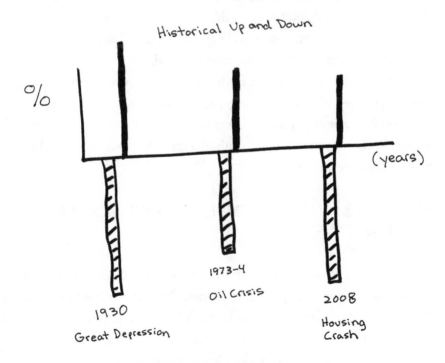

Figure 6: Stock Market Rebounds Example

After the Great Depression that began in 1929 and lasted throughout much of the 1930s, the market rebounded nicely. Care to take a guess how much? More than 45%.[29] Do you know how long the market was down during the Great Depression? Four years. The economy is what struggled to recover.

There will be bull and bear markets. The market is not good or bad. As an individual, you need to have an overall plan and strategy that accounts for market risk. Here is a simple example that shows how market performance and the economy intersect in your life. If you were thirty years old in 2008 and planned to work for the next thirty years, would the 2008 drop in the market have changed your daily life, your economy? No, because you were investing in your retirement account and not going to touch that money. Same scenario, but now you were seventy in 2008 and living on a retirement account that was still in the market. Did the 2008 drop in the market change your economy? Absolutely, because you were pulling money out of your retirement account to live on even when the market was down.

Is the market good, bad, or performing differently than it always has? Nope. The difference is where you are in your life. Would you say an umbrella is not worth having because it rarely rains? Or are you glad to have it when you need it? An umbrella is neither good nor bad, but it does its job at the right time.

MYTH #3: YOU SHOULD TAKE SOCIAL SECURITY EARLY

SOME PEOPLE BELIEVE THEY NEED to take Social Security as soon as they can, before it runs out of money. Remember how I shared that myths usually contain grains of truth? This is a perfect example. Social Security is a bedrock of our system in the United States, but it is not a pension. In 1935, President Roosevelt created Social Security as a federal safety net for elderly, unemployed, and disadvantaged

Americans.[30] The main stipulation of the original Social Security Act was to pay financial benefits to retirees older than age sixty-five based on lifetime payroll tax contributions.[31] It was designed to protect against the expenses of illnesses that may otherwise use up savings.

For a lot of Americans, Social Security is a significant source of retirement income, so it is distressing to hear that it may be in jeopardy. According to the Social Security and Medicare Boards of Trustees' 2021 annual report, the fund that pays retirement and survivor benefits will be okay until 2034. After that, the reserve will be depleted and tax income will be able to pay about 76% of benefits.[32]

History shows that our lawmakers are not inclined to let Social Security fail. In fact, Social Security has already been rescued—in 1983, when taxes were increased and benefits curtailed in a bipartisan solution between the House, Senate, and then-President Reagan.[33] This happened again in 1993 under the Clinton Administration.[34] The trustees point out in their 2019 report that lawmakers could shore up the fund. They could raise the tax rate, change the cap on how much individuals can be taxed, change the age at which you receive full benefits, or reduce future benefits.[35] None of these are choices politicians running for office want to make, but Social Security can be secured. You must decide for yourself whether you believe Congress will continue to protect Social Security or let it fail. If you believe that Social Security is probably going to be okay for your lifetime, please read this scenario, which is representative of many of my clients.

Alicia came to me when she was sixty-two. Just like Judy, whom you met in Chapter 1, Alicia wanted to retire because all of her friends were retiring. She'd been running the numbers herself and figured that if she took her small, $300-per-month pension from a previous job and started her Social Security, between her and her husband, Felix, they'd have enough to live on. Felix was already sixty-six and had started his Social Security when he was sixty-two, so a precedent had been established.

I had to break this down into several parts. First, did she understand that there are three big milestones when it comes to the Social Security benefit? Recall that we talked about this in Judy's story as well. Most people don't realize that you can take Social Security early, on time, or later. Today, you can take it at sixty-two at a reduced benefit amount. If you take it early, you lock in this lower payment. I asked if she realized that Felix had locked in his benefit at a lower rate forever because he took it early. She did not know that. I asked how much her Social Security benefit was according to her report. She said it was $1,800. I asked, "At what age?"

She had to look and then said, "Oh, I see. It's $1,800 when I'm sixty-seven, my full retirement age."

I then asked what her benefit would be if she took it early, at sixty-two.

She replied, "$990."

I then asked what it would grow to if she waited until she was seventy. She raised her eyebrows.

"A lot more than Felix is getting—$2,850."

I recapped. "So right now, you have the choice between $990, $1,800, and $2,850, correct?"

"Yes," she replied. "I like the bigger number, but I really want to retire now, and I need the money to do it."

I then asked, "How long did your mom and grandma live?"

She said, "A long time, eighty-six and ninety-four, respectively."

I said, "There's a pretty good chance you are going to live another twenty or thirty years. If you consider waiting eight years to retire, you could increase your income by almost $2,000 a month for, potentially, another twenty years." Her brow furrowed.

Then I asked, "What happens if you start your Social Security today and then decide you want to keep working part-time?"

"What do you mean?" she asked.

I explained, "If you continue to work when you've taken your Social Security early, you may have to pay extra taxes on the Social Security depending how much you make. But if you wait until your full retirement age, you will not have to pay those taxes. You can do what you want to do, but it's better if you have all the facts so you know the second- and third-order effects of your decisions."

Alicia's decisions started with whether she believed the myth that Social Security might run out and she should start as early as possible. Then she had to know the rules about taking Social Security early or on time and how each decision would affect her benefits. She had to consider how long-lived her family was because this is the best predictor of how long she may live. Obviously, the longer you live, the more advantageous it is to have the higher benefit. She also realized that if she waited, her benefit would be larger than Felix's benefit, so that could be extra money in her pocket, too.

What would you do? Fear is a powerful driver, and it would be a loss if Social Security was not part of your retirement equation. But what if Social Security remains solvent? Would you feel frustrated that you didn't make a choice that would benefit your family?

Like it or not, Congress plays a role in your retirement decisions. Legislation impacts taxes, how we save money, and even how we decide to manage our Social Security benefits. I believe it is always best to have as much information as possible when making decisions. Don't take the myth at face value. Make up your own mind about what is right for you and your family.

MYTH #4: YOU'LL NEED LESS MONEY IN RETIREMENT

MANY PEOPLE BELIEVE THEY WILL be able to live on much less money in retirement because they'll have paid off their home mortgage. The kids will be on their own. They'll be able to eat at home and live frugally.

This could be true if you controlled all the expenses in your life. This could be true if nothing unexpected ever happened.

In our first meeting, Jamal told me he only needed $40,000 a year to live on. "I don't need any insurance," he said. "My house will be paid for when I retire, so I won't have a mortgage. I don't like the stock market, but I'm afraid I may run out of money. I don't do much and I don't like to travel, so I won't need much."

Right away, I was struck by how Jamal was living in a place of lack, scarcity, and austerity in his head. He had not even retired yet, but he was mentally making his life as small as possible because he was afraid he wouldn't have enough.

I enjoy working with clients like Jamal because, if they are open-minded, I can share some strategies that will help them find peace of mind. But I can tell you, Jamal and I had to work through some doubts. Let's walk through just a few of the assumptions we addressed.

Jamal was making $110,000 a year, so I asked him if we could talk about his assumption that he would be able to live on $40,000 a year. He had done some rough accounting in his head, the kind of accounting we will talk about in Chapter 7. The numbers didn't really add up, but the rounding errors worked out well for what he wanted to be true.

Most people convince themselves they will be able to live on less because they make assumptions that nothing will go wrong. This is why I talk about plugging holes in your retirement plan. Holes exist where assumptions you make about how things will work out turn out differently. For example, one client's wife developed a rare, early onset form of Alzheimer's in her early fifties. Not only did this start costing them money, but it also cut short ten years of high expected earnings they had anticipated she would make between the ages of fifty and sixty.

Jamal and I talked about insurance first because this is a hole a lot of people do not plug in their retirement plans. It turned out he was a widower who had lost his wife many years earlier, and they did not have children. We talked about long-term care and what his options would be since he did not have children to take care of him as he got older. He didn't like this conversation and didn't want to discuss it. Unfortunately, ignoring a problem does not make it go away. The challenge here was that he would have to spend some of his nest egg on health care if he decided not to protect himself with insurance. He could certainly make that choice—and it would drive another series of calculations about running out of money.

Here's the thing to consider. Insurance allows you to enjoy and spend your money. If you do not have insurance, you need to conserve your money because you don't know if you may need it.

INSURANCE

ANY KIND OF INSURANCE WORKS BECAUSE A LARGE GROUP OF PEOPLE PAY A NONREFUNDABLE PREMIUM IN EXCHANGE FOR THE PROMISE OF A PAYOUT IF A TRAGEDY STRIKES (LIKE A CAR WRECK, HOUSE FIRE, OR DEATH, FOR EXAMPLE).

Next, we talked about Jamal's mortgage. I said it was great that he would not have this expense during retirement, but what about taxes and insurance? He looked confused for a minute.

I reminded him, "You live in a nice neighborhood, and your taxes alone are $10,000 a year. Did you already account for that expense?"

Right away, $10,000 of the $40,000 he said he could live on was gone. I didn't poke him further with the fact that a paid-off home still needs to be insured as well.

Then we talked about how he wanted to manage his money. I introduced the Rule of 100 to him and pointed out that, although he didn't like the market, he had almost 90% of his money in the market at the time. We discussed how to balance his money between risk (GA) and guaranteed (SMA) accounts. I ran some models to show him how different mixes of market and guaranteed money could potentially grow over the next thirty years, assuming he lived to be ninety years old. It was his money; he needed to decide how he wanted to allocate it so he could sleep well at night.

This brought us to the last big consideration. What about life's unexpected curveballs? Jamal had already planned not to do much traveling or invest in expensive hobbies to keep his expenses down to a $40,000-a-year budget, which had been reduced to a $30,000-a-year budget after accounting for property taxes. His situation required almost everything to work out in his favor.

In his first year of retirement, Jamal needed to replace the sewer line from his house to the street, which cost $8,000. This was 20% of the $40,000 budget he'd allowed himself that, as discussed, did not even include the $10,000 tax bill he needed to cover. But he was a good saver and had money in his emergency fund.

A few years later, he called me in a panic. "I need $15,000 to pay off the central air conditioning I bought on credit. It was six months same as cash and I need to pay it off. We need to pull more money from my retirement account."

Jamal had holes in his retirement plan because it was not resilient. Any problem that required money was going to upset the house of cards he'd built. Solutions were available because he was healthy and a good saver. But because he had elected not to use some advanced-planning strategies to plug the holes in his retirement, he had created a reality that was making his life smaller and smaller each time an emergency happened.

TO WRAP UP

You now know that you make the best decisions you can with the information you have at the time. Recognize that, when you hear something contrary to what you believe to be true, it is human nature to dismiss the new information. However, if you can consider the new strategy and evaluate how it may apply to your situation, you may garner benefits for your financial world. Financial myths persist because they contain grains of truth. Consider these questions:

- You may need less money in retirement, but do you want to plan that way?
- Do you want to stick with black and white decisions, like taking your Social Security as early as possible, or maximizing the amount of Social Security you can receive instead?
- Do you want to cross your fingers and hope you don't need long-term care, or have a plan in place in case you need it?
- Do you want to learn strategies that will allow your money to have more than one job, so you have more flexibility and control when life throws curveballs at you?

KEY TAKEAWAYS

- You make the best decisions you can with the information you have.
- Allow yourself to course-correct when better information is available. Spending time feeling frustrated does not help you in the end.
- Find out and learn from what wealthy people are doing.
- Money is more emotion than math. You work with people you trust first, and then math proves the concepts.
- Studies show that the pain of shame or embarrassment is almost physical and we will avoid it at all costs.
- Be a critical thinker to see beyond the grain of truth a myth may contain.
  - Myth #1: The stock market will make you rich.
  - Myth #2: The stock market is the economy.

- Myth #3: You should take Social Security early.
- Myth #4: You'll need less money in retirement.

TAKE ACTION CHECKLIST

CHECK ALL THE ITEMS THAT apply and add more beliefs about money if you have them. Remember, there is no judgment here. This is another opportunity to realize how you make choices about your money. The more self-aware you are, the better choices you will make.

I still feel like this is true, even if the numbers show something different:

- ☐ Black and white options feel good.
- ☐ I'm uncomfortable with shades of gray or "it depends" answers.
- ☐ I should pay off all my debt before I start investing.
- ☐ I should make paying off my mortgage a priority.
- ☐ Fees are bad and should be avoided at all costs.
- ☐ I should start taking my Social Security as soon as I can.
- ☐ If the stock market is good, the economy must be good.
- ☐ Life insurance is bad.
- ☐ Life insurance is good.
- ☐ Annuities are bad.
- ☐ Annuities are good.
- ☐ The market is bad.
- ☐ The market is good.

CASE STUDY: SOCIAL SECURITY—NOW OR LATER?

GETTING COMFORTABLE IN THE GRAY area: Should Joe take his Social Security as soon as he can?

Joe is sixty-four, enjoying his work, and wants to keep working until he is at least seventy. Unfortunately, an unexpected health issue is driving him to retire at sixty-five. Because of this, he is medically unable to qualify for life insurance, so his wife, Jill, is in danger of living below the poverty line if he passes first. Jill was a homemaker, so she does not qualify for her own Social Security. Key details:

- Joe's Social Security at sixty-five: $1,800 per month.
- Joe's Social Security at seventy: $2,900 per month.
- Joe's retirement money is tied up in a business deal with no foreseeable liquidation date.
- Joe has a $120,000 traditional IRA that earns 4% after fees.
- Joe will have a pension from his company of $800 per month.
- Joe's house is paid off.
- Joe owns land and has dabbled in RV storage. There is potential to expand this income source.

Should Joe start his Social Security immediately to handle this unexpected retirement?

Let's unpack this case. It is easy to say, "Just take it, he could have started when he was sixty-two," but in case you don't already know, Jill will keep receiving Joe's full Social Security amount after he passes. Joe cannot qualify for life insurance, so if they can wait until he is seventy to start, they will ensure that Jill receives $2,900 a month versus the $1,800 a month she will get if he starts his Social Security right away. That is more than a thousand dollars a month more.

But what are they going to live on in the meantime? I'm glad you asked. Joe's IRA is earning about 4%. If he waits, his Social Security will increase 8% each year after his full retirement age of sixty-seven. There are few guarantees in life, so it is important to see what the government is offering when it's time to make your own decision. The market will go up and down, but it is impossible to guarantee a specific rate of return, especially in such a narrow time frame. Joe is old enough to start spending his IRA. The $100,000 is not a large enough amount to grow substantially, because Joe is in retirement and needs to use the money. But the IRA is enough to provide income for the five years until Joe's Social Security is maximized.

Changing where your money lives changes how your financial world grows. By thinking strategically, Joe is able to make choices that plug the hole in his financial plan: no income protection for his wife. Joe is leveraging his IRA to increase his future passive income and protect his wife. In the near-term, he has the potential to expand his rental business and bring in more money, but as Joe and Jill get older, they may not want to manage a business. Waiting until seventy for his maximum benefit will provide the most security.

CHAPTER 3

WEALTH CREATION IS NOT A STRAIGHT LINE

May all your wishes be granted instantly

—Ancient curse

- Do you feel like you should have more of your life figured out at this point?
- Do you wonder if you are on track for a successful retirement?
- Have you ever been frustrated by the answer "It depends?"
- Have you ever been frustrated when you get different answers to same question from different people?

WHEN THE AIR FORCE SENT me to pilot training, I incurred a ten-year commitment to serve in exchange for this training. Because I went to pilot training as a captain, having already served five years, the option to separate from active duty came after fifteen years of service for me, and it only takes twenty years of service to start receiving a pension. I spent a large chunk of those flying years going to and from the Middle East, living in a tent, and putting on shoes to go to the bathroom in the middle of the night. A lot could happen in five years.

I thought to myself, "I could get hit by a bus tomorrow. I can choose security, stay in the Air Force, and finish my twenty years, or I can take a big leap out into the unknown and start a business." Making this kind of decision depends on how you're wired. For me, it was terrifying. But it was more terrifying not to try. I did not have my life figured out. By all rights, I should have been setting myself up to go fly for the airlines and, at the very least, finish my twenty years of active duty. But I took that leap into the unknown, choosing adventure over security.

Overnight, I left my nice XY graph life and entered something more akin to the board game Candy Land or Chutes and Ladders. You think you're winning, and then you roll the dice and land on the space that sends you back to the beginning again. You have all these pitfalls in life, and then you have the amazing times, too. This is how it felt to me in terms of my future retirement plan. I walked away from a guaranteed pension in five years. I cashed out all my savings and IRAs, attended workshops, and learned about business. My thought was, "I'm already old to be starting a business, so I'm going all in on my education now instead of trying to spend time figuring things out." It got dark for a while, and I felt panicked. I actually created a countdown showing the number of months I had before I ran out of money and would have to move back in with Mom.

Luckily, I was able to log more time with the Air Force Reserve that I hadn't planned on, opening a path to my Air Force retirement that I hadn't considered and some immediate income. I was grateful to have the ability to keep earning, but this slowed down my business growth, which was frustrating to my type A personality. Life has these twists and turns you don't expect, so it really is important to understand your larger plan. Instead of feeling derailed, I decided to call these events my little side trips. Planning helps you always figure out how you're going to come back to your desired path when life pulls you in other directions.

Wealth creation is not a straight line because life does not happen in a neat and orderly fashion. Some things happen to you, and some things you do to yourself, like starting a business in your forties. You need a holistic plan that adjusts for the curveballs. The financial world tries to offer one-size-fits-all solutions because, as humans, we like simplicity. When we boil our decisions down to black and white, yes or no options, we feel more in control. However, life is messy and does not tend to follow the steps we think it should.

Now let's consider other known variables. How many employment decisions are made from the need for health care? I am grateful that my husband is retired military, so we have affordable health care. This really allowed me to take time to start creating the business I wanted versus being forced to do a job I didn't like. I firmly believe that universal health care would allow for an explosion of small business creativity. So many people I know stick with jobs they loathe because they need the health care plan for their family. Covering an entire family's health premiums can cost as much as a mortgage payment.

Here's an example of life throwing a curveball: When I was teaching biology at the Air Force Academy, one of my fellow instructors had surprise twins in his late forties. I once heard him muttering loudly to himself, "I don't know how this happened, I don't know how this happened." I laughed, because where kids come from should be a basic concept for a bio instructor. But I can empathize with his plight.

He said, "We were about to be empty nesters, the kids off to college, and now I'm shopping for diapers three times a week." He had already created a retirement plan that included getting his kids through college—and just when he was about there, the game reset almost back to the beginning, just like Candy Land. Real people, real life.

Planning must start somewhere, so it begins with math and modeling. In this chapter, I share how to calculate some key numbers. I show you what variables are most important for your wealth creation. In Chapter 9, you will apply my step-by-step process to tailor a plan for you specifically. Math is the logical place to start because you identify the numbers you're working with and the assumptions you're making to arrive at an answer. To get past the "it depends" answers, you must agree on the goal you want to reach, the assumptions you will make, and even level-set when it comes to what words and terms mean. For example, a variable annuity is very different than a fixed annuity. You need to understand that the word "variable" means risk is involved, whereas "fixed" indicates a contract with guarantees.

Starting with a simple XY graph will help determine whether you feel like you need $500,000 or $5 million as your target. Are you going to work your government or corporate job with a W-2 income for thirty-five years, or are you going to become an entrepreneur? If you say you want $5 million in your retirement account, is that before or after-tax dollars? In this chapter, we will explore the variables that must be considered ahead of time so that you can start answering the questions "How much is enough?" and "Am I on track to get there?"

HOW MUCH IS ENOUGH?

STOP FOR A MOMENT AND ask yourself: How much is enough? If you can answer that question, you are the rare exception. When you are close to retirement, it is a bit easier to come up with a number because you have been paying on your student loans, mortgage, cars, and other lifestyle expenses. You have an idea of what it costs for you to live and this is the best estimate for retirement.

If you are currently in your earning years, you most likely have no idea what your number is right now. To wrap your mind around the complexity, we'll start with simple assumptions and then add in the "what-ifs." The visual we begin with is the XY graph, where you start at zero and go up to infinity. It's such a nice, pretty graph (Figure 7). I see this on a lot of financial documents, proposals, and projections. Math is, well, simple and straightforward.

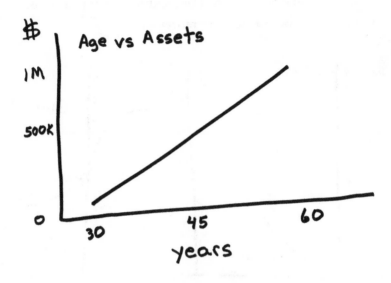

Figure 7: $500,000 IRA in 30 Years

The XY graph, the formulaic approach to money planning, is a correct beginning step because you must have some kind of measuring stick to plan with for retirement. When you are still figuring things out, we can work backwards to give you an idea. Here is where you can say, "I want to have $500,000 in my IRA by the time I'm sixty." Let's say this will be in thirty years. Assuming no growth, just savings, $500,000 in thirty years is $16,666.66 a year. This breaks down to $1,400 per month. For most thirty-year-olds, $1,400 a month is a mortgage payment. It's good to start a conversation with an understanding of what it takes to create a retirement, but most thirty-year-olds are going to say, "No way I can do that!"

A bell curve graph is a little more realistic for most people who do not inherit money or have parents who can buy them their first home (Figure 8). It's important to build your saving muscle when you're young, even if it's just a few hundred dollars a month, but please understand that you must save more as you earn more. The bell curve concept shows that you can start out a little slower by necessity and then catch up as you get closer to retirement.

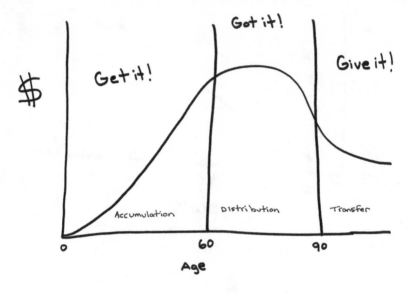

Figure 8: Realistic Savings Profile

AM I ON TRACK?

A FEW THOUGHTS YOU MAY have had or overheard in conversations about money priorities:

- I don't make enough money to start saving and investing.
- I'm only twenty-eight; I don't need to worry about retirement yet.
- I need to find the best broker so I can get good rate of return.
- We lost half of our retirement account in 2008. The market is a scary place.
- I'm closing in on retirement and need some aggressive growth strategies so I can catch up.
- I'm never going to be able to retire.

You've seen some simple math that will generate a ballpark number which tells you how much is enough for you. For a number that makes sense for you right now, multiply how much you are earning today by how long you plan to live in retirement. For example, if you make $100,000 a year, plan to retire at sixty-five and then live for twenty more years, your target number should be at least $2 million.

If life moved along a predictable path, figuring out if you're on track would be simple. However, you are most likely in the situation of having to catch up with saving in order to achieve your target number. It's important not to get down on yourself at this point. You may have been saving diligently, right on track, and then had a job opportunity that required you to move across the country and take a loss on your house. Or you may realize that you should have been saving but still haven't gotten around to it. No matter where you find yourself, figure out your number and start moving forward. Think about being on track as being on a literal racetrack. You'll want to reassess your progress with each annual lap.

After you have your target number, you need to figure out how to reach it. The next thing to examine is this: What's more important for growth—money, time, or rate of return? Go ahead and decide which one you think is most important. Remember, if you commit now, the lesson will anchor deeper in your brain. This is important because your understanding of what matters will contribute to your success at creating and sticking to an investment plan that reaches your goals. I meet many people who are in their fifties and haven't really saved for retirement. They shop around for the highest rate of return different advisors allude to making for their clients. They have an edge of desperation and want an advisor to promise an investment that will make them rich, or at least okay. Remember, if someone promises you something that sounds too good to be true, investigate. An old Chinese proverb says, "The best time to plant a tree was twenty years ago. The second-best time is now." In the context of the conversation here today, this means that if you want success and growth in the future, the best time to act is now.

This discussion is getting into a layer of complexity when it comes to money. There are three primary variables when you are trying to grow your nest egg: money, rate of return, and time.

A quick aside here: Learning styles (visual, verbal, and kinesthetic) reflect how you best process information. For example, if you are a visual learner and I try to talk numbers and expect you to keep them straight in your head, you will not understand the point of the conversation. I mentioned this in the introduction, and I want to reemphasize here that cocreating a good financial plan means speaking up about how you want to receive your information. I will use a mix of presentation styles so you can think about what your preference is for numbers.

Money: If you increase your account size from one dollar to ten dollars, you clearly have more money saved.

Rate of return: 5% of a dollar is a nickel. 10% of a dollar is a dime (Figure 9).

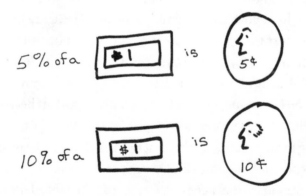

Figure 9: Visual Percentages

Here is where it becomes interesting. If you have a 10% rate of return, one dollar would become one dollar and ten cents and ten dollars would become eleven dollars. The rate of return is the same, but 10% of a bigger number is a bigger number.

Think about how you manage your savings. Assume you want to have $10,000 in your emergency fund. A bank may pay 0.1% interest, so your $10,000 account would earn ten dollars. But what if you changed where your money lived, and you had $5,000 in the bank earning 0.1% and $5,000 in a different account earning 3%? You would earn five dollars plus $150. Changing where your money lives can allow your money to work better for you while still solving the problem of emergency savings. In this example, you earned more than thirty times the money you would have from one simple bank account. I'm speaking to you if you have a significant amount of money on the sidelines, not adding value for you because it's in a bank account. If you have time working for you, you will see the benefits of compounding interest, too.

It's important to grasp the concept of being intentional about where your money lives for two reasons I have seen with my clients.

One, I have the clients who come in with $300,000 in their savings accounts because they don't know what to do with it. Once we define what problem that money is trying to solve—i.e., the need to establish an emergency fund, fund a down payment for a house, or create a retirement nest egg—then we can decide where it should live based on growth and access needs.

Two, I have clients who are in their seventies and have 100% of their money in aggressive growth funds in the market. If this is intentional, that is a decision. However, I find that many of these people don't really know what's going on. This money may have been sitting in an old 401(k) plan since retirement, and they've just never considered what problem the money is there to solve. Do they want 100% of their money positioned to experience a 2008-style market drop and lose up to half of their nest egg, like we saw with Joe in Chapter 1? Or would they like to protect some of it so they can leave money in the market to do its thing and live off some guaranteed accounts? As an advisor, my job is to make sure you know the options available to you and the pros and cons of each option so you can make an informed choice.

Figure 10 is an apples-to-apples example for visual comparison, so you can begin to think about the truth of which is most impactful in your situation—money, time, or rate of return for growth. Walk through Figure 10 so you understand the numbers.

- The first line of the table assumes you have $10,000, earning a 10% rate of return annually, for ten years.
- The second line answers the question: "What if you start with more money, such as $20,000 instead of $10,000?" You can see that the amount basically doubles in ten years.
- The third line answers the question, "What if you earned a 20% rate of return?" You can see that the amount more than doubles.
- The fourth line answers the question, "What if you had more time?" You can see that the amount grows the most with more time.

$$$	Rate of Return	Time	Expected Growth
$10,000	10%	10 years	$25,937
$20,000	10%	10 years	$51,875
$10,000	20%	10 years	$61,917
$10,000	10%	20 years	$67,275

Figure 10: Comparison of Money, Rate of Return, and Time on Growth
(NOTE: This chart has a baseline example of $10,000 earning 10% for ten years. Each number is doubled individually so you can compare which factor—money, rate of return, or time—has the biggest impact on growth.)

Let's extrapolate some meaning. First, time is your best friend. Compounding your money over time is how you get it working for you. Saving when you are younger will always be a good idea, but you cannot start any sooner than today.

Second, a good rate of return will grow your money the most over time. Are you surprised that time has a bigger impact than a good rate of return? And here's what I want to say while you visualize me stomping my feet with each word: *While rate of return does grow your money, you can see that simply increasing the amount of money you are investing is super important.*

Investing will not make you rich. Investing will grow the money you save to keep up with inflation, but without a good savings habit, you will never see real growth in your accounts. Therefore, I recommend that you contribute to your retirement accounts on a regular basis. We can run the numbers based on any amount of money, different rates of return, and different periods of time to see where you may end up. This is also a great exercise to do to answer the question, "Am I better off paying down debt first or starting to invest?"

This table is a simple "what-if" machine where you can input your numbers today and get an idea of whether you are on track to reach your goals.

Time is your biggest ally when it comes to building your wealth. And you can play with the variables of savings amount and rate of return to catch up if you are not on your path. If you are goal-oriented, it can be especially frustrating when you are on track to reach your number with your investment strategy and life happens.

Katie is a newly divorced mom taking a time-out from work to stay at home with her two-year-old daughter, Beth, so there are a few missing years in the savings part of her timeline. Compounding over time and rate of return have continued to work, but she will have to increase her savings to catch her account size up to where she would be if she had stayed on a steady schedule. Figure 10 gives you an idea how that works.

Being on track for success and then falling off the wagon is very much like when you're dieting. Trying to hold things together by willpower alone is a sure way to fail; diets don't work if you try them for a while and then go back to your old ways. Building your financial world is sustainable when you have a plan that's working toward a goal you want to achieve and is broken down into doable steps (as we will do in Chapter 9).

So far, this chapter has taken you through the math behind reaching a savings goal. The remainder of this chapter introduces the mental work necessary to create a plan that is meaningful for you—instead of a vague hope that you'll eventually make enough, marry enough, or get lucky enough to win the lottery.

HOW DO I START?

AT THIS POINT, PLANNING STARTS to become a web of interrelated decisions, but I am going to keep it as linear as possible for the remainder of this chapter. You will build your plan in Chapter 9. First, you need to reflect on your values, your dreams, and the reasons why you make your money. Focus on these questions, in this order:

- What is your number? (How do you know when to get off the treadmill? How much is enough?)
- What are your values, your why? (Are you keeping up with the Joneses? Creating meaningful life experiences? Supporting a cause?)
- What problem are you trying to solve? (Are you trying to retire early? Set up a business? Get kids to college?)
- What risk strategy appeals to you? (How much are you willing to lose?)

- What are your emotional triggers ? (Fear of the future or of not having enough control? Feeling less than or behind?)
- How well do you communicate? (Do your partner, spouse, and/ or family know what enough feels like to you?)

What Is Your Number?

What is your number? Your brain needs a target before it can start to help you reach your goal. I like to target two levels of "What's my number?" to achieve. Your first decision point addresses your basic requirements. This is what you need for food, clothing, and shelter. You should feel like, "If I just had this much money, I would be okay." And then there's the "Okay, this is really where I'd love to get to" level. You want to identify a stretch goal because it's almost impossible to achieve a goal you don't set. The Take Action Exercise at the end of the chapter shows you how to calculate this stretch goal number for yourself.

Zack works for the telephone company in Colorado. He sees the inside of a lot of houses. He told me, "You would not believe how many of these McMansions, these gorgeous, beautiful houses, have little to no furniture. They even have sheets hanging up on the windows instead of curtains or blinds." All appearances point to success.

The reality is, everyone is just doing the best they can. I remember my high school math teacher telling us, "Never compare yourself to other people. You're either going to feel superior or you're going to feel inferior; either way, it's not the truth." This stuck with me because I wasn't sure why my math teacher was sharing this philosophical point. And it sticks with me because I seem to have to relearn this lesson every so often, even now. What works for someone else may not be right for you. Figure out your number and don't worry about anyone else's.

What Are Your Values?

What are your values, your why? You may be thinking, "Values? I thought we were talking about numbers!" Wealth is different for each person. For a lot of you, the number of zeros in your bank account is not important in and of itself. What's really valuable about money is that it allows you to have experiences with your families, travel, and participate in life. What do you value? It becomes much easier to reach your goals when you understand what drives you. As author Simon Sinek would say, find your why.[36] If you have a goal to save $1 million but you don't know why, it is a meaningless goal. I used math (the discussion around Figure 2 and 7) to break the big number into smaller amounts you save today so your brain can help you stay on course. If $1 million seems abstract or unreachable, for example, you will struggle to maintain good savings habits.

What Problem Are You Trying to Solve?

The question I repeat in this book is, "What problem are you trying to solve?" Do you want to make sure you have enough food, clothing, and shelter money to pay the bills so that you can be an artist, so you can travel? Are you trying to build up a good nest egg so you can send your kids to college? Are you trying to save $100,000 or $1 million? This may seem arbitrary, but I have clients who either have a personal goal of being able to call themselves a millionaire or having "FU" money in the bank, over and above their personal needs. Problems are not always simply tied to physical needs, but often emotional needs. Do you have a career that will support your goals?

A common thing I see happen is that people tend to lump everything they want to do into the category of savings. You could pull money out of your 401(k) to pay for a wedding and intend to pay it back, but will you? Life happens, and you can do what you need to do, but it's powerful for you to understand the detour this kind of decision creates.

If you determine your get-well plan when you borrow the money, you will be more likely to stay focused and on track.

Risk

What about risk? You also need to ask, "How do I balance growth risk and safety?" This is an important question. Have you ever filled out one of those questionnaires for an investment where you answer about ten questions and get a ranking from zero to ten at the end? This number is supposed to tell you whether you are conservative, moderate, or aggressive in your approach to risk. I think this is a very clinical way of getting at a very emotional state of mind. Everybody is okay with making money. The real question is always, "How much money are you willing to lose?" And that's a different question for everybody because it's also about how much money you can afford to lose. Kidding on the square, I prefer to ask, "On a scale of stuffing money under your mattress to investing in cryptocurrency, where do you see yourself?"

As I discussed in Chapter 2, the market is not good or bad; it simply goes up and down. Figure 11 shows some key ups and downs of the past hundred years. John Steinbeck's *The Grapes of Wrath* sticks with me as my impression of the Great Depression, and how it impacted so many people over almost a decade—the Dust Bowl, the misery.[37] The market downturn, however, only lasted about four years, and then it recovered by almost 66%!

In fact, historically, the market tends to recover within six to eighteen months after a big drop. Figure 11 shows historical drops in 1930, 1973-4, and 2008.[38] When the market drops, many people wait a few months or maybe a year, and when they cannot take it anymore, they pull their money out. Then they miss the recovery, so it's like losing twice. This is why you need to have both a GA and a SMA—it allows you to invest without risking losing everything all at once.

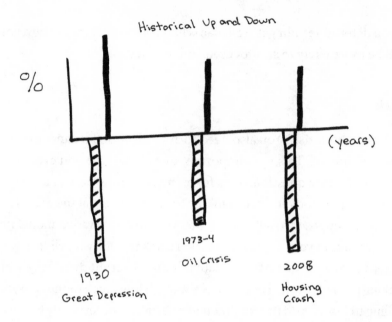

Figure 11: Historical Ups and Downs

It makes a big difference where you are in your financial life cycle, as well. Let's take a look at the "Financial Life Cycle" chart again (Figure 12).

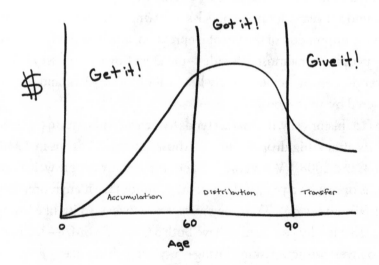

Figure 12: Financial Life Cycle

In the "Get it" phase, the volatility of the market does not have as great an impact because you are still working. You can let your money recover and continue to work for you. This table shows how a million dollars performed from 1973-77. The performance wasn't great, but it still ended up close to $1 million after a couple years of recovery from the 1973 oil crisis.

Beginning of Year	Year	Rate of Return	End of Year
$1,000,000	1973	-14.66	$853,400
$853,400	1974	-26.47	$627,505
$627,505	1975	37.2	$860,936
$860,936	1976	23.84	$1,066,184
$1,066,184	1977	-7.18	$989,632

Figure 13: Market Volatility Impact on Growth (1M 1973-1977)

Your risk tolerance changes in the "Got it" phase, when you are not working and are spending your savings. Looking at the same time period, but adding an $80,000 per year withdrawal, you can see how the account gets smaller (Figure 14).

Beginning of Year	Year	Rate of Return	End of Year	Withdrawal	After Withdrawal
$1,000,000	1973	-14.66	$853,400	$80,000	$773,400
$773,400	1974	-26.47	$568,681	$80,000	$488,681
$488,681	1975	37.2	$670,470	$80,000	$590,470
$590,470	1976	23.84	$731,238	$80,000	$651,238
$651,238	1977	-7.18	$604,480	$80,000	$524,480

Figure 14: Market Volatility Impact with Withdrawal (1M 1973-1977)

You can see the major impact on investments from withdrawals made when the market is down. Your strategy needs to adjust as you get to retirement and want to start drawing money out of the market.

Please make a mental note here about why you get so many different answers and opinions about how to manage your money in the market. People will tell you, "You need active management." "You need the lowest fees." "You need an index fund." "You need a bond fund." No one is trying to lead you astray; a lot of brain power is dedicated to creating models, identifying patterns, and coming up with strategies to win in the market. However, looking at strategies without knowing where you are in your financial life cycle, or defining your personal risk tolerance and your family needs, can allow good intentions to go awry for you. A holistic planning approach that looks at all of your financial decisions, not just your 401(k), will align your efforts toward your goal. Investments all have inherent risk (which I discuss in Chapter 5). You mitigate risk with education so you can make intentional choices for your peace of mind. Reading this book is a good step toward taking control of your money.

What Are Your Emotional Triggers?

Are you aware of your emotional triggers? I discussed the fact that wealth creation is not a straight line, and you must remember that emotion is part of the picture as well. When you're young and don't have much money, ups and downs are not a big deal. Losing 10% of $25,000 drops your account down to $22,500. When you have $500,000 a 10% drop leaves you with $450,000, so it stings more. Therefore, no matter how idealistic and liberal we are in college, we all move a little closer to fiscal conservatism when we have something to lose. Seeing your account drop by $50,000 can make you feel ill and do things to feel better on impulse, like pull your money out of the market. You may feel better in the moment, but have you really helped yourself? I recommend having a proactive plan so you will already have decided how to react when the market drops.

How Well Do You Communicate?

How well do you communicate? Money becomes more challenging when you have a spouse or partner who gets to vote on how decisions are made. Rarely do you both agree on risk, for example. You want to be in the market with an aggressive strategy to grow; your partner would love to just stuff the money under the mattress. Balance is the key. This doesn't mean each person should get full control of half the money. It means that you should have conversations and make decisions in the context of your life situation.

Communication is also key because you don't know what you don't know. I can't emphasize this enough: There can be a lot of financial baggage (I delve into this in Chapter 7) and myths you grew up with mixed in with the truth. And you will make the best financial decisions you know how to make depending on the kind of baggage you picked up.

At the end of the day, it's your money and you are the decider. But it doesn't hurt to get a couple of opinions while you're working your way toward what "right" looks like. Through conversation, you'll learn more about pros and cons. If you thought of it, great. But maybe there's something out there that you haven't thought of yet.

TO WRAP UP

YOU NOW KNOW THAT WEALTH creation is not a straight line because life is not a straight line. It would be nice if money was black and white and we could just focus on our passion projects.

The reality is that money is woven into the fabric of your life, so you need to understand the basics. This does not mean you have to figure it out on your own. Progressing up the ranks in my military career, I've learned that making good decisions is more about asking good questions than knowing all the answers. Life can be messy, but good, bad, or ugly, it's better to have your eyes wide open and make intentional choices that move you toward a defined goal.

KEY TAKEAWAYS

- Your money does not grow in a neat, straight line on an XY graph. Life is messy and you will go through ups and downs on your way to retirement.
- Successful planning will require you to come up with a target amount. You must know how much is enough for your lifestyle.
- After you have a plan in place for your lifestyle, you need to review annually to see if you are on track to reach your number.
- A holistic approach to financial planning will account for the surprises in life that can move you off course. As a pilot, I know it's essential to correct for drift—the longer you fly without a correction, the further off course you will be.

TAKE ACTION EXERCISE

- If you had to guess right now, what is your number? $_____
  (Remember, this is the number you accumulate during your working years that will allow you to retire with the lifestyle you want.) If you have no idea what your number is, take what you earn now and multiply it times the number of years you think you might live after a retirement age of sixty-five. For example, if you earn $100,000 a year and you think you might live to be eighty-five, multiply 100,000 times twenty and you will see that $2 million should be your target number. It's time to get over sticker shock and get comfortable with reality. After you have this number, you can get an idea of what your stretch goal will

be. I'd recommend you sit down with a professional to calculate your stretch number.

- Would you like help to create a plan? Yes or no (circle one)? There is no right or wrong answer. This is about knowing yourself.

If your answer is yes, start making notes about what qualities are important to you in a trusted advisor.

If your answer is no, check all the reasons below that resonate with you and add more items as needed.

- ☐ My partner or spouse manages our money.
- ☐ I don't make enough money or have enough money.
- ☐ I'm expecting an inheritance.
- ☐ I'm a financial geek and I'm taking care of it.
- ☐ I had a bad experience once before, so I'm not sure who to trust.
- ☐ I plan to start planning when I have time.
- ☐ I have a 401(k) at work, so I'm good.
- ☐ I have a pension and will adjust my lifestyle accordingly.

CASE STUDY: WHAT'S MY NUMBER?

WHAT IS JOHN'S NUMBER? $_____.

- John is fifty-five years old, and both of his grandparents lived to be almost one hundred.
- He makes $100,000 a year.
- He has been contributing to Social Security diligently, even though he hasn't always had a W2 job, so expects to have $2,500 a month ($30,000 a year).
- He expects to inherit $1 million from his parents as a beneficiary of their life insurance.

(ANSWER KEY)

WHAT IS JOHN'S NUMBER? $1.1 million.

Because he expects to receive $30,000 a year from Social Security, we can adjust his annual planning factor from $100,000 down to $70,000.

Based on his current income, to continue living his current lifestyle, John would need $2.1 million ($70,000 x thirty years).

Because he is expecting a $1 million inheritance, he can safely reduce his planning number down to $1.1 million.

CHAPTER 4

STRATEGIC THINKING VS. CONVENTIONAL THINKING

Choose courage over comfort.

—*Brené Brown*[39]

- Have you ever chosen to stay in your comfort zone rather than try something new (and possibly better) on the off chance that you might not like it?
- Do you think holistically, creating synergy amongst your money decisions, or do you feel that separating your financial decisions spreads out risk?
- Have you ever heard, "There's no reward without risk?" What if education could mitigate this fearsome adage?
- How much is enough for you?
- What if you could have some balance with your money like you do with a good work/life balance?
- Have you ever struggled with the difference between a need and a want? A requirement versus a solution?

PICTURE A WILD WEST SALOON scene: The double doors swing open. The bartender wears a white long-sleeved shirt with a black band around his upper arm. He has a handlebar mustache. You can hear the music in the background. I'm thinking of the movie *Tombstone*, with Val Kilmer as Doc Holliday, saying, "I'll be your huckleberry," and his funny shot glass-twirling scene. And *Wyatt Earp* and the line that hit home about money, Kevin Costner as Earp saying, "No man ever got rich working for another man."[40] This is the spirit of the American West, a feeling of freedom, control, and self-determination. The moment planted a seed deep in my brain. I was a kid in West Virginia, watching a moving on the couch with my four brothers, thinking about entrepreneurship before I knew the word. What did Wyatt Earp mean? Getting rich? Movies leave impressions on me, and the strategic thinking of the West resonated more than the safety of conventional thinking.

After hearing the line, "No man ever got rich working for another man," I talked with a neighbor, Cal, and he said, "Forget starting a business. Find the highest-paying hourly job you can and have a life."

I was confused. Cal explained that his dad had owned a cabinet-making business and nearly killed himself working. He never had time off or time with his family. It seemed to me that all the adults in my life spent a good amount of time at work, so I wasn't sure what Cal was driving at in terms of actual freedom.

I know now that Cal was telling me how to live a safer life based on his own paradigms. Who were some of your trusted role models in your own formative years? Your mom and dad? A teacher or family friend? What money stories did they tell you? It's amazing how our dreams can be squashed early in life by trusted adults who try to protect us from disappointment or struggle. Some ask us questions that mean, "Who do you think you are to want that?" Or worse, they can teach us to tell ourselves, "Well, I didn't want that anyway."

I was taught to work hard, get an education, get a good job, be reliable and steady, and keep my head down. This story I was taught did not jibe with what I observed. Some of my classmates' parents were CEOs or managers, in charge of stuff; I happened to be surrounded by adults who did not want to be in charge at work. I wanted to be in charge and to make money. I didn't realize it at the time, but I was already envisioning something beyond the conventional when it came to my expectations for my life and my earning potential.

The next time I saw Val Kilmer was in *Top Gun*.[41] I liked everything about the movie and the idea of being a pilot: doing something challenging, being tested, making a difference. When I went to pilot training, the process had changed, so there were three potential tracks for us after flying the initial T-37 trainer—flying heavies, fighters, or helos. Of course, I wanted to fly a fighter like in *Top Gun*. Our flight commander, Major Kim, said that we needed to be okay flying a helicopter if that was how it panned out in our stratification after T-37s. In the previous class, one student who didn't get selected for fighters had quit. Major Kim said that the Air Force was spending a lot of time and money on our training, and we were there to do a job for our country, not to satisfy our romantic dreams. Still, I wanted that fighter. I did feel like I'd want to quit if I didn't get one. The Catch-22 was, I had to go all in to see if I could get the fighter, but would still be on the hook for ten years if I didn't. When you're only twenty-two years old, ten years is a long time to commit for one gamble.

I did not get a fighter.

The only day I felt like crying on the flight line was during our first preflight training in the T-1, when I saw that there was a button I had to push to illuminate passenger "fasten seat belt" signs. I also felt depressed about the fact that the career path for non-fighter pilots was to fly for the airlines. I did not like the idea of my entire life being planned out; nor did I look forward to driving a bus, albeit a flying one. Conventional paths did not inspire me.

When Elon Musk appeared on *Saturday Night Live*, he explained that as a kid, he was kind of like he is now. Regarding his gaffes, he said, "I'm reinventing the electric car and trying to send people to Mars— whatever made you think I would be a normal guy in person?"[42] Musk is not a conventional thinker, and he does not fit neatly into a niche.

An example of strategic and unconventional thinking came from the Air Force commandant of cadets, General Redden, during his address to the parents of incoming cadets in 1990. My mom told me that during his talk, he said, "What kind of men come to a military academy? Your conservative and conventional men. What kind of women come to a military academy? Not your most conservative or conventional thinkers."

My mom, who went to Woodstock when she was eighteen, shared with me, "That was when I decided it would be okay for (you) my daughter to go to a military school." Looking back, I see this as a strategic thought for General Redden to express because it voiced the value of tapping into the strength of young women as military leaders. As a woman who chose the military, I relate to making unconventional, strategic choices.

Conventional thinking was around making safe choices. In 2020, of the 10,964 pilots in the Air Force, only 708 were women—6.5 percent.[43] Why was I considering giving in to conventional thinking about my career path so many years after I went to pilot training as I transitioned from active duty military service to civilian life?

Perceived safety and security are powerful incentives, but conventional thinking can be an illusion. You need to understand what you want, but know that there are many different ways to get there.

Thinking strategically without getting mired in conventional thinking depends on how you receive new information. Are you open-minded? Most people believe they are open-minded, independent, and make their own decisions. This may be true, except for their unconscious biases and the myths they believe to be true. I believe it is nearly impossible to choose a different thought when you're unaware of what influences your feelings or beliefs.

I grew up in a community of people who didn't really like the military—they believed in peace, not war—but I was encouraged to think for myself at the same time. I attended a military school because I wanted to fly airplanes, not because I wanted to wear a uniform and march around like some of my high school classmates had done. However, an unexpected side effect of my time at the Air Force Academy was finding that serving my country had become a desire that rivaled wanting to fly. I realized that people in uniform follow orders given by civilian leadership, as outlined in the Constitution. It is a gross stereotype to think that all military people are warmongers. Being open-minded about a belief you've been raised with can be hard, but personal growth is usually positive. And I was able to share what I'd learned with my community and shift the thinking of an entire group.

I ask you to accept that when you are on the way to something better in life, you'll go through change. Just as my notion of what I wanted to be when I grew up changed, your world has experienced changes. Saving and planning for retirement has changed from how it was for your grandparents and parents. My crystal ball is a little vague about what the future may bring, but change will come. My question is, "Do you like change?"

In a talk he gave about connecting with people, bestselling author and motivational business speaker Phil M. Jones shared a brilliant way to test how open you are to change.[44] I'd like you to give this exercise a try right now, while you're reading this chapter. Seriously, put your book down for a second and just do it.

Step one: Cross your arms.

Step two: No, not that way, cross your arms the other way.

It's super weird, right? It's as if you're being hugged by a stranger. It is one of the simplest changes I could ask you to make, yet it alone is uncomfortable at best. Could you even do it? Or did you stay in your comfort zone and keep reading because I couldn't see you or hold you accountable to try?

Here's my request: For the remainder of this book, can you be open to change and accept that you're in rookie mode? Does that sound okay?

Helping you achieve and retain the lifestyle you want is my obsession. This book is designed to help you help yourself think differently. I'm asking you to accept that change is uncomfortable. I selected Brené Brown's quote, "Choose courage over comfort," to begin this chapter because I want you to think about how you normally handle uncomfortable things. Facing money head-on takes courage because it's woven into so many parts of our lives. Conventional thinking is comfortable and feels safe because it's what everyone is doing. There is social proof. Most marketing drives us toward conventional thinking. On the other hand, strategic thinking challenges you to get outside your box. I'm not asking you to take a giant leap of faith. Even Ronald Reagan was known to say, "Trust but verify." I'm asking you to consider if you hold any conventional beliefs that keep you isolated from people who may think differently than you. Investigating the motivations that drive you to make decisions can free you to make better choices for yourself.

In this chapter, you'll learn about strategic thinking and how it can help you achieve your financial dreams more easily than blindly following the path of conventional thinking. The more you understand your options, the better choices you can make. Conventional thinking will have you use one or two tools to save for retirement. Strategic thinking will lead you to define what a good retirement looks like for you and then help you select the strategies that will get you there, not just use the tools you may already be familiar with.

COMMON MISCONCEPTIONS

BELOW ARE THREE THINGS I find my clients believe to be true about their lives that turn into big problems. I share these because I want you to know you are not alone. There is no need to spend time feeling embarrassed or beating yourself up. Now is the time to make a different choice.

The first thing a lot of my clients used to secretly believe is that someone else would take care of them. Clare's husband, Rick, divorced her after twenty-one years of marriage. She was a teacher and had always worked. They had been unable to have kids. Rick married his mistress, the ten-years-younger version of Clare, when she became pregnant.

In a moment of honesty, Clare told me, "I'm not going to train another one. And I never really understood how poor he kept me."

"What do you mean?" I asked.

"Rick was always starting some harebrained side hustle, and drained our savings without asking me on more than one occasion. And somehow I thought he was the head of our household, taking care of me."

I have another client, Ruth, who has a PhD in math and a great job. She's in her fifties now and still single. She confessed to me that she always thought there would be a man to take care of the money stuff. The princess finds her prince and they live happily ever after is a common fairy tale we grew up on. Whether we're married or single, it is a way for us to mentally abdicate from our financial responsibilities.

It's very common to split up household chores in a relationship. One person might do the cooking and grocery shopping while the other pays the bills, for example. This can become dangerous when, in addition to splitting up the chores, you also divide the knowledge about your resources. This hole in your planning is usually illuminated by an emotional, stressful life event like divorce or death. Such circumstances are not the best time to figure out your money situation.

The second thing nearly all my clients used to believe is: "I have a great 401(k), I'm good for retirement." There is much more to financial success and security than a 401(k). I have so many people in their fifties and sixties who come to me with $1 million in their retirement accounts and think that's enough to live on for the next twenty or thirty years. I can help you make it work, but I challenge you to think bigger! A traditional 401(k) comes with a tax problem and doesn't offer any income stream protection or a long-term care plan. Many of you are closing in on retirement with a good nest egg, yet still have the same investment growth strategy you did when you were forty. How do you think the investment practice of a forty-year-old might be a different from that of a sixty-year-old?

The third thing a lot of my clients buy into when they first come to me is the idea that they don't have enough money to invest. It's true that many planners won't work with someone who has less than $5 million to invest—if that is the case, find a different planner. The fallacy is thinking that investment is only for wealthy people. Pensions are almost extinct in America today, and you need to have a retirement. What I want you to realize, reading this book, is that you start where you are right now. Compounding growth and time will allow you to achieve more than you will if you wait to arrive at some arbitrary future state of success before you start taking care of yourself.

Conventional thinking is powerful. You may not even realize how fairy tales have impacted your idea of happily ever after. Your family, your faith, or your desire for it to be true may have you convinced that if you play your role, someone else will take care of you. This may happen sometimes, but wouldn't you like to have your financial plan account for worst-case scenarios, too? Strategic thinking will ensure that you consider as many variables as possible while living your best life. You can live your life according to the roles or within the boundaries you prefer and still be prepared to step up when life takes unexpected turns. The key takeaway is, you want to be conscious and intentional about the decisions you make.

HOLISTIC PLANNING

IN 1994, I LOOKED AT what it would take to provide combat capability from my Air Force base in Florida to the Middle East. F-15 fighter airplanes provided air support to ensure no enemy aircraft would fly into the airspace where Americans and allies worked; the footprint of the extra support needed to get the planes in the air was the puzzle. The planning vision moved combat capability from the US to the Middle

East. The strategy revolved around prioritizing what needed to be in place first in a comprehensive, beginning-to-end list. Planners got tunnel vision focusing on the major equipment, like airplanes, and forgetting basics like water and bathrooms. This happens in financial planning when people focus on 401(k)s and forget that they also need life and long-term care insurance to protect their families.

Logistics planning in the military requires success. An almost good enough solution can be one course of action, but my boss always needed a conservative plan that guaranteed success (as much as that is possible in life). Some financial planning relies on Monte Carlo simulations that predict rates of success. A prediction that says you have a 75-85% chance of not outliving your money is considered good. How does that feel? Are you comfortable with probably not running out of money? Likely, you are not. That is why I recommend using strategic thinking that includes a comprehensive approach, with the goal of eliminating gaps or holes in your plan. Empirical evidence makes me believe that Murphy's Law is real and we need to try to plan for it with our finances.

The final planning step to move troops to the desert identified the types of airlift needed to transport them. All airplanes are not the same. For example, a tanker aircraft is designed for in-flight refueling, so it carries a lot of gas and just a few people. A tanker will help drag fighter airplanes across the ocean, but who's going to receive the fighter airplanes in the desert, park them, fix them, and prepare them for mission flights? A cargo airplane can carry things like pallets of water and porta-potties. While it's exciting to plan for the flashy things like fighter airplanes that gin up visions of Tom Cruise in *Top Gun,* wars are won with sound logistics planning.

People have this kind of tunnel vision with their investment decisions all the time. If you cherry-pick different solutions, like focusing on a 401(k) while ignoring your whole picture, you may not really solve your entire retirement problem. Ed, your coworker, invests in SuperAmazingFundX, so you think, "I'm going to invest in

SuperAmazingFundX, too!" Does Ed from work also have five kids he wants to get through college? Maybe SuperAmazingFundY would be a better option for you. Conventional thinking is not bad, but it leans toward a one-size-fits-all solution set.

Strategic thinking zooms out to a bigger picture, identifies gaps in your plan, and fills them in. It is not your fault if you have believed some of the conventional wisdom out there, but now you can make a different, better choice to look at your financial world in a holistic way.

EDUCATION MITIGATES FEAR

IN CHAPTER 2, WE DISCUSSED the myth that the stock market will make you rich. Conventional thinking supports the idea that if you have enough money in the market, you can live off the interest. This is true if you assume that the market will not drop at an inopportune time for you.

Tina, a new client, called me up and said, "I want to invest in the market."

I said, "I can help you do that. I begin by sitting down with you and your husband, Ray, and discussing what your goals are."

"We really just want to be in the market. Can't we just take care of this over the phone? Ray's not really involved in our money side of things."

"I'd recommend we sit down together so we can level-set expectations and our investing terminology face-to-face, but we can do this online, if that's your wish."

I asked Tina about her goals and risk tolerance. She was in accounting and worked for herself. Her mother-in-law, Pam, had recently passed away and had accounts in the market that had grown enough to cover her long-term care costs. Tina had $600,000 sitting in a savings account because she didn't want to lose money in the market. But she wanted more growth than a bank will pay to ensure that she and Ray had enough money for future long-term care needs.

"Tina, you have some conflicting desires here. You are afraid of losing money and you are also insisting on investing in the market, an option that will go up and down. Can we discuss savings and investment options that will build in some guaranteed money for you?"

"No," Tina said.

I created three different investment options for her in the market that balanced different risk categories. I emphasized, "Tina, I know the risk tolerance questionnaire is designed to determine if you prefer conservative, moderate, or high-risk investments. But I think a more honest question is, 'How much are you willing to lose?' It sounds to me like you are not willing to lose any of your $600,000."

She didn't answer my question but replied, "I need to be in the market, and I'm also concerned about fees."

The *Oxford English Dictionary* defines "cognitive dissonance" as "the state of having inconsistent thoughts, beliefs, or attitudes, especially as relating to behavioral decisions and attitude change."[45] Tina wanted to be sure not to outlive her money. Conventional thinking made her believe that she had to accept risk in the market to grow her money, even though she was highly risk-averse. However, she had enough money to invest in an SMA that would grow more slowly but never lose a dime. She had already done the work of being a good saver and did not need market exposure at this point in her life. Tina would be spending her money soon, so she did not have a lot of time for it to grow in the market. The fees and exposure to risk were not recommended at this point in her life. If she were in her forties, the strategy would be different. Close-mindedness and the inability to trust drove Tina to make a suboptimal choice based on emotion.

Investing is necessary, but your product choice must be balanced with where you are in your life span. Are you in your thirties or your fifties? What is your personal risk tolerance? A 1994 study by financial planner William Bengen resulted in what is now known as the "Four Percent Rule." It says that the highest withdrawal rate retirees can use if they want their money to last thirty years is 4%, given the historical rates of stocks and bonds up to the time of the study.[46] So for every million dollars you have, you can use $40,000 to live on each year if you are invested in stocks and bonds. That's great, except for the fact that the market does not come with guarantees about how much you will earn in a given year. Strategic thinking allows for the shades of gray that happen in real life.

Winning is more than just having a bigger account balance. Winning is when you are enjoying your life, too. Do you want to start out every day listening to the Dow Jones Industrial Average and let that direct how you feel? Abundance is more than just money. Money can help us enjoy life, but money is not life.

HOW MUCH IS ENOUGH?

FRED HAS $647,000 TODAY. ALMOST ten years ago, he had $892,000. I know this because he proudly showed me the older statement. Fred is seventy-six years old. His house and car are paid off. He lives very conservatively, so he barely pays taxes. Fred could bury his money in the backyard and have enough to live on.

When I asked Fred how I could help him, he said, "We're here to figure out who's going to take care of my wife, Donna, when I pass."

"You have enough money that you could protect all of it and not have to worry about the market ever again," I said.

"Oh no, that's not an option."

Donna shared, "Fred's up every morning, tuned in to the market. He stresses about it every day and I like the sound of that not being part of our morning routine."

I said, "Fred, what gives?"

He talked round and round, telling me about how he'd made different investment choices. He said, "Look how good this bond fund I picked did last year."

"I see that the market is stressful for you, but you love it. You love making choices and enjoy the thrill when your picks go up in value. It sounds like you would be happy joining an investment club to have these kinds of conversations. I don't think I can help you."

Donna interjected, "I like the idea of having some money we cannot lose!"

I presented a few options to balance their at-risk money in the market with some guaranteed investment options. We discussed how they had done an amazing job of creating a large nest egg and becoming debt-free, too. We talked about how, at seventy-six, it was a good time for Fred to consider a more balanced approach to risk.

Fred said softly, "I want to be a millionaire."

I replied, "Ahh, you have been very close a couple of times. You said you came here to discuss how to take care of Donna, but you have an overriding goal of hitting $1 million in your account."

To bring a little levity to a serious conversation, I added, "I will tell you that what you are doing is strongly AFA (against financial advice), just like a doctor would only let you sign out of the hospital AMA (against medical advice) if you were not well. If we experience another 2001 or 2008, you could lose almost 50% of your assets and never be close to a million bucks again."

Fred replied, "My research tells me that I should be in an index fund with the lowest possible fees. It's the best way for me to make money."

"Fred," I said, "I would agree, that is one way to make money when you're younger. You've done a great job growing your account, and you don't have to be exposed to 100% risk anymore." I struggled to find a tactful way to say, "Why don't you consider finding a new hobby beyond playing Risk with your entire savings?"

Fred was plugged into the conventional thinking that he needed to be in the market to grow a nest egg big enough to pull 4% a year to live on. Because he was fixated on seeing $1 million on his statement, he was not even pulling money from his investment to live on comfortably. He was not ready to be a strategic thinker and bring balance to their lives.

Fred and Donna came to see me because they knew Fred's personal management in the market would not work for Donna if Fred passed first. Strategic thinking for your financial plan includes a course of action that adapts to a changing environment, as does military planning. There is no such thing as a one-size-fits-all solution.

NEED VS. WANT

WHAT IS THE DIFFERENCE BETWEEN a requirement and a solution, a need and a want? One former boss, a military commander, Colonel Smith, shared a story about dealing with strong-willed children. He'd recently read in a book that you do not issue ultimatums to a strong-willed child because you will lose every time. You must, instead, offer alternatives. Option A or B? Just imagine a tall, imposing man with an almost permanently furrowed brow. At work, people snapped to attention when he entered a room. Now here he was at home with his thirteen-year-old daughter, Kaylee, in the dad zone.

Kaylee shouted, "Dad, I need an iPhone10. Everyone has one. Do you want me to be the only one without an iPhone? People will think we're poor!"

Chagrined by being so instantly drawn into a dramatic conversation, Colonel Smith stated evenly, "You do not need an iPhone10."

Kaylee retorted, "You may as well just start homeschooling me if you're going to be a tyrant like this!"

Through gritted teeth, he said, "Would you like to have my old iPhone8, or would you prefer to be grounded for two weeks?"

A requirement is something you need that does not change. For example, you need a way to communicate with your family. This has always been a requirement. In the beginning, it was snail mail, then the telegraph, then the telephone, then cell phones, and now the internet.

If your kid says they need an iPhone10, they are confusing a solution with a requirement. Your kid has a requirement (need) to communicate. The solution they want is an iPhone10.

Strategic thinking about money includes understanding the difference between requirements and solutions. You want to understand this distinction when it comes to your finances. Watch any financial commercial and you will be told to buy an insurance, mutual fund, or other product. These are solutions. To avoid being sold a solution that may not be the best for you, you must define your retirement requirement so you know the problem you are trying to solve. Do you want to retire with the current lifestyle you've grown accustomed to? Do you want to be able to travel the world during your retirement? Do you want to have the ability to leave money to your family and your favorite charity?

I implement strategic thinking with my clients using this three-step framework (Figure 15), and I think it will work for you too.

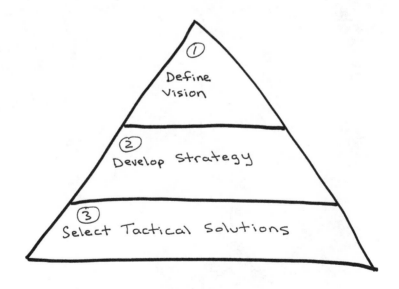

Figure 15: 3-Step Financial Plan Framework

First, I help you define your vision. What problem are you trying to solve? In financial terms, your vision is what you would like your retirement to look like. If you had a cartoon bubble above your head, what would be in it? A beautiful beach? Time with the grandkids? Amazing travel?

The second step is for us to develop the strategy to achieve your vision together (Figure 16). Are you going to get the best high-paying job you can and work until you get there? Are you going to start a business? Is there a certain age at which you'd like to retire? Think back to the Rule of 100 that deals with risk. How aggressively do you want to invest? How much guarantee do you want in your plan? There will be multiple ways to achieve your vision. Your strategy allows you to map out a way to get to your vision that works for you.

Figure 16: What Is Your Vision?

Third, select tactical solutions to execute your strategy. This will probably feel very different to you from what you've experienced in the past. Stocks, bonds, mutual funds, exchange-traded funds (ETFs), insurance, annuities, real estate, and so on are the last step of your financial planning process, not the first. Marketing ads and commercials sell you solutions. Imagine that you see an ad for an amazing pair of basketball shoes with highly-rated ankle support, a cool design, and recommendations from serious athletes. You buy them for your son. Then your son comes home and says he's decided to play football and needs a pair of cleats. You bought a great pair of shoes for the wrong sport. This kind of thing happens with investing all the time.

Each of these solutions (stocks, bonds, mutual funds, ETFs, insurance, annuities, real estate, etc.) fall into categories with characteristics like flexibility, liquidity, tax status, risk, and so on that I will discuss in Chapter 6. If you define your vision first—the problem you're trying to solve—you can select a solution that helps you achieve your vision. If you start with a solution and try to work backwards, you may not address your requirement or, in other words, solve your problem. Here is another financial example: If your need is to ensure that your family is cared for in the event of your untimely death, buying stock in GameStop is not the most suitable solution available to help you address your requirement. Kaylee demanding that her dad, Col. Smith, give her an expensive iPhone10, was not the best or only solution to their communication problem. Marketing had convinced Kaylee it was the only solution.

TO WRAP UP

YOU NOW KNOW THE DIFFERENCE between strategic and conventional thinking. It may be uncomfortable to challenge some of your beliefs, but being open-minded can lead you to more efficient gains. There are common misconceptions to be aware of and they are tricky because, like myths, they contain grains of truth. A holistic planning approach supported by strategic thinking is your best chance to plug the holes in your retirement plan. When you understand the difference between a need and a want, you achieve clarity for your financial plan. You can select solutions that change where your money lives so you can change how your financial world grows.

KEY TAKEAWAYS

- Strategic thinking fills in gaps left by conventional thinking.
- You are not alone, but you are now aware. Common misconceptions when it comes to your retirement plan can give you a false sense of security.
- Holistic planning will set you up for success better than picking individual solutions as you would from an à la carte menu. Spreading your money across different investment products or advisors does not reduce your risk. Without an integrating advisor, you cannot be sure that all of your efforts and decisions are working together synergistically.
- Conventional thinking feels safe because everyone is doing it. Strategic thinking ensures that you align your decisions to create the best outcome for your family.
- The ideal 3-Step Financial Plan Framework is Vision → Strategic Planning → Tactical Execution.

TAKE ACTION EXERCISE

IF SOMETHING YOU THOUGHT WAS true really wasn't, when would you want to know about it? This exercise demonstrates a common misconception that many people have about which numbers matter in the real world.

Average Return vs. Actual (Real) Return

NOTE: This exercise is presented in a format for read/write learners and visual learners like me who like pictures. The answer key immediately follows the questions.

What is the average return on one hundred dollars in the stock market? Assuming you start with one hundred dollars, fill in the dollar amount you think your account will grow or shrink to each year.

- Year 1: + 100% = $_____
- Year 2: - 50% = $_____
- Year 3: + 100% = $_____
- Year 4: - 50% = $_____

If you add up your return from each year and then divide by four, what do you get?

Average return is _____

Do you have more money after four years in the market?

Actual return is _____

Often, your investment statement will show quarters with high, exciting-feeling rates of return. At the end of the year, though, your account may not have grown very much at all.

Here is the same example using bananas to demonstrate the concept. (Even if you do not like numbers, you can understand the concepts and strategies behind how your money is managed. Find an advisor with the ability to adjust to your preferred learning style.)

Assuming you start with four bananas, how many bananas do you have at the end of each year?

Starting with 🍌🍌🍌🍌

- Year 1: + 100% = _____ bananas
- Year 2: - 50% = _____ bananas
- Year 3: + 100% = _____ bananas
- Year 4: - 50% = _____ bananas

What is the actual number of bananas after four years? _____

(**ANSWER KEY**)

What is the average return on one hundred dollars in the stock market?

- Year 1: + 100% = $200
- Year 2: -50% = $100
- Year 3: +100% = $200
- Year 4: -50% = $100

Average return is 25%

Actual return is 0%

Average return is 25% (you add up the percentage of return for each year and then divide by four years). Actual return is 0% because you started with one hundred dollars and ended with one hundred dollars.

How many bananas do you end up with? (What is the real return?)

Starting with ᙦᙦᙦᙦ

- Year 1: +100% = ᙦᙦᙦᙦᙦᙦᙦᙦ
- Year 2: - 50% = ᙦᙦᙦᙦ
- Year 3: +100% = ᙦᙦᙦᙦᙦᙦᙦᙦ
- Year 4: - 50% = ᙦᙦᙦᙦ

The actual number of bananas you have after four years is four. (You've ended up where you started.) This visual example really highlights why the average return is a meaningless number. Do you care about the average number of bananas you had, or how many real bananas you have today?

CASE STUDY: SAVE VS. SMART TACTICAL EXECUTION

AN IDEAL FRAMEWORK FOR YOUR financial plan is Vision → Strategic Planning → Tactical Execution.

Julio just retired. He has a $1 million 401(k). It is still with his company, sitting in a money market fund because he does not trust the market. Julio is only sixty, and his parents are still alive at eighty-nine and ninety-seven. He is afraid he will run out of money because his family is blessed with longevity. He wants to dip his toe in the water and put $10,000 in a growth fund. Why would he want to do this? Does it make sense?

Julio is worried about losing money in the market. He thinks he can minimize his risk by seeing how investing just a little money might work out. Figure 17 shows how $10,000 grows to $136,767 over twenty-five years with 2% fees using historical returns.

YEAR	BALANCE AT BEGINNING OF YEAR	RATE OF RETURN	FEES OF 2%	BALANCE AT END OF YEAR
1	$10,000	-14.67%	($200)	$8,333
2	$8,333	-26.31%	($167)	$5,974
3	$5,974	37.13%	($119)	$8,073
4	$8,073	23.82%	($161)	$9,834
5	$9,834	-7.19%	($197)	$8,930
6	$8,930	6.52%	($179)	$9,334
7	$9,334	18.45%	($187)	$10,869
8	$10,869	32.45%	($217)	$14,179
9	$14,179	-4.88%	($284)	$13,204
10	$13,204	21.50%	($264)	$15,778
11	$15,778	22.46%	($316)	$19,006
12	$19,006	6.22%	($380)	$19,809
13	$19,809	31.64%	($396)	$25,680
14	$25,680	18.62%	($514)	$29,948
15	$29,948	5.18%	($599)	$30,900
16	$30,900	16.61%	($618)	$35,415
17	$35,415	31.69%	($708)	$45,929
18	$45,929	-3.10%	($919)	$43,587
19	$43,587	30.47%	($872)	$55,996
20	$55,996	7.62%	($1,120)	$59,143
21	$59,143	10.08%	($1,183)	$63,922
22	$63,922	1.32%	($1,278)	$63,487
23	$63,487	37.58%	($1,270)	$86,076
24	$86,075	22.96%	($1,722)	$104,116
25	$104,116	33.36%	($2,082)	$136,767

Figure 17: $10,000 Growth in 25 Years with 2% Fees

Here are some of the problems Julio does not understand as he tries to tactically execute his money management plan in a vacuum, with no strategy: He doesn't account for all the variables that impact the growth of his money in the market. He doesn't understand the difference between active management for large accounts versus an index fund that simply follows the market. He doesn't understand how to follow the money to see how money managers are paid. Typically, they are paid by a percentage of assets under management. It is the same amount of work to set up and manage a small account as it is to set up and manage a large one. Therefore, smaller accounts usually have larger initial setup fees and charge a larger percentage to manage the money. Break points vary, but most companies will not manage accounts smaller than $100,000. The larger the account, the smaller the management fee. Because $10,000 is such a small account, Julio pays a $250 account setup fee and 2% each year. In the example in Figure 18, you can see that the setup fee reduces the growth.

YEAR	BALANCE AT BEGINNING OF YEAR	RATE OF RETURN	FEES OF 2%	BALANCE AT END OF YEAR
1	$10,000	-14.67%	($450)	$8,149
2	$8,149	-26.31%	($163)	$5,885
3	$5,885	37.13%	($118)	$7,909
4	$7,909	23.82%	($158)	$9,597
5	$9,597	-7.19%	($192)	$8,728
6	$8,728	6.52%	($175)	$9,112
7	$9,112	18.45%	($182)	$10,577
8	$10,577	32.45%	($212)	$13,729
9	$13,729	-4.88%	($275)	$12,798
10	$12,798	21.50%	($256)	$15,238
11	$15,238	22.46%	($305)	$18,287
12	$18,287	6.22%	($366)	$19,036

13	$19,036	31.64%	($381)	$24,558
14	$24,558	18.62%	($491)	$28,549
15	$28,549	5.18%	($571)	$29,427
16	$29,427	16.61%	($589)	$33,628
17	$33,628	31.69%	($673)	$43,399
18	$43,399	-3.10%	($868)	$41,213
19	$41,213	30.47%	($824)	$52,695
20	$52,695	7.62%	($1,054)	$55,576
21	$55,576	10.08%	($1,112)	$59,955
22	$59,955	1.32%	($1,199)	$59,531
23	$59,531	37.58%	($1,191)	$80,265
24	$80,265	22.96%	($1,605)	$96,720
25	$96,720	33.36%	($1,934)	$126,406

Figure 18: $10,000 Growth in 25 Years with 2% Fees + Setup Fee

Another market problem Julio doesn't understand is that the market is not personal i.e., it does not take your feelings and needs into account and does not always perform as predicted. Figure 19 shows a twenty-five-year performance with the market returns shown in reverse order of Figure 18.

YEAR	BALANCE AT BEGINNING OF YEAR	RATE OF RETURN	FEES	BALANCE AT END OF YEAR
1	$10,000	33.36%	($445)	$12,891
2	$12,891	22.96%	($258)	$15,593
3	$15,593	37.58%	($312)	$21,141
4	$21,141	1.32%	($423)	$20,997
5	$20,997	10.08%	($420)	$22,694
6	$22,694	7.62%	($454)	$23,969

7	$23,969	30.47%	($479)	$30,793
8	$30,793	-3.10%	($616)	$29,223
9	$29,223	31.69%	($584)	$37,899
10	$37,899	16.61%	($758)	$43,436
11	$43,436	5.18%	($869)	$44,817
12	$44,817	18.62%	($896)	$52,266
13	$52,266	31.64%	($1,045)	$67,757
14	$67,757	6.22%	($1,355)	$70,617
15	$70,617	22.46%	($1,412)	$85,065
16	$85,065	21.50%	($1,701)	$101,653
17	$101,653	-4.88%	($2,033)	$94,659
18	$94,659	32.45%	($1,893)	$123,483
19	$123,483	18.45%	($2,470)	$143,795
20	$143,795	6.52%	($2,876)	$150,295
21	$150,295	-7.19%	($1,503)	$137,986
22	$137,986	23.82%	($1,380)	$169,474
23	$169,474	37.13%	($1,695)	$230,705
24	$230,705	-26.31%	($2,307)	$167,700
25	$167,700	-14.67%	($1,677)	$141,421

Figure 19: $10,000 Growth in 25 Years with Reverse Sequence of Returns

If you take the same twenty-five years and just reverse the sequence of returns, see how it differs from the final number in Figure 18? If Julio tested out the market with the returns from Figure 19, he would feel pretty comfortable. However, if he invested with the returns from Figure 18, he might not like the results. Further, see what happens when you adjust the numbers (see Figure 20) to show annual withdrawals (of $500) as you would make in retirement, spending your money. The account shrinks much more quickly (down to $34,515).

YEAR	BALANCE AT BEGINNING OF YEAR	RATE OF RETURN	FEES	WITHDRAWAL	BALANCE AT END OF YEAR
1	$10,000	-14.67%	($450)	($500)	$7,649
2	$7,649	-26.31%	($153)	($500)	$5,024
3	$5,024	37.13%	($100)	($500)	$6,252
4	$6,252	23.82%	($125)	($500)	$7,086
5	$7,086	-7.19%	($142)	($500)	$5,945
6	$5,945	6.52%	($119)	($500)	$5,706
7	$5,706	18.45%	($114)	($500)	$6,123
8	$6,123	32.45%	($122)	($500)	$7,448
9	$7,448	-4.88%	($149)	($500)	$6,443
10	$6,443	21.50%	($129)	($500)	$7,171
11	$7,171	22.46%	($143)	($500)	$8,106
12	$8,106	6.22%	($162)	($500)	$7,938
13	$7,938	31.64%	($159)	($500)	$9,741
14	$9,741	18.62%	($195)	($500)	$10,824
15	$10,824	5.18%	($216)	($500)	$10,657
16	$10,657	16.61%	($213)	($500)	$11,678
17	$11,678	31.69%	($234)	($500)	$14,572
18	$14,572	-3.10%	($291)	($500)	$13,338
19	$13,338	30.47%	($267)	($500)	$16,553
20	$16,553	7.62%	($331)	($500)	$16,959
21	$16,959	10.08%	($339)	($500)	$17,795
22	$17,795	1.32%	($356)	($500)	$17,169
23	$17,169	37.58%	($343)	($500)	$22,649
24	$22,649	22.96%	($453)	($500)	$26,792
25	$26,792	33.36%	($536)	($500)	$34,515

Figure 20: $10,000 Growth in 25 Years with $500 Withdrawals

Another problem for Julio is that the rest of his account is sitting in the money market fund. Not taking action is a decision. While Julio is deciding if he feels comfortable putting money into the market, his $900,000 is in a conservative account but not a guaranteed account. The assumption is that because it is conservative it should not lose money, but it could because it is still in the market. A cheeky financial advisor might call this a "buy and hope" strategy.

Strategic thinking focusing on tactical execution deserves a deeper dive. You want to grow your retirement nest egg so you don't run out of money. You are probably conditioned to believe that greater risk is needed to realize a greater reward. You may fear the uncertainty of the stock market with good reason because you have friends or family who lost half of their retirement accounts in 2000 or 2008. Your account from work (TSP, 401(k), 403(b), 457, etc.) may be your single biggest source of income in retirement. During your "Get it" phase, you didn't think much about the 401(k) because you were working and assumed the company was taking care of your retirement fund. Life creeps up on you quicker than you think, though. Suddenly, you are retiring and trying to decide what to do with this precious nest egg. You are the exception if this one account is enough for you to live on in retirement for the next twenty to thirty years. Stuffing the money under your mattress is not a good plan if you need some growth to keep up with inflation.

You may feel like you need to be in the market because conventional thinking says you grow money in the market, but this is terrifying because you don't understand or control the market. A natural, and common, baby step you might consider is investing a small amount of your nest egg to "see how it works out"—essentially running a little scientific experiment to see if the market is going to help you or bankrupt you. This will always be a faulty experiment, as you saw with

Julio, because you cannot control the market to try out your hypothesis. You will either prove to yourself that the market makes money if you use a snapshot sequence of returns that produce a positive result (Figure 19), or you will prove to yourself that the market is a poor bet if you use a snapshot that includes a bad year or two (Figure 18). Remember, these two tables use the same real return numbers from the market; the only thing that changed is the sequence of the returns. Your takeaway here should be that the market will go up and down, and this is why the longer you are in the market, the better your returns will be. You need time for the ups and downs to average out so you feel overall growth. Planning to invest in the market for only five to ten years is a short time horizon, so longer is better.

HOW DOES JULIO AVOID A CATCH-22?

JULIO WANTS HIS MONEY TO grow but fears losing it. Crafting an intentional plan using strategic thinking to direct tactical execution looks like this: Julio's vision is to have enough money to last until he passes. Julio now needs to determine, strategically, how much risk he can accept to sleep well at night and also have some growth in his account. According to the Rule of 100 that I discussed in Chapter 1, because he is sixty years old, Julio would ideally have only 40% of his money in the market and exposed to risk. However, because his family is so long-lived, we are going to keep 60% in GA and 40% in SMA (60% of $1 million is $600,000). Now Julio has $400,000 growing in a guaranteed account. This addresses his concern about losing all of his money.

Figure 21 shows how $600,000 would grow over the same twenty-five years in the market shown in Figure 17.

YEAR	BALANCE AT BEGINNING OF YEAR	RATE OF RETURN	FEES	BALANCE AT END OF YEAR
1	$600,000	-14.67%	($12,000)	$501,740
2	$501,740	-26.31%	($10,035)	$362,340
3	$362,340	37.13%	($7,247)	$486,954
4	$486,954	23.82%	($9,739)	$590,887
5	$590,887	-7.19%	($11,818)	$537,417
6	$537,417	6.52%	($10,748)	$561,004
7	$561,004	18.45%	($11,220)	$651,198
8	$651,198	32.45%	($13,024)	$845,267
9	$845,267	-4.88%	($16,905)	$787,942
10	$787,942	21.50%	($15,759)	$938,228
11	$938,228	22.46%	($18,765)	$1,125,956
12	$1,125,956	6.22%	($22,519)	$1,172,084
13	$1,172,084	31.64%	($23,442)	$1,512,052
14	$1,512,052	18.62%	($30,241)	$1,757,734
15	$1,757,734	5.18%	($35,155)	$1,811,828
16	$1,811,828	16.61%	($36,237)	$2,070,510
17	$2,070,510	31.69%	($41,410)	$2,672,086
18	$2,672,086	-3.10%	($53,442)	$2,537,480
19	$2,537,480	30.47%	($50,750)	$3,244,452
20	$3,244,452	7.62%	($64,889)	$3,421,825
21	$3,421,825	10.08%	($68,436)	$3,691,416
22	$3,691,416	1.32%	($73,828)	$3,665,368
23	$3,665,368	37.58%	($73,307)	$4,941,939
24	$4,941,939	22.96%	($98,839)	$5,955,052
25	$5,955,052	33.36%	($119,101)	$7,782,848

Figure 21: $600,000 Growth in 25 Years

His \$600,000 grows to \$7.78 million after twenty-five years. The \$400,000 in a safe money account (SMA) earning 3% grows to \$837,511, as shown in Figure 22.

YEAR	BALANCE AT BEGINNING OF YEAR	RATE OF RETURN	BALANCE AT END OF YEAR
1	\$400,000	3.00%	\$412,000
2	\$412,000	3.00%	\$424,360
3	\$424,360	3.00%	\$437,091
4	\$437,091	3.00%	\$450,204
5	\$450,204	3.00%	\$463,710
6	\$463,710	3.00%	\$477,621
7	\$477,621	3.00%	\$491,950
8	\$491,950	3.00%	\$506,708
9	\$506,708	3.00%	\$521,909
10	\$521,909	3.00%	\$537,567
11	\$537,567	3.00%	\$553,694
12	\$553,694	3.00%	\$570,304
13	\$570,304	3.00%	\$587,413
14	\$587,413	3.00%	\$605,036
15	\$605,036	3.00%	\$623,187
16	\$623,187	3.00%	\$641,883
17	\$641,883	3.00%	\$661,139
18	\$661,139	3.00%	\$680,973
19	\$680,973	3.00%	\$701,402
20	\$701,402	3.00%	\$722,444
21	\$722,444	3.00%	\$744,118
22	\$744,118	3.00%	\$766,441

23	$766,441	3.00%	$789,435
24	$789,435	3.00%	$813,118
25	$813,118	3.00%	$837,511

Figure 22: $400,000 Growth in 25 Years at 3%

Figure 22 shows that Julio's $400,000 grows to $837,511 in twenty-five years. Please note that SMA rates can range from 0-6% depending on the market conditions at the time. Although SMAs are not in the market, insurance companies use the stock market as a ruler to determine what rates they will offer in their contracts.

Let's take this a step further and show why having a balanced plan based on the Rule of 100 works. Figure 23 shows the $600,000 in the market with $40,000 a year to live on. The account reduces to $431,624.

YEAR	BALANCE AT BEGINNING OF YEAR	RATE OF RETURN	FEES	WITHDRAWAL	BALANCE AT END OF YEAR
1	$600,000	-14.67%	($12,000)	$40,000	$461,740
2	$461,740	-26.31%	($9,235)	$40,000	$293,453
3	$293,453	37.13%	($5,869)	$40,000	$354,376
4	$354,376	23.82%	($7,088)	$40,000	$390,013
5	$390,013	-7.19%	($7,800)	$40,000	$314,720
6	$314,720	6.52%	($6,294)	$40,000	$288,533
7	$288,533	18.45%	($5,771)	$40,000	$294,921
8	$294,921	32.45%	($5,898)	$40,000	$342,813
9	$342,813	-4.88%	($6,856)	$40,000	$279,563
10	$279,563	21.50%	($5,591)	$40,000	$292,886
11	$292,886	22.46%	($5,858)	$40,000	$311,488

12	$311,488	6.22%	($6,230)	$40,000	$284,249
13	$284,249	31.64%	($5,685)	$40,000	$326,697
14	$326,697	18.62%	($6,534)	$40,000	$339,780
15	$339,780	5.18%	($6,796)	$40,000	$310,236
16	$310,236	16.61%	($6,205)	$40,000	$314,530
17	$314,530	31.69%	($6,291)	$40,000	$365,915
18	$365,915	-3.10%	($7,318)	$40,000	$307,482
19	$307,482	30.47%	($6,150)	$40,000	$353,150
20	$353,150	7.62%	($7,063)	$40,000	$332,457
21	$332,457	10.08%	($6,649)	$40,000	$318,649
22	$318,649	1.32%	($6,373)	$40,000	$276,401
23	$276,401	37.58%	($5,528)	$40,000	$332,666
24	$332,666	22.96%	($6,653)	$40,000	$360,863
25	$360,863	33.36%	($7,217)	$40,000	$431,624

Figure 23: $600,000 Growth in 25 Years with $40,000 Withdrawals

Look what happens if you do not pull the $40,000 from this GA after each negative market year in Figure 24. The account grows to more than $2.9 million! You may ask, "Why after the bad year and not in the down year?" This is because we don't have a crystal ball to tell us ahead of time when a bad year will occur. So, following bad years (you can refer to Figure 25), we do not pull money from Julio's GA. Instead, we pull money from his SMA, which allows time for his GA to recover from the drop. If your GA drops and you take a withdrawal while it's down, you will have a bigger loss because there are fewer shares to increase in value when the market goes back up.

YR	BALANCE AT BEGINNING OF YEAR	RATE OF RETURN	FEES	WITH-DRAWAL	BALANCE AT END OF YEAR
1	$600,000	-14.67%	($12,000)	$40,000	$461,740
2	$461,740	-26.31%	($9,235)	$0	$333,453
3	$333,453	37.13%	($6,669)	$0	$448,133
4	$448,133	23.82%	($8,963)	$40,000	$503,780
5	$503,780	-7.19%	($10,076)	$40,000	$418,193
6	$418,193	6.52%	($8,364)	$0	$436,547
7	$436,547	18.45%	($8,731)	$40,000	$466,732
8	$466,732	32.45%	($9,335)	$40,000	$565,826
9	$565,826	-4.88%	($11,317)	$40,000	$487,452
10	$487,452	21.50%	($9,749)	$0	$580,426
11	$580,426	22.46%	($11,609)	$40,000	$656,562
12	$656,562	6.22%	($13,131)	$40,000	$643,459
13	$643,459	31.64%	($12,869)	$40,000	$790,097
14	$790,097	18.62%	($15,802)	$40,000	$878,474
15	$878,474	5.18%	($17,569)	$40,000	$865,509
16	$865,509	16.61%	($17,310)	$40,000	$949,082
17	$949,082	31.69%	($18,982)	$40,000	$1,184,832
18	$1,184,832	-3.10%	($23,697)	$40,000	$1,085,147
19	$1,085,147	30.47%	($21,703)	$0	$1,387,481
20	$1,387,481	7.62%	($27,750)	$40,000	$1,423,334
21	$1,423,334	10.08%	($28,467)	$40,000	$1,495,473
22	$1,495,473	1.32%	($29,909)	$40,000	$1,444,920
23	$1,444,920	37.58%	($28,898)	$40,000	$1,908,155
24	$1,908,155	22.96%	($38,163)	$40,000	$2,259,333
25	$2,259,333	33.36%	($45,187)	$40,000	$2,912,795

Figure 24: No Withdrawals After Down Years

Now let's look back at the SMA in Figure 22. Growing steadily at a guaranteed rate, it grows to $837,511. This account is what gives you choice in how you manage your money. Following down years, Julio pulls from his SMA and allows time for his GA to recover in the market. You can see in Figure 25 that the SMA still grows to $501,703. If he'd continued to pull $40,000 each year from the GA and leave the SMA alone, he would have had $1.2 million (add Figures 22 and 23). Thanks to good money decisions, he ended up with $3.4 million (add Figures 24 and 25). When you look at all of your money together, instead of individual, stovepiped accounts, the alignment of your decisions become clear.

YEAR	BALANCE AT BEGINNING OF YEAR	RATE OF RETURN	WITHDRAWAL	BALANCE AT END OF YEAR
1	$400,000	3.00%		$412,000
2	$412,000	3.00%	(40,000.00)	$384,360
3	$384,360	3.00%	(40,000.00)	$355,891
4	$355,891	3.00%		$366,568
5	$366,568	3.00%		$377,565
6	$377,565	3.00%	(40,000.00)	$348,891
7	$348,891	3.00%		$359,358
8	$359,358	3.00%		$370,139
9	$370,139	3.00%		$381,243
10	$381,243	3.00%	(40,000.00)	$352,680
11	$352,680	3.00%		$363,261
12	$363,261	3.00%		$374,159
13	$374,159	3.00%		$385,383
14	$385,383	3.00%		$396,945
15	$396,945	3.00%		$408,853

16	$408,853	3.00%		$421,119
17	$421,119	3.00%		$433,752
18	$433,752	3.00%		$446,765
19	$446,765	3.00%	(40,000.00)	$420,168
20	$420,168	3.00%		$432,773
21	$432,773	3.00%		$445,756
22	$445,756	3.00%		$459,129
23	$459,129	3.00%		$472,903
24	$472,903	3.00%		$487,090
25	$487,090	3.00%		$501,703

**Figure 25: $400,000 Growth in 25 Years at 3%
with $40,000 Withdrawals After Down Years**

I would also continue to adjust the balance of Julio's SMA (guaranteed) and GA (at-risk) accounts according to the Rule of 100; for example, when Julio is seventy years old, he should only have 30% of his money in the market. We will evaluate his health at that time to determine our GA/SMA balance. The Rule of 100 is a guide; we adjust as needed for other variables like longevity.

Julio is in a much better position to survive retirement than he would be if he had acted piecemeal, without a strategy. By changing where his money lived, using the Rule of 100 as a strategic guide, Julio was able to tactically select products (stocks, bonds, mutual funds, annuities, etc.) to manage his risk.

Why didn't Julio's strategy of 'trying out" investing in the market with a small amount of money work so well? If you refer back to Figure 18, you can see that Julio paid a $250 setup fee for his small $10,000 investment, which meant he had a smaller amount of money working for him right from the beginning. Smaller accounts tend to have larger fees, and a ten-year period is almost always too short to see growth in any account, especially a small one.

In Julio's example, he did not make an intentional decision with the money sitting in the money market fund. Using the Rule of 100 as a strategic guide for risk, Julio could expect this outcome. Figure 22 shows how $400,000 would grow over twenty-five years at 3%, assuming no fees.

In Figure 17, it is not until year seven that Julio's account is more than the initial $10,000 he invested. In this scenario, it is likely that Julio would have pulled his money out of the market after two or three years and felt frustrated about having lost half of his initial investment.

The market goes up and down. The sequence of returns matters a great deal at the beginning of an investment cycle. If the market has a few down years when you first start investing (Figure 17), it will take longer to see growth in your account. Conversely, if you luck into a bull market (good returns, as in Figure 19), your account will start growing sooner.

Chapter 6 will discuss what kinds of tactical tools (stocks, bonds, mutual funds, etc.) typically have fees and how the fees are applied. Fees are not bad if you are getting value. You want to avoid paying unnecessary fees. However, paying a fee for a service that sets you up for success is smart.

CHAPTER 5

THE CHARACTERISTICS OF A GOOD INVESTMENT

Any investment in knowledge pays the best interest.

—*Benjamin Franklin*[47]

- Have you ever wondered why you must accept risk to get a good rate of return?
- Do you ever feel pressured to be a do-it-yourselfer with your money, like everyone else has it figured out and you should too?
- What is a traditional versus a Roth individual retirement arrangement (IRA), and why do I care?
- Liquid or illiquid—why are there so many choices?

WHEN I TAKE ON A new horseback riding student, the first thing I have them do is tell me their goals. Then they capture the three new things they learn after each ride in a notebook.

Because I know it works, I've created a notes page for this chapter (Figure 26) to accompany your reading. If you are one of those people who does not want to think about money and investing details, it may have as much to do with your preferred learning style as anything. To maximize your experience with this information, I invite you to answer the questions in Figure 26 by circling answers in the "What would you prefer?" column. If you aren't sure how to answer, take your best guess because you will retain the information as you read if you commit to an answer now. (At this point, you are learning in sponge mode; you do not need to act on anything right now.) This knowledge is foundational to the "What problem are you trying to solve?" question. This chapter will help you start to define what is good for you so you don't feel pressured to do what everyone else is doing.

DEFINITION OF A GOOD INVESTMENT

Directions: Circle your preference

Characteristic	What would you prefer?
Rate of Return	High or Predictable
Risk	High or Low
Easy /Systematic or Research/Heavy	Systematic or Research Heavy
Pay the Taxes as money grows	Low as possible or ordinary rates
Pay Taxes as money is distributed (i.e. retirement)	Low as possible or ordinary rates
Money access	Flexible or Locked in
Money availability	Liquid or illiquid or penalties
Protected from Lawsuits	Yes or No
Self-completing if disabled	Yes or No

Figure 26: Definition of a Good Investment

It can be a relief to learn that some things you thought were immutable laws are really only conventional thinking.

RATE OF RETURN

WHO DOESN'T WANT A GOOD rate of return (ROR)? How about a good return on investment (ROI)? I want these things. I ask you, tongue in cheek, "Doesn't conventional wisdom say you have to accept risk if you want reward?" Playing the lottery means you accept a low risk with a cheap ticket, knowing you have a better chance of getting hit by lightning twice than winning. The message still is: You cannot win if you don't play. I like to have a plan that's more intentional and less play. This is why I talked about strategic versus conventional thinking in Chapter 4: You can get boxed into thought forms that may not be true, just familiar!

When I first started investing in real estate, I quickly found out that banks do not like to loan money to people who are remodeling a home for resale. It's not a good risk for the banks because if you do not complete the remodel, the bank is stuck with a property they cannot sell. This is where hard money lenders come in. These people are willing to lend you money at much higher interest rates than a bank because they will have to take over your project to recoup their investment if you fail in your remodel.

In my first year as a real estate investor, my hard money lender made more money than I did; after I'd paid the closing costs, realtor fees, and hard money fees, there was not a lot of money left over. I continued because I was at least offsetting the cost of my education. I learned that the people who control the cash (banks and hard money lenders) make the rules. And they make the rules in their favor, meaning you accept the risk in any deal. When you are cash-poor, you contribute sweat equity and accept less of a return.

When you invest in the market, market forces drive the rates of return. You take a questionnaire to determine your risk tolerance and get an answer of conservative, moderate, or aggressive. The market choices we have reflect the truth that we must take more risk to have a chance to earn more of a return in the market. When you invest in guaranteed products, a contract drives the rate of return. An annuity with an insurance company is a contract, so you agree up front to what kind of return you will make. This is a very conservative approach. The question is: Do you have to accept risk to reach your personal financial goals? If so, how much? Are you looking for a product solution or a strategy solution? What if you could select a strategy that uses a product instead of buying a product that dictates your strategy?

The way you mitigate your risk is through education about both products and strategy. It is so important to understand that a product and a strategy are not the same thing. I point this out because most of the marketing you see online and on TV drives you to buy a product—this mutual fund or that annuity. There are many good products available, and the key to selecting a product is knowing first what problem you are trying to solve.

A fixed annuity product does not require much education because it is a guaranteed contract that ensures you will not lose any value in your account. Annuity companies use the market as a ruler of performance to determine how much interest they will pay during a given year, but your account will never earn less than zero. This product serves our human desire for safety and security. The market has a lot of product options, such as stocks, bonds, mutual funds, and ETFs, and study is needed to make educated choices.

You can research different options in the market. Blue chip companies, defined as financially stable and dividend-paying, like Apple Inc., Coca-Cola, and GE, have a long history of steady performance and are viewed as less risky. Conversely, junk bonds are issued by companies that are struggling financially and have a high risk of not making their interest payments, so this debt security is rated poorly by credit agencies. If you don't do your research, the market can feel a bit like gambling. After you decide how much risk you want to assume, research will allow you to make the best choices supporting your planning goals.

Real estate is a good example when thinking about the need for education about investing. So many shows on TV make real estate seem as easy and simple as a makeover. Reality is quite different. If you're going to invest in real estate, it requires a good education, and many people get burned because they do not even know *how* to do their due diligence.

You make your money when you buy in real estate. This concept seems a bit counterintuitive, but it's important. Success requires analysis of a property to account for rental vacancy months, the cost of new paint and carpet between tenants, a maintenance budget, and so on— essentially, planning for the expected *and* the unexpected. If you buy a property and just hope it will grow in value, you may get lucky, but a more analytical approach will go a long way toward ensuring that you don't lose money. Many people struggle with their real estate investments because they pay full market value and then hope the value of the property will go up in time. This may happen—or it may not happen for a long time, or even ever. Also, a lot of novice real estate investors do not realize that they need an exit strategy. For example, if you buy a property to remodel and then sell, will you be able to rent out the property if it does not sell? Can you charge enough rent to pay your hard money lender? Will you be able to refinance with a bank for a more reasonable note?

The market is more complex than real estate because there are a lot of options to choose from and different strategies to use. Most people do not have the time for the due diligence required to pick investments that have a chance of performing as desired, much less identify a strategy. They end up listening to the radio or watching money shows on TV and making their selections based on fairly old news. People tend to give themselves credit for being a genius if their investment rises and attribute a drop to bad luck or bad advice. You usually hear the good news stories, or the wistfulness—"If I'd only purchased Amazon when they were first on the market…" Likewise, most people use the buy and hold (hope) strategy because they feel like it's saving them money on fees. When you're young, buying an index fund to follow the market can work because you have time to recover from big market downturns. You would be wise to consider more active management as you get older, though. Active management can range from a quarterly rebalancing of your accounts to a 60/40 equity/bond ratio to having a manager actually move your money to cash or cash equivalents when it looks like the market may be headed for a big drop.

As in real estate, you need to consider your exit strategies when you write up your financial plan. For example, you don't want to put money into a tax-advantaged account and then need the money before you reach retirement age. Pulling money out of these accounts early incurs penalty fees. A holistic plan has a balance of emergency, liquid, and illiquid investments so you retain flexibility to respond to life's unexpected issues.

Part of your research should include fees, so you know how professionals get paid. The simple buy and hold strategy should have very few fees attached. You should verify this. Active management will have fees attached. It usually costs 1-3% of assets under management to have more focused attention on your accounts.

Here is the key thing to remember about investing: You always pay a fee. No financial manager or company is running a charity, so there is always a cost. In the case of annuities, you pay with a commitment of time. You agree to leave your money in the annuity for seven to ten years, generally, and the insurance company agrees that your account will never lose value. Your money can grow, but you will never lose value. Why would a company would offer this deal? The insurance company agrees to cover your annuity value in the down years because you agree to let the company have your money to invest for seven to ten years.

Long-term investments are more reliable, and because insurance companies are able to invest billions of dollars (the pot of money from all the collective investors), they can make more secure long-term investments. Because the sums of money invested are so big, they do not need to make huge returns to gain big profits. I mentioned assets under management percentages earlier. 1% of $1 billion will keep the lights on for a while, so insurance companies agree to guarantee your money in order to make a whole lot of money themselves. This is similar to what banks do. Banks do not generally offer good returns because they do not have surrender fees over long periods of time. However, banks will incentivize keeping more money in savings—for example, by offering no-fee savings accounts if you agree to keep a minimum balance of $25,000. We are trained to avoid any and all fees, and the bank's offer is more convenient; doing nothing is easier than doing something. But this is a perfect example of how changing where your money lives—to an account that pays some interest—can change how your financial world grows.

So, does a good investment have a high or predictable rate of return? You must answer this question with a question. What problem are you trying to solve? If you are young, have time for growth, and can weather a few market downturns, a more aggressive approach is doable. If you are nearing retirement and have already grown a large nest egg, you may elect to protect part of those savings with some predictable returns. If you grew up in a family with money stress, you may want to have a predictable rate of return so there is more stability in your life. Having a high or predictable rate of return is not as important as having a plan. High risk without a plan can make you a larger pot of money, but how do you know when you have enough? Predictable investment is, well, predictable, but how do you know if you're on track to reach the number you need? Think about your investment dollars like arrows in a quiver. If you are shooting blindfolded, you will run out of arrows and have to hope a few of them hit the target. However, if you remove your blindfold and aim at your target, you have a much higher chance of hitting the bullseye.

RISK

How much money are you willing to lose? Have you ever filled out the investment questionnaires (that remind me of a beauty magazine quiz)? You know, the ones that ask a few questions with an assigned point value and have you tally the points to determine if you are conservative, moderate, or aggressive? A lot of potential options are summed up in these simple assessments. If your magazine quiz told you that you are fun and flirty or serious and stoic, would you make a life choice based on this result?

I don't expect you to remember every kind of risk that exists, but I do want you to know that there are layers of complexity involved in the seemingly simple question of risk. If you are making your own investment choices, it's good to understand some of the driving factors behind different options. If you are working with a financial planner, it's beneficial to have some solid background so you can ask informed questions about your money.

How many kinds of investment risk do you know about? If you google "types of investment risks," you will come up with a potential laundry list that includes market, inflation, reinvestment, investment rate, currency rate, unsystematic, business, financial, default, political (for example, trade wars with China), investment management, liquidity, and tax. You're probably familiar with inflation as part of market risk, and I will go into that in a moment. How about unsystematic risk, including political risk? Why should you care? Risk is about so much more than the result of some short investment questionnaire that tells you are either a conservative, moderate, or aggressive investor.

Systematic risk, or market risk, is just part of the market. You have probably heard that diversification is good. You shouldn't put all your eggs in one basket. Including five different kinds of mutual funds in your portfolio does not get rid of market risk because they are all in the market; they are all in one basket.

Inflation risk is included in market risk. It is the chance that the real value of your assets can change. One way to think about this is with soft drinks. How much did a can of Coke cost when you were a kid? In the 1980s, I could get a can of soda for about fifty cents. In 2021, a Coke from a vending machine costs me at least $2.50, and it's usually in a bottle, not a can. The takeaway here is that the basic things you're used to buying will probably cost more in the future. This is why the myth that you can use 75% of your current income as a planning factor for retirement is flawed. If you plan to live on a reduced amount of money, I will ask you to consider what basics you plan to give up in the future. If you plan to give up soda, this plan might work out for your health.

Unsystematic risk is a type of risk you may not have considered but makes perfect sense once you think about it. An example of unsystematic risk is when you have all your money in one spot. If you have only SuperGreatFundX, you might end up rich or a pauper depending on how it performs. This can apply to any single-focus effort, for example, if you only buy and sell low-flow toilets. I met an investor once who used his Roth IRA to bulk-purchase low-flow toilets. He made himself known to builders and they would purchase these toilets from him because even with his price markup, it was still cheaper than buying retail toilets one or two at a time. Toilet guy made money because he solved a niche problem, but he had little margin if the environment changed. Just imagine if all of a sudden people decided they wanted to go even greener and have outhouses. What good would a storage shed full of toilets be then?

Political risk is a type of unsystematic risk. It was a big "aha" for me when I first learned about it. I thought, "What could politics have to do with money?" As the world becomes more connected, events on the political stage impact what happens here in America more and more. Think about how the trade wars with China beginning in 2018 were in the news. Farmers in Iowa felt the effects because of the amount of soybeans China was buying. Do you remember the old saying, "What does that have to do with the price of tea in China?" It turns out, China matters more than we might like.

Legislation has impacted pensions. Congress has a huge impact on how you are allowed to save and grow your money. Here are a few examples. You don't have to memorize them, but I want you to be aware that legislation impacts risk in your retirement planning.

The Employee Retirement Income Security Act (ERISA) established the traditional (regular) IRA, among many other things.[48] The traditional IRA allows you to save a certain percentage of earnings in an account that earns a tax deduction right away, and the money grows tax-deferred. You pay taxes on this money at your ordinary tax rate when you pull the money out. An IRA makes sense to the government because allowing your money to grow means more tax dollars for them when you pull your money out. Traditional IRAs have required minimum withdrawals, so the government is guaranteed to collect tax dollars. 5% of $500,000 is more attractive than 5% of $5,000. Encouraging Americans to save creates a future pot of money to support the government. Remember, investment laws are not created out of the goodness of anyone's hearts; there's always a motive. "Follow the money" is a catchphrase for a reason.

According to Peer Fiss, the Deficit Reduction Act of 1984 revised the tax code so as to deny tax benefits to "excess" golden parachutes. Golden parachutes for executives were limited to about three times an executive's base compensation. However, instead of curbing excessive parachutes, the law had the perverse effect of legitimizing payments up to this threshold, and it became the norm.[49] This is an example of how the legislation benefitted the top 1%.

The Roth IRA was introduced as part of the Taxpayer Relief Act of 1997.[50] This act of legislation again changed how Americans saved money. A big attraction of Roth IRAs is that you pay taxes when you fund your account, so the money grows tax-free and you can pull the money out of your account tax-free. Congressional decisions can change how you save for retirement. How attractive is it to have a Roth account that is not subject to changes in tax rates? You could argue that Congress could change the Roth IRA rules. But if you had to bet, would you expect Congress to get together to make this change? I wouldn't take that bet.

Does it seem farfetched that this political risk could really make a difference for you personally? It did to me. I was a young Air Force captain in 1997. I had had a traditional IRA for a few years. I asked Phil, my financial advisor at the time, if I should get a Roth. He was not very helpful and, knowing what I know now, did not really act as a good fiduciary, either.

Phil's first response was to shrug his shoulders and say, "Do you want a Roth?"

I was confused because I thought he was the expert. I didn't know why he was throwing the question back at me.

"It seems like a Roth makes sense based on what I've read, but you're my advisor," I said.

What I did not connect the dots on at the time is that Phil was paid a percentage of assets under management. If I converted my traditional IRA to a Roth IRA, my account would probably be smaller after paying taxes and result in a smaller paycheck for Phil. Follow the money.

Phil replied, "You're going have to pay some taxes."

He left me hanging again, like I was supposed to pick up on some subtext.

He then explained that I could pay the taxes inside or outside of the account. What I took from that was, I could write a check to pay the taxes right away or just pay from my account. While this was true, Phil did not explain the impact of the different choices. If I paid outside of the account, I would be able to convert the full amount of my traditional IRA to a Roth IRA. I had $45,000 in my account; if I paid taxes outside of my account (approximately 26%, or $11,700), $45,000 could have grown to $145,952 by the time I was sixty (assuming a 4% average rate of return). Instead, I paid the taxes from my account, so I only transferred $33,300. This option projected growth to $108,005 by the time I was sixty, assuming a 4% average rate of return in the account. It was frustrating not to have this explained to me.

The takeaway here is that, in addition to time being your best friend, legislation drastically affects how much of your money is yours at the end of the day. It's not necessary for you to become a history buff and research legislation. The important thing is, you now know that there are different types of risk that impact how you make retirement planning choices. When you understand the pros and cons of different kinds of investments, as I share in Chapter 6, you can build a plan in which the whole is greater than the sum of its parts.

HOW MUCH MONEY ARE YOU WILLING TO LOSE?

NOW FOR THE CLOSER, MORE personal risk question that taps into the human drivers of fear and greed. You might remember Tina, back in Chapter 4, and our conversation about how much money she was willing to lose. Figure 26 asked you to pick either high or low risk. Everyone wants high rates of return. Conventional thought assumes we must then accept higher risk, which pushes our fear button.

You can select some risky investments and potentially have a high rate of return, but you must know that you could also suffer a big loss. If you want to be in the market with a growth strategy but want professional management, you will have to pay for this service. Paying for a service pushes our greed button because, by nature, we do not want to pay for anything we feel we could get for free. Active management can be as simple as having your portfolio rebalanced every quarter to a 60/40 balance of equities and bonds. For example, if your bonds perform well and your ratio shifts to 50/50, a rebalance will sell some bonds and buy more equities to achieve your desired 60/40 balance.

Active management with downside protection should include experts watching the market every day and making decisions about when it's time to move out of the market, to cash or cash equivalents, and then go back into the market when it looks like there is an upswing. If you are paying for this service, your accounts should perform better than a simple index fund over a five-to-ten-year period. In any given period, a simple index fund can provide better returns than a managed account simply because the index fund does not have an associated management fee. A managed account should not drop as low as an index fund because a manager should be identifying risk and moving your money out of the market when necessary.

Back in Chapter 1, I discussed why it is important not to lose money, especially as you are approaching retirement. In that chapter, I defined accounts in the market, or any accounts associated with risk, as growth accounts (GAs). Blue chip stocks are fairly conservative and predictable, but they still have some risk. Annuities are often characterized as safe money accounts (SMAs). Annuities are guaranteed contracts, so the risk of loss is not associated with them. However, annuities have surrender periods and will charge fees if you pull your money out of your accounts sooner than agreed upon in the contract.

Without context, there are no right or wrong, good or bad ways to invest your money. It's all about using investment options that solve your particular problem. For example, if you are seventy-five and have a terminal illness, it would be illogical to put your money into an annuity with a seven-to-ten-year surrender period.

So, how much are you willing to lose? This is closely tied to the age question. Risks you take during your earning years are very different from recommended risks when you are retired. Many different factors drive risk, and you now know that it has layers of complexity. You are starting to see why decisions are interrelated. Legislative risk can affect taxes, which is why you want to move as much of your money as possible toward tax-free environments. Risk also depends on how much money you have, the lifestyle you lead, and other factors. Risk is an individual question. What is good for your neighbor may or may not be good for you.

EASY/SYSTEMATIC OR RESEARCH-HEAVY

ARE YOU A DO-IT-YOURSELFER WHEN it comes to money? I want you to think about this for a minute and be honest with yourself. Some people truly are finance geeks. They subscribe to multiple financial blogs. They watch TV shows and YouTube videos about money. They have subscriptions to *Money* magazine. I find that a lot of people want to believe they are do-it-yourselfers. It's the American way.

At this point, you may realize that I connect a wide variety of stories with valuable lessons that have helped me understand financial decision-making. For instance, I have a German friend, Stina, who gave me dressage horseback riding lessons. I shared with her that I never had a formal riding lesson until I was in my mid-thirties. (When I was a kid, my neighbor would buy horses from the local sale and put me up on them, as much for entertainment value as horse training. I was always happy to sit on a horse, even one trying to dump me in the dirt.)

Rolling her eyes, Stina said, "Typical American." I asked her what she meant. She said, "You also see this on the ski slopes. The Americans are obvious because you are the ones having all the crashes. We have to ski around you like obstacles. Would it kill you all to take a lesson once in a while?"

I thought about it, and it's true—it's really not the American way to take a lesson. Cowboy symbolism is all about doing it yourself. You had what you could make happen.

We Americans can be a little suspicious of easy or systematic processes. Mass marketing affirms that we should all be do-it-yourselfers and avoid fees. "What's it going cost me?"

My husband, Kris, and I went through this when it came to hiring a housekeeper. When we were first married, the idea of having a housekeeper felt highly indulgent, and we really couldn't afford it. We were also establishing the ground rules of our relationship, and I knew that I was not interested in being either the nag or the maid. The rub was, I didn't want to live in a messy bachelor pad either. We compromised by getting a housekeeper to come in and do all the deep cleaning once a month. We still pick things up, and knowing our housekeeper is coming helps us keep things in check during the weeks between cleaning times. We pay for something we could easily do ourselves. But with both of us working full-time, we now head out for a hike on Saturday morning and come home to a clean house instead of spending a large chunk of the weekend cleaning and then being too tired for anything else. We've provided someone with a job, and we have time to work on our relationship instead of being grumpy about who's doing more than their fair share of work.

The housekeeper's fee is an expense we pay because we get something of value in return. When you are considering the type of investment process you want to use, it's important to think about more than just the fees. If the cost associated with an easy or systematic process is adding value and a sense of well-being to your relationships and your life (even if you're single), it may very well be worth it. Please note that "easy and systematic" can be as simple as having 10% of your paycheck go directly into a savings account.

Now, if you are one of those people who will dig in, do your research, and feel good about it, you *should* do it yourself. But if, in reality, you are one of those people who would *like* to do it yourself but find that you do not follow through, be honest. Not taking action because you're not doing the mental task you've assigned yourself is making a decision. This is very much like the mental gymnastics we go through with eating. "I'll start eating better after Thanksgiving is over." "Christmas is just around the corner, so I'll start eating better after that." And so it goes.

It's important to remember that time is your best friend, as I discussed in Chapter 3. Please don't be suspicious of easy or think that easy is the enemy of good. A systematic investment you actually make will grow your wealth. So many people have an ideal in their head that never makes it into action. Coulda, shoulda, woulda—we've all been there. A systematic investment process will almost always pay dividends—your future self will thank you.

In summary, "Would you prefer an investment that is easy and systematic, or research-heavy?" is really a question about time and personality. If you enjoy all things money and have time, do it yourself. If you enjoy all things money but are a doctor starting a new practice, get help until you have time to research your investments. If you feel concerned about paying too many fees, you should invest on your own *if* you will follow through with your research. If you feel concerned about paying too many fees but understand that fees are okay if you are getting some value, work with a professional. The key is to know yourself, be honest with yourself, and take the actions that will best help you reach your financial goals.

TAXES: AS MONEY GROWS

"Do I want a traditional or Roth IRA?" This question has an "it depends" answer. If you use an IRS status like a Roth IRA, you pay taxes on your money when you deposit it into your account. This is a no-brainer when you're young. You're not making that much, so the tax break is minimal. The money in this account can now compound over time and, based on today's rules, you will be able to pull it out tax-free after you are fifty-nine and a half. Would you rather pay tax on the seed or the crop? Usually you want to pay tax on the seed because it's a smaller amount. For example, 5% of $5,000 is $250, while 5% of $500,000 is $25,000. The real question is, why would you want a traditional IRA?

This is a question that your financial planner and CPA may have different opinions on. A CPA's role is to save you money each year. A financial planner's role is to save you money in retirement. As your taxes get more complicated, there are more considerations, which is why you want your CPA and financial planner to work together. This decision should not be a guessing game; you should know why you select the account.

TAXES: AS MONEY IS DISTRIBUTED DURING RETIREMENT

RULES, RULES, RULES. YOU MAY consider a traditional IRA if you make too much money to qualify for a Roth IRA, or if your accountant identifies that the traditional IRA tax deduction in a given year will benefit you more than putting money in a Roth. In both a Roth and traditional IRAs, you pay taxes at your ordinary income rate. The conventional thinking is that you will be in a lower tax bracket when you retire, so you will pay less in taxes and therefore a traditional IRA makes sense. This is not always the case. First of all, many people choose to continue working well past a normal retirement age because they enjoy what they are doing. Some of them are making more money during their last few working years than they did previously.

My mom, Jeanne, went to medical school in her forties, after I left for college, and retired from practice at sixty-five. However, she continues to teach at the medical school as a contractor and is making good money. She is older than seventy, so she's collecting her full Social

Security. However, because her IRAs are traditional, she is required to take out required minimum withdrawals even though she doesn't need the money. It's always better when you have full control over your money and IRS rules don't dictate when you have to spend it.

You want to understand your financial goal and pick an account that supports it. Taxes have a significant impact on how much spendable money you have in your retirement accounts. I recommend working toward having as much of your money in tax-free vehicles as possible so you have better access to it.

FLEXIBLE OR LOCKED-IN

WOULD YOU PREFER TO HAVE flexibility when it comes to your money? Probably. Most of us would. It's nice to have an investment that allows you to adjust how much you invest. There are times when you may want to have a little more cash on hand, like when you're switching jobs. The counterpoint is, you may prefer structure and invest more diligently knowing your investment is locked in with monthly or quarterly contributions, for example. While it can be seductive to stop investing this way and play, you may be more likely to stick to a plan if it is mandatory.

You will probably enjoy having a mix of both flexible and locked-in investments. For example, if you set up a monthly contribution from your paycheck or savings account to your Roth IRA, you'll have a structure that supports a good habit. It is also nice to have some flexibility so you can temporarily adjust your investment amounts if life throws you unexpected curveballs.

LIQUID, ILLIQUID, OR PENALTIES

"LIQUID OR ILLIQUID" IS NOT an either-or proposition, but rather a question of balance. Your emergency fund should be liquid, meaning that you can access the money easily and quickly. An example of an illiquid investment is real estate. If you have a rental property but need to pull the money out of it, you will have to sell. You cannot walk into your spare bedroom and take cash out of it. Real estate depends heavily on the housing market. Being forced to sell a house can result in losses for you. IRAs and annuities can have penalties for early withdrawal, so they are considered illiquid.

A couple came to see me because they were getting close to retirement and worried. In their early fifties, they had cashed out their traditional IRA and joined with a partner to purchase some real estate. Think about this. They took $450,000 and liquidated it early, so they paid $45,000 in penalties. They paid almost another $100,000 in taxes based on their ordinary income tax rate, higher in their fifties than it would be in retirement because they were still working. They only had $305,000 in spendable money. They put this into real estate, another illiquid investment. They came to me at sixty-two, wondering how they were going to retire because the bulk of their money was tied up in a piece of property for the foreseeable future.

It's good to have balance in your portfolio. You need long-term investments like your retirement accounts—money you will not touch for twenty to thirty years. In the meantime, life keeps happening, so you need an emergency fund and access to some investments that are growing with a better rate of return than a bank account. Liquid money protects your retirement accounts. It also prevents you from using the worst option when you need quick cash: credit cards.

PROTECTED FROM LAWSUITS

DO YOU PREFER THAT YOUR money grow and also be protected from lawsuits? Not all accounts are protected from lawsuits, but some are, and this is good information to have. This goes back to intentionality. You do not need to be an expert in picking stocks, but you should understand why you have your money in different kinds of accounts.

Advertising focuses our attention on growing our accounts as much as possible, and accumulation is important; however, little to no marketing attention is devoted to protecting your nest egg as you grow it. You want to enjoy the fruits of your labor in retirement. In Chapter 4, I talked about strategy. This characteristic of a good investment addresses the fact that you want to have both offensive and defensive components as part of your overall strategy. As I discussed in Chapter 4, conventional thinking tends to concentrate most on the "Get it" phase but rarely addresses the need to protect your money as it grows.

SELF-COMPLETING IF DISABLED

THIS IS ANOTHER QUALITY OF an investment to be aware of while you are in the "Get it" phase. Some investments will include disability protection as an option, and some will not. This is a good question for you to consider. If you are the sole breadwinner for a family, it may be more important to you than if you are single. However, a good friend of mine ran a financial practice that focused on surgeons. It was very important for his clients to have disability insurance because if something happened, particularly to their hands, they would not be able to make a living in their trained profession. You must keep asking, "What problem am I trying to solve?" The answer is much more nuanced than just growing your savings as much as possible.

TO WRAP UP

PLANNING FOR YOUR FINANCIAL FUTURE has layers of complexity. It is human nature to want to boil things down to simple yes-or-no decisions. The reality is, there is so much more to consider than the math needed to calculate a good rate of return. I've discussed factors that can color choices you make, like political risk and your personal idiosyncrasies. All the information you could want is available; the real limitation is how much time you have to digest it and decide what you will do. Now that you understand some basic parameters of a good investment, you are prepared to ask a professional financial advisor educated questions. You don't have to be a financial expert to be in the driver's seat of your financial world, you just need to be able to judge whether you are getting advice that moves you forward in a positive direction.

KEY TAKEAWAYS

- When it comes to rate of return, select a strategy that uses a product rather than buying a product that dictates your strategy.
- Honest conversation about risk includes the question, "How much are you willing to lose?"
- Unless you are truly doing in-depth research, work with a professional to create a systematic approach to building your financial security.
- Your financial strategy should drive your money toward tax-free accounts.
- Have a balance of flexible and structured investments to allow for life's ups and downs.
- Think about protecting your money as it's growing, not just in the "Got it" phase of your financial life cycle.

TAKE ACTION EXERCISE

Now that you've gone through this chapter, revisit the "What would you prefer?" column of Figure 26. Have any of your answers changed? In Figure 27, jot down a quick reason for your preference. Remember, your reason can be based in fact or emotion. What is important is that you understand yourself. This will help you with the next chapter, where I start covering different investment products and what may be a fit for you and your lifestyle.

Characteristic	What would you prefer?	Why?
Rate of Return	High or Predictable	
Risk	High or Low	
Easy /Systematic or Research/Heavy	Systematic or Research Heavy	
Pay the Taxes as money grows	Low as possible or ordinary rates	
Pay Taxes as money is distributed (i.e. retirement)	Low as possible or ordinary rates	
Money access	Flexible or Locked in	
Money availability	Liquid or illiquid or penalties	
Protected from Lawsuits	Yes or No	
Self-completing if disabled	Yes or No	

Figure 27: Definition of a Good Investment—Fillable Table

After you've done this exercise, you've completed Chapter 5 and have the foundational knowledge to start thinking about what is important for you. It is normal to feel a bit lost or confused when people around you talk about investing, money, and retirement, throwing around terms you may not be familiar with or things you have not thought much about. However, people will speak with authority even when they really don't know much about a subject. In my military career, being around people in the medical profession, and especially while learning finance, I have found that once I know some of the lingo, people I used to think were geniuses do not seem as smart as I initially thought. You can feel confident in your decisions. I want you to see that you have options to pick from.

CHAPTER 6

HOW YOUR MONEY WORKS

Successful investing is about managing risk, not avoiding it.

—*Benjamin Graham*[51]

- Should you get a Roth IRA?
- Have you ever felt either overwhelmed or uninterested in the plethora of investment options?
- Are you fee-focused or value-focused?
- Have you ever wondered how to link your financial decisions to the freedom and security you want for your life?

BY NOW, I HOPE YOU recognize that it is more important for you to ask good questions than it is for you to know lots of answers. So much information is available on the internet today. Getting access to ideas is not a problem. Sifting through it all is the challenge. In the last chapter, I talked about the characteristics of a good investment. Now I build on that foundational discussion. In this chapter, I look at the most common types of investment options and see how the characteristics of good investments do or do not apply to them.

I hope you'll come away from this chapter with a better understanding of why good advice varies so much. "It depends" is not a cop out. "It depends" is important because a plan should be very specific to you. I have yet to meet the average American. We all have things in common, but an individual plan is put together based on many factors.

SHOULD I GET A ROTH?

I GET THIS QUESTION A lot, especially on my radio show[52]: "Should I get a Roth?" We need to unpack this a bit because I think the real question is, "How can I pay less in taxes?"

A Roth IRA is just an IRS tax status that I like to think of as a gym bag. You can put a lot of different things into this bag: a soccer ball, a football, a baseball mitt, or cleats.

We have another bag called a traditional IRA. You can put the same equipment into it. So what's the difference? With the Roth, you pay taxes when you put your money in the bag. With the traditional IRA, you pay taxes when you pull the money out.

Now for the real question: "How can I pay less in taxes?"

There are more bags that can give tax advantages.

Can you see how the question, "Should I get a Roth?" needs more context? To keep this simple, I will ask you, "What sport are you trying to play?" I

TRADITIONAL IRA

A TAX-ADVANTAGED ACCOUNT THAT LOWERS YOUR TAXABLE INCOME WHEN YOU CONTRIBUTE. YOU PAY ORDINARY INCOME TAX RATES WHEN YOU WITHDRAW YOUR MONEY LATER.

ROTH IRA

A TAX-ADVANTAGED ACCOUNT THAT REQUIRES YOU TO PAY TAXES WHEN YOU CONTRIBUTE. YOU PAY NO TAXES WHEN YOU WITHDRAW YOUR MONEY LATER.

cannot tell you whether you need a soccer ball, a baseball, or a mitt until I know your sport. This question requires more context because you have more options. You may get hung up trying to find the magic equipment, the amazing baseball mitt the guy at work is going on and on about. The problem is, you need to pick your sport first, and *then* select your equipment.

SPORTS ANALOGY

WHAT PROBLEM ARE YOU TRYING TO SOLVE? = WHAT SPORT ARE YOU PLAYING?

STOCKS, BONDS, MUTUAL FUNDS, ETFS, ETC. = "EQUIPMENT."

DO YOU PICK YOUR BALL OR YOUR SPORT FIRST? WOULD YOU BUY A SOCCER BALL AND THEN REALIZE YOU'RE ON THE FOOTBALL TEAM?

This is what happens so often with investing. A client came in with a burning question. He really wanted to use municipal bonds for his emergency fund because his friend at work told him the bonds were great. They are tax-free.

I said, "Tax-free is good, but did you say you wanted an emergency fund?"

"Yeah, that's right!"

"Are these bonds liquid? Can you easily access your money if you need it in a hurry?"

"Well, I don't know," he said with a sheepish look and a shrug.

In this scenario, the emergency fund is his sport. Are the municipal bonds the right "equipment" for his gym bag?

As you learned in Chapter 5, there are pros and cons to each investment tool, the equipment you select. An emergency fund needs to be liquid so you have immediate access. Bonds can be set up different ways and have different setup fees, so they may not be liquid or great for short-term cash needs. There are other kinds of "equipment" that work better for emergency funds.

You want to be successful; I want you to be successful, and this is where we must create context and understanding around how to get there. When you understand what an investment vehicle does, you can start to understand why it may or may not be a fit for you. My expectation is not that you will now go and create your own financial plan; my goal is for you to feel a new level of comfort and have a resource you can refer to quickly when you begin building your unique plan. I walk through the steps to build your strategy in Chapter 9.

MY HOLISTIC FINANCIAL BUBBLE

I'M INTRODUCING A NEW CONCEPTUAL model, "My Holistic Financial Bubble," (Figure 28) to accompany the holistic approach (the 3-Step Financial Plan Framework) I introduced in Chapter 4. A key takeaway from this book is that different investment tools have contracts, legislation, and other impacts to your bottom line beyond fees.

Many of you are familiar with simple ledger math. Here's what I put in: Subtract fees and what I have left over is mine. I've noticed over and over that many people—to their detriment—get hung up on fees. Overpaying fees is a problem. Paying for a service that adds value is smart. Almost all accounts have fees, even savings accounts. Sometimes, for example, banks make introductory offers of free savings accounts for veterans, firefighters, and people in other specific categories. But, generally even savings accounts have fees because the account is a service the bank is providing to you. In the upcoming sections, I include a financial bubble example to go with each account type from Figure 29. I ask you to start thinking about your money in a different way. Add your numbers to your financial bubble, Figure 28, as best you can off the top of your head. You will refine your numbers later. Identifying what you have in your financial bubble before we define all the benefits of each account will allow you to begin to see how a holistic view of your money, versus a restricted and separate (stovepiped) organization of it, gives you more control and freedom. Now you're ready to learn Figure 29.

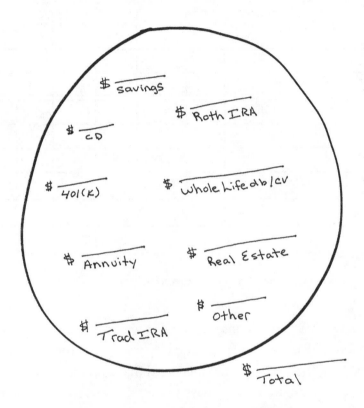

Figure 28: My Holistic Financial Bubble
Directions: Add the types of accounts you have to your financial bubble (Figure 28). Add any additional assets you may have, such as real estate or other business investments.

INVESTMENT TYPE COMPARISONS

FILL OUT THE TABLE IN Figure 29 as you read the chapter. The key thing is for you to gain basic financial understanding. Having this table to refer to is almost like having the letters of the alphabet so you can spell words.

CHARAC- TERISTICS	ACCOUNT TYPES								
	SAVINGS	CD	ROTH IRA	TRAD. IRA	401(K), 403(B), TSP, ETC.	NON- QUAL.	WHOLE LIFE	TERM LIFE	ANNUITY
FEES*									
INTEREST EARNED									
TAXES									
GUARANTEES									
DISABILITY									
LAWSUIT PROT.									
CAN BORROW									
DEATH BENEFIT									

Figure 29: Comparisons of Basic Investment Types Based on Rules

I created this table to consolidate a lot of information on one page. I have found that my clients' eyes quickly glaze over when they have to look at multiple pages of numbers, and that communication stops at that point. I also want you to have an easy way to reference different investment options and avoid confusion when you hear marketing messages or advice from friends.

As I discussed in Chapter 5, there is always either a product solution or a strategy solution. Figure 29 lists the account types that are the most common product solutions. Take a minute to digest these account types so you will be better able to understand and retain the strategy discussion in the upcoming chapters, particularly in the end-of-chapter case studies. This is a learning styles note, if you prepare your brain with a framework of information, the details will have a place to go.

My chemistry teacher at the Academy wanted us to preread the end of chapter questions before we had our lesson discussion. He said it was like putting hooks up on the wall to hang your coats by the door. If there are no hooks, then all your coats (in his analogy his lesson) will just fall on the floor. I discuss the characteristics each investment tool includes. First, you need to understand the account types so you can think strategically. Strategy is where you change where your money lives to change how your financial world grows.

Have your pen ready so you can add "yes" or "no" to the boxes in Figure 29—depending on whether an account type has a particular characteristic—as you go through the material. Some of the answers will be a qualified yes or no because this stuff is complicated and hangs out in the shades of gray. As I discussed in "How to Use This Book," the physical act of writing while you read anchors concepts for better retention (even if you never look back at your notes). I go through each account type one by one and identify the characteristics of each. You will find a yes or no in bold at the end of each discussion so you can circle it and complete the table.

Please note that this table will look the same for everyone because this information is factual. The IRS defines the tax-advantaged rules for a Roth or traditional IRA. Whole life, or permanent, insurance provides a tax-free death benefit. A savings account at a bank is FDIC-protected. What will vary is the "equipment" you choose. For example, you can set up a savings account at almost any bank, but each bank will pay different interest rates and have different account fees.

Whole life insurance is a contract between you and an insurance company and can be designed for your portfolio in many different ways. IRAs are like empty gym bags that provide either tax-now or tax-later options. You can put many different kinds of sports equipment in your bag. You can have mutual funds or ETFs, or own property or other businesses inside your IRA "gym bag." Figure 29 helps organize the most common account types or "gym bags" so you have a frame of reference for financial discussion. A more in-depth explanation of each account type follows if you want to learn more.

Figure 29 is not going to make you a financial wizard, but it will arm you with some good questions to ask when you're speaking with a financial advisor. I will highlight right up front that while I am trying to keep this as simple as possible, it is complex. You may need to mix accounts with different IRS (federal) and state regulations, market rules, and contract rules to support your desired outcome in the best possible way. I believe that once you complete this table, you will have the working knowledge to advocate for yourself and know if you are being presented with good options.

When I bought my first home and signed the paperwork, they kept going on about the points and what a good deal I was getting. I asked what a point was and got a peculiar look. There was a momentary pause in the conversation, like, "Why are you asking such an incredibly stupid question?" It turns out a point is just a percentage. I had two semesters of calculus, so I understand percentages. But I was feeling small and stupid after the look I got, so I just did as I was told and was unable to advocate for myself in that moment.

With these basic building blocks, you will be able to understand what makes sense, ask good questions, and feel more comfortable and confident as you build your custom financial plan. In Chapter 5, you learned about the characteristics of a good investment. Now I'm going to define which of these characteristics are included in some very common investment vehicles.

THE WAY AHEAD: CONNECT FINANCIAL DECISIONS TO LIFE DECISIONS

IN CHAPTER 3, YOU VISUALIZED what financial success looks like for you. You should be getting an idea of how much risk you are comfortable having in your financial plan that will drive your specific strategy. Tactical execution involves picking the investment tools (account types) you want to use from Figure 29. I want to introduce you to this table now because the account types listed in it are what you are probably familiar with from advertisements and conversations with friends and coworkers. This is your reference document, right here. After you have defined your vision and strategy to include risk tolerance, you can start to move from plan to action.

Now I go through each account type, one by one, to determine its characteristics. After you fill out the table, you will see if you have good alignment in your own financial world. Or you may discover that you are using municipal bonds for your emergency fund account. Either way, you will be better positioned to make wise choices.

At the end of each discussion, you will find the answer to add to the table in bold type.

SAVINGS

FEES (Y/N)?

Savings accounts with most banks have either no fees or small fees; this usually depends on the size of the account. Some accounts have a minimum balance requirement in exchange for a reduction in fees. For example, if you have $25,000 in a savings account at the bank, you may not have any fees. **(Qualified No)**

INTEREST EARNED (Y/N)?

Right now, savings accounts do not earn very much interest. It's always fascinating because at times, these accounts have earned more interest. For example, in the 1960s, the average savings interest rate was 7-8.5%. **(Qualified Yes)**

Taxes *(Y/N)?*

Do you pay taxes on a savings account? Well, yes, but you only pay taxes on interest earned. The bad and the good news about savings accounts is, they don't earn much interest, but then you don't pay much tax. **(Yes)**

Guaranteed *(Y/N)?*

Are savings accounts guaranteed? Banks have Federal Deposit Insurance Corporation (FDIC) protection.[53] The standard insurance amount is $250,000 per depositor per account and the coverage is automatic. That is why having a savings account is a little bit better than just stuffing your money under your mattress. **(Yes)**

Disability *(Y/N)?*

Is there any kind of disability coverage? No. There's no disability coverage for your savings. You have what you have; that's it. **(No)**

Lawsuit protection *(Y/N)?*

Is there lawsuit protection for your money in a bank account? **(No)**

Can you borrow *(Y/N)?*

Can you borrow your money from a savings account? No, but the money is your money, so you don't borrow it; you just spend it. **(N/A)**

Death benefit *(Y/N)?*

And is there a death benefit? No death benefits. Again, you just have what you have. **(No)**

Savings are foundational to financial success. No advisor can make money appear for you; advisors help you maximize the protection and growth of money you have saved.

I had a couple stop in for a complimentary meeting. They shared that they made about $550,000 a year, but didn't keep a regular savings account. They had one IRA with about $6,000 in it. And they had heard on the radio that it was reasonable to expect a rate of return of at least 15% on investments.

First of all, there is never a guarantee of growth, or rate of growth, for money in the market. Second, 15% of $6,000 is only $900. Such a small nest egg was not going to grow very much or very quickly. Plus, investment accounts (unlike savings accounts) do have fees. The bank is the place to grow your money until you establish your emergency fund—then you can look for other places to invest your money for growth. Remember, success in your financial world really begins with diligent saving habits. This may feel a bit redundant, but I want you to internalize this concept.

Jerry and Sue came to see me for holistic help. One thing we looked at was the $350,000 they had in their savings account. I asked them what six to twelve months of expenses would be. They said $60,000.

Then I asked why they had so much in their emergency fund. "Well, we feel comfortable with $100,000 at the ready."

Again I asked why they had such a large savings account balance. They thought some more and said, "We didn't know what else to do with it."

"Okay, got it," I said.

I showed them how to put their money to work with multiple benefits for them while they were sleeping, right away. I will highlight two of them.

We moved $250,000 to a modified endowment contract (MEC) with an insurance company (Figure 30). They still had access to their money inside the MEC if needed, just like a bank account. However, instead of just being liquid, their money was now doing much more for them. One, the money earned much more in dividends than it had in savings account interest. Two, the money now had a tax-free death benefit. So the same money that was in the bank—simply moved to a different account (MEC), but still inside their holistic financial bubble—now made Jerry and Sue more secure without adding risk to their lives or affecting their monthly budget. They realized how changing where their money lived changed how their financial world grew.

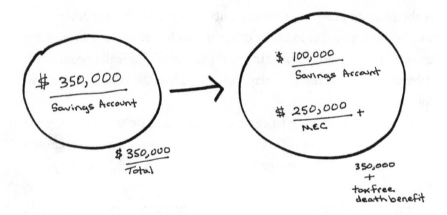

Figure 30: Holistic Financial Bubble—Savings Example

Some of you might say, "Well, there were small fees associated with the savings account, but the MEC is going to have a premium to pay. That feels like paying a fee." This is where you need to meet with your financial advisor about numbers personal to you. For the purposes of this discussion, a fairly typical MEC will have an annual premium of $200 to $750 a year or seventeen to sixty-two dollars a month. You be the judge if the value is worth the impact to your monthly budget. Your feeling is okay. Think of a feeling in your gut as an internal warning system to gather more information. Keep an open mind as you do a side-by-side comparison of the numbers to see if the benefits of the MEC outweigh your preconceived idea that all fees are bad. Figure 30 shows you the money is still in the same bubble.

CDS

Fees (Y/N)?

   CDs do not generally have associated fees, but they do have different time considerations. CDs are usually one-year or three-year contracts. If you take the money out before the contract end date, you pay a penalty. You agree to let the bank have your money for a specified time period and the bank guarantees that it will pay the agreed-upon interest and that your account will not lose value. (**No**)

Interest earned (Y/N)?

   Do CDs earn interest? They can, but you should note that a higher interest rate often accompanies higher inflation, so your money doesn't go as far as you might think. In the 1980s, CDs paid more than 8% in annual percentage yield. As of this writing, they pay under 1%.[54] While CDs do pay interest, they are primarily a tool used for their guarantee not to lose value. (**Yes**)

Taxes (Y/N)?

   What about taxes? You pay taxes on interest earned. The bad news is that CDs do not earn a lot of interest, but the good news is that you won't have to pay much in taxes. (**Yes**)

Guaranteed (Y/N)?

   Are CDs guaranteed? CDs are in banks, so they are FDIC-guaranteed.[55] (**Yes**)

DISABILITY OR LAWSUIT PROTECTION (Y/N)?
CDs do not have disability or lawsuit protection. (**No**)

CAN YOU BORROW (Y/N)?
As with your savings account, you don't borrow from your CDs, you just have the money. (**N/A**)

DEATH BENEFIT (Y/N)?
Likewise, there is no death benefit. (**No**)

CDs are attractive because they are in banks and have guarantees. It's nice to feel that your money is safe and secure. A CD is a product to keep your eye on, but until they start paying a higher interest rate, there are other products that provide both guarantees and higher returns.

Carrie was recently widowed. As we went through her financial junk drawer in our initial meeting, we found that she had $1.2 million in CDs—safe, guaranteed money. A hole we subsequently found in her plan was no long-term care coverage. Carrie's children were spread across the country, and she did not want to be a burden to them. Moving $200,000 a year into a whole life policy over ten years did three things for her (Figure 31). First, she was able to convert taxable money into tax-free money. Second, she created a contract that had an accelerated death benefit rider (ADBR), which will allow her to access some of her money if she needs long-term care. Third, even better, if she remains healthy and does not develop a chronic or terminal illness requiring her to use the money in her policy, the money will go to her children tax-free. Carrie was able to take $200,000 that was sitting in a CD earning 2.5% interest and move it to a whole life policy, still inside her holistic financial bubble, and garner multiple benefits. All things being equal, two to three benefits are better than one.

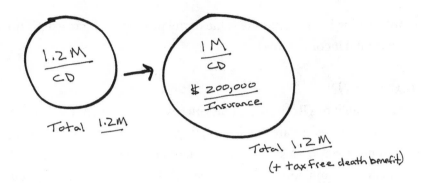

Figure 31: Holistic Financial Bubble—CD Example

ROTH IRAS

FEES (Y/N)?

Earlier in this chapter, I discussed Roth IRAs. Remember, this is just a tax status, so "it depends" is a viable answer here. When you set up a Roth IRA, you will pay some kind of fee to set up and manage the account. You can have it in a mutual fund, for which you will pay account setup fees and potentially some management fees. A different example is, I own a piece of real estate inside my Roth IRA and pay a company that manages self-directed IRAs. I paid an account setup fee and annual management fees because you are not allowed to manage your own IRA and keep the tax benefit. (**Yes**)

INTEREST EARNED (Y/N)?

Is there interest earned in a Roth IRA? Hopefully. That's why you have the investment. And again, that's all just going to depend on what kind of investment you have inside the account. Remember, your Roth IRA is just the tax status or "gym bag"—you can put a lot of different things into it. It goes without saying that an investment should provide some kind of return; otherwise, you may want to ask yourself why you have an investment that is not earning or growing. My rental property is not earning interest, but the value of the property is increasing, and I earn rental income. (**Yes**)

TAXES (Y/N)?

The benefit of a Roth IRA is that you pay taxes as you put assets into it, but after the assets are inside of it, they grow tax-free. The thinking is, you pay taxes on a smaller investment and then your investment grows tax-free and you are able to spend it tax-free. An overall goal is to make as many of your retirement accounts tax-free as possible. Then you do not have to worry about legislation in Congress or changes in tax rates. Your money should be your money. There is no guarantee that Congress will not change the rules about Roth IRAs, but it is highly unlikely. (**No**)

GUARANTEED (Y/N)?

Are Roth IRAs guaranteed? It depends on what investment vehicle you put into your Roth IRA. If you have something in the market or in real estate, there are no guarantees. But if you own an annuity inside your Roth IRA, you will have guarantees associated with that annuity contract. Are you starting to see the layers of complexity, and why you get "it depends" as an answer a lot? (**No**)

DISABILITY (Y/N)?

There is no disability protection for a Roth IRA. (**No**)

LAWSUIT PROTECTION (Y/N)?

Lawsuit protection for a Roth IRA depends on your state and the judgment in question. There are no federal protections in place. It is important to check with an attorney or CPA as rules vary from state to state. (**Yes**)

Can you borrow (Y/N)?

Usually, no. There are a few exceptions outlined by the IRS that you can research, such as for first-time homebuyers and for people in some extreme medical situations, but a safe bet is to plan on not being able to borrow money. (**Qualified Yes**)

Death benefit (Y/N)?

There is no death benefit for a Roth IRA. (**No**)

Remember the farmer analogy. Would you rather pay tax on the seed or the crop? Taxes on the seed will be much less than paying on an entire crop, so it's usually advantageous to pay taxes up front.

Jack retired and had $2 million in his 401(k). His question was whether he should make it a Roth IRA; he was concerned about the tax bill he would get due to the conversion. Jack had a pension and Social Security that was going to be taxable. Remember, a traditional IRA and Social Security benefits are not shielded from taxes and current amounts received each year drive the tax bill. When required minimum distributions (RMDs) kicked in, Jack was going to have to take money from his 401(k) and pay taxes on it, whether he needed the money or not. Working with his CPA, we made a plan to spread out his tax burden from the conversion to minimize his bill. Moving money to a Roth sooner allowed the Roth IRA account to grow tax-free (Figure 32). This gave Jack more control. He is now able to take his money out only when he wants to. And he will not pay taxes on the Roth IRA in the future, so he doesn't have to worry about tax increases changing his available money in retirement.

What you have to understand is that money in a non-Roth account grows, but the taxes grow, too. If you make the conversion, you pay a known amount of tax and then your account grows tax-free. Some people want to leave their money alone because they assume that they will be in a lower tax bracket when they retire, for example, 22% versus

28%. But this may not happen, and it is less likely to happen for people with pensions and Social Security. If you had to guess, do you think taxes will go up or down in the future? Do you want to take control of your money now or hope the future will work out for you?

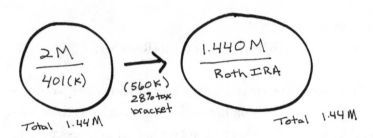

Figure 32: Holistic Financial Bubble—Roth IRA example

TRADITIONAL IRA

FEES (Y/N)?

Similar to the Roth IRA, a traditional IRA will have account setup fees. (**Yes**)

INTEREST EARNED (Y/N)?

This will depend on what you put inside your account because, again, it is just an IRA tax status. You can put a lot of different things inside a traditional IRA. (**Yes**)

TAXES (Y/N)?

You want to remember: You pay taxes when you pull the money out. Many CPAs really like to use the traditional IRA as a vehicle, especially if you're making a lot of cash right now and need a place to put money to reduce your tax burden today. But the money will be taxable in two ways. One, if you convert your traditional IRA to a Roth IRA, you'll have to pay the taxes. Two, if you let the account grow and then start pulling your money out when you're fifty-nine and a half or seventy, you'll pay taxes when that money comes out. And you want to remember that the money will be taxed at the ordinary income tax rate, not the capital gains tax rate. For most people, the ordinary income tax rate is a little higher than the capital gains tax rate. A popular example comes from an interview with Warren Buffett, in which he explained that his secretary pays a higher tax rate than he does.[56] In United States tax code, wages are taxed more than wealth. Like it or not, this is why you want to understand different types of investment products. This will help you create a strategy to make your money work for you as much as possible *and* avoid extra taxes. (**Yes**)

GUARANTEES (Y/N)?

There are no guarantees. (**No**)

DISABILITY (Y/N)?

There is no inherent disability protection. (**No**)

LAWSUIT PROTECTION (Y/N)?

Lawsuit protection is the same as for a Roth. (**Yes**)

CAN YOU BORROW (Y/N)?

It is safe to assume probably not—and even if you can, it is not a good idea. There are some different rules for 401(k) or other retirement savings accounts with your employer. A financial advisor can help you set up business retirement accounts if you own your own business. (**Qualified Yes**)

DEATH BENEFIT (Y/N)?

There is no death benefit. (**No**)

During one recent year, Hasan accrued a lot of overtime and was right up to his 24% tax bracket. Instead of funding a Roth IRA, he decided to put $6,000 into a traditional IRA so he didn't have to move up a tax bracket (Figure 33). He knew that the next year, he would be well below the 24% limit and could convert the traditional IRA to a Roth IRA at the lower tax rate. Understanding the IRS rules allowed Hasan to keep more money in his bubble.

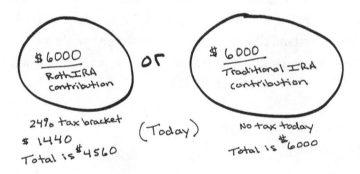

Figure 33: Holistic Financial Bubble—Traditional IRA example

401(K), SIMPLE, SEP, TSP, 403(B), 457, ETC.

THIS IS A LIST OF tax-advantaged accounts that business owners may establish. Each account type offers different advantages. The type you select will be based on how much you want to save, what kind of tax benefits you want, how much you can contribute to your employees, and how flexible you need your required contributions to be each year. For example, consider an architect with one employee. She wants to provide a retirement account to support her employee and encourage loyalty; however, the cash flow in the business varies from year to year, so it is important for her to have flexibility in required contributions for both herself and her employee. The kind of account she uses will probably evolve as the company grows.

NON-QUALIFIED MONEY

FEES (Y/N)?

Are there fees for non-qualified money? Yes. A non-qualified investment is an investment that does not have any level of tax-deferred or tax-exempt status. Investments of this sort are made with after-tax money.

You will always pay fees with non-qualified money, but the question is, how much? And for what? Fees are based on the type of investment strategy you use. Typically, if you have stocks or mutual funds in the market, you're going to pay fees associated with the investment you select. Some accounts are very simple, so you pay very minimal fees. If you want any kind of active management, fees will generally be 1-2% of assets under management. (**Yes**)

INTEREST EARNED (Y/N)?

Are you going to earn interest or a rate of return? I hope so, because that's generally the point of having non-qualified money—that and the fact that non-qualified money is liquid, meaning you can access it without paying any kind of penalty. (**Yes**)

TAXES (Y/N)?

Yes, you will pay taxes in a non-qualified account. Returns from these investments are taxed on an annual basis. It's always just taxes on the money you earned. If you put $100,000 into your account, you won't have to pay taxes on $100,000. But if the account grows to $110,000, you will have to pay taxes on the $10,000 (Figure 34) . (**Yes**)

GUARANTEED (Y/N)?

There are no guarantees with non-qualified money. (**No**)

Disability (Y/N)?
There is no disability. (**No**)

Lawsuit protection (Y/N)?
There is no protection from lawsuits with non-qualified money. (**No**)

Can you borrow (Y/N)?
There's no borrowing. It's just your money; you can take it if you want, so it's liquid. (**N/A**)

Death benefit (Y/N)?
Because this is just your money, there is no death benefit. (**N/A**)

You may be asking yourself why you would want non-qualified money when there are no tax advantages. There are a few reasons. You may have maxed out your allowable contributions to your employee accounts, like your 401(k) or IRA. You may want a blue chip stock like GE that will pay a dividend. You may like your Tesla Model 3 and want to own some stock in the company. The reasons will be your own, and you'll want to know the pros and cons so you can make the best decisions to reach your goals.

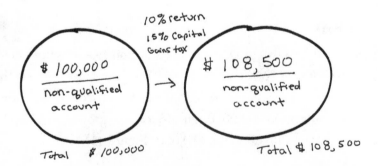

Figure 34: Holistic Financial Bubble—Non-qualified Example

Taxes are only paid on growth. Meanwhile, this money grew more than it would have in a savings account. And it's liquid, meaning that it's readily accessible. The risk with a non-qualified account is that you could lose value in the market; for example, your $100,000 could drop down to $90,000 or less. In the case of a loss, you would pay no taxes.

WHOLE LIFE POLICIES

FEES (Y/N)?

Are there fees with a whole life insurance policy, also known as a whole life policy? Whole life policies do not have fees, but you will pay premiums. The amount of the premium will be the same for the rest of your life. A whole life policy is different from an investment in the market. It's in the name: it is a contract with a life insurance company to receive a tax-free death benefit and some guaranteed amount of growth in cash value. **(Qualified No)**

INTEREST (Y/N)?

Maybe. However, whole life policies do grow the cash value inside the policy, and you may earn dividends. Because a whole life policy is a contract, you can design the policy to do different things. For example, you can add levels of long-term care planning factors, usually called accelerated death benefits riders (ADBRs). Or you may elect to design a policy that will self-complete if you become disabled and are unable to work and pay premiums. **(Qualified Yes)**

TAXES (Y/N)?

It depends. The cash value inside a whole life policy grows tax-deferred. You will pay taxes if you withdraw cash value. The death benefit will go to your heirs, tax-free. **(Qualified No)**

GUARANTEED (Y/N)?

The death benefit defines the guaranteed payout for your beneficiary. You can also design a policy to self-complete if disabled. Some policies also have long-term care type benefits associated with them as I discussed earlier. (**Yes**)

DISABILITY (Y/N)?

There is no disability unless the policy is specifically designed to include it. (**No**)

LAWSUIT PROTECTION (Y/N)?

Life insurance death benefits are generally protected from lawsuits. The life insurance industry is regulated at the state level. State insurance departments maintain strict oversight and verify independently that life insurance companies have the resources to meet their financial obligations. (**Yes**)

CAN YOU BORROW MONEY (Y/N)?

This is one of the great things about whole life policies: You can borrow the cash value and pay it back. As with credit cards, this option can be used to create opportunity or to dig yourself into a hole of debt. If you access money from your cash value, your death benefit is reduced until you pay the loan back. No problem here. However, if you borrow from the cash value and do not make your premium and interest payments, you can cause your whole life policy to implode and lose the death benefit. I've spent a lot of time talking about the emotions around money and financial baggage, beginning in Chapter 2. This is a case where you need to know and be honest with yourself. If you borrow money from yourself, will you hold yourself accountable and pay it back? Or will the voice inside your head rationalize why you don't need to pay yourself back? Do not judge yourself as good or bad. Success is driven by action. Reflect on how to make the best choices for you.

Because life insurance is a contract and policies can be designed to include different features, you want to do your research. You want to know what problem you are trying to solve first. This is how you ensure that you select a policy that meets your needs. You also want to understand what is in the realm of the possible. For example, if you intend to use its cash value, you'll want to know the difference between direct and non-direct recognition when it comes to your policy. (**Yes**)

DEATH BENEFIT (Y/N)?
Is there a death benefit with a whole life policy? (**Yes**)

Beyond its usefulness for protecting one's family or business, whole life is a tool used by wealthy people, business owners, and others who are interested in growing their assets in a tax-advantaged way. Because of the complexity of the tax code, I've heard it said that whoever knows the most rules wins. I've talked about product versus strategy solutions; whole life is a product used to support advanced planning strategies.

Here's a real-world example: During the pandemic, my husband, Kris, and I were able to make a cash offer on the property next to us and double our horse pasture acreage. We borrowed money from our whole life policy. We didn't have to go to a bank and ask for a loan. We were able to repay the loan to our policy at our convenience. And because our policy is a non-direct recognition, we kept earning dividends while the policy loan was out. Instead of just having $100,000 we didn't need at the time, we added an asset, land, to our financial bubble (Figure 35). The note to ourselves allowed us to control how and when we repaid the cash value in our policy. Now we have increased the size of our financial bubble because of the flexibility provided by our whole life policy contract.

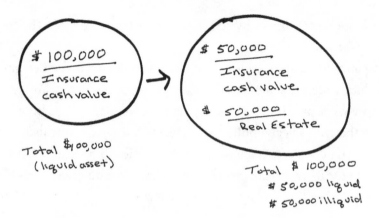

Figure 35: Holistic Financial Bubble—Whole Life Policy Example

TERM INSURANCE

FEE (Y/N)?

There are no fees with term insurance, but you do pay a premium during the specified term. Term policies last for specific time periods and include ten-, twenty-, and thirty-year policies. A term policy is a contract with a life insurance company, so you determine exactly the term you want. (**No**)

INTEREST EARNED (Y/N)?

Term policies do not earn interest or grow cash value. (**No**)

TAXES (Y/N)?

You do not pay any taxes. (**No**)

GUARANTEED (Y/N)?

There is a guaranteed death benefit within the agreed-upon terms of the policy. Some term policies have guaranteed conversion options that allow you to convert to a whole life policy without getting a new medical exam. (**Yes**)

This worked out well for Kris and me when Kris's health put our insurance to the test. We purchased convertible term insurance for Kris when we were launching our business because all of our money was going back into the business and we did not have extra cash to pay the whole life policy premiums.

One morning, we had our usual breakfast of oatmeal and took our daily two-mile walk. We were downtown checking on our rental properties when, suddenly, Kris started looking pale and clammy. He leaned his seat back and said he was going to nap on our drive home. I drove straight to the emergency room. The intake nurse walked Kris back before we even filled out the paperwork. By the time I had parked the car and got back to the front desk, Kris was being wheeled upstairs to the cardiac catheterization lab for a stent. His right coronary artery was 100% blocked. Kris was forty-eight at the time. This is why you would have convertible term insurance (Figure 36).

DISABILITY (Y/N)?

Normally, there is no disability coverage with a term policy. But again, insurance products are contracts. You can actually design them in different ways when you set them up, so you can ask about disability coverage during the setup process. (**No**)

LAWSUIT PROTECTION (Y/N)?

Lawsuit protection does not really apply because there is no inherent value to a term policy, just a death benefit. (**N/A**)

CAN YOU BORROW (Y/N)?

You cannot borrow from a term policy because there is no cash value. (**No**)

DEATH BENEFIT (Y/N)?

Term life insurance does have a death benefit for the specified period. (**Yes**)

Planning ahead with a convertible term increased the size of our financial bubble. We now have an ADBR to use for long-term care if we need it. Meanwhile, we have access to cash value to use at our discretion. If Kris had had regular term insurance, he may not have qualified for a good rating, meaning insurance would be more expensive—or worse, a hole in our financial bubble. Without our whole life policy, we would have to set aside money just for unexpected medical expenses—one pot of money doing only one job.

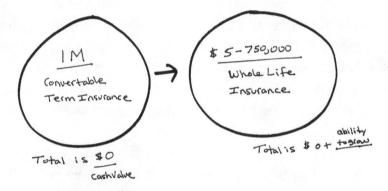

Figure 36: Holistic Financial Bubble—Term Insurance Example

FIXED OR FIXED INDEX ANNUITIES

FOR THE PURPOSES OF THIS discussion, when I refer to annuities, I mean fixed or fixed index annuities. Variable annuities are a whole different thing and come with a different set of questions.

FEES (Y/N)?

Do annuities have fees? No. You may be thinking, "Wait, you already said no one is in this business for free. What's the catch?" Annuities have what is called surrender periods, which generally last from seven to ten years. What this means is, you basically agree to let the insurance company have your $100,000 for ten years while you leave it there, untouched. This allows the insurance company ten years to invest your money. Because they know your money is going to be there, they can choose safe, long-term investments. With large amounts of money to invest, they only need a low rate of return to make a lot of money and guarantee your contract. If you pull your money out early, you will pay a surrender charge because you have broken the annuity contract. You pay for an annuity by agreeing to leave your money there for a period of time. In this example, the insurance company guarantees that your balance will never fall below $100,000 and that they will pay growth per the contract.

You may be thinking, "Why would I want an annuity when whole life insurance grows and allows me access to my cash value?" Whole life requires a medical exam, and not everyone qualifies. Annuities are contracts with guarantees that do not require you to be in good health.

Now you should be asking, "So how does my financial planner get paid?" Insurance companies pay commissions to financial planners. You could almost think of them as finders' fees for matching customers with insurance company products. The commission is paid to your financial advisor outside of your account. If you have $100,000, $100,000 will go into your annuity. You will not pay additional fees. (**No**)

INTEREST EARNED (Y/N)?

Annuities will grow per their contracts. Usually, the amount an annuity can grow will be adjusted each year based on the market. Annuities are guaranteed not to lose money. (**Yes**)

TAXES (Y/N)?

Do you pay taxes on annuities? Yes, but annuities grow tax-deferred. The rules are like those for a traditional IRA. You pay ordinary income tax rates when you start taking money out of an annuity. Do you remember how I said there can be layers of complexity when it comes to investing? Here is a twist. You can put an annuity inside of a Roth IRA. I explained before that a Roth IRA is just a tax status, and you can think of it as a gym bag into which you can put whatever equipment you want. I shared that I own a rental property in my Roth IRA. You can also own an annuity in a Roth IRA. The annuity gives you the guarantees that a contract gives you, so you don't lose money. When you put the annuity into a Roth IRA, you do not pay taxes when you pull the money out at age fifty-nine and a half. If you are one of those people who would gladly bury your money in the backyard with a treasure map but also want tax advantages, consider an annuity. It is a tool that provides guarantees and can be tax-advantaged, too. **(Yes)**

GUARANTEED *(Y/N)?*

Do fixed index and fixed annuities have guarantees? Yes, it is guaranteed that your account will never lose value. You may have years where the market is negative and you earn zero, but you are never going to earn less than zero; in other words, you will not lose money.

Here it starts to get a little more complicated. There are guarantees with a fixed index annuity or a fixed annuity. The word "variable" indicates risk. Make a note here. Variable annuities can involve risk and are not 100% guaranteed. I urge you to do a lot of research on variable annuities: They can be much more confusing and can have investment fees. And, all annuities may add additional contract options (called riders). **(Yes)**

DISABILITY *(Y/N)?*

Is there disability coverage with fixed or fixed index annuities? Typically, no, but it is possible. It depends on how you design the contract. **(No)**

LAWSUIT PROTECTION *(Y/N)?*

Do annuities come with lawsuit protection? Annuities and life insurance policies are considered protected assets in many US states.

Different states may protect different amounts in these policies. In some states, the cash value of the policy is protected. In others, only proceeds paid to beneficiaries are protected. Finally, in the best states, all the funds from the policies are protected. If an annuity is inside a Roth or traditional IRA, it will have the same protections those retirement accounts have. (**Yes**)

CAN YOU BORROW (Y/N)?

Kinda sorta. Per your contract, most annuities will allow you to withdraw 5-10% of the account value each year without penalty. An annuity is considered illiquid money and should be a place to protect money that you do not need for seven to ten years (or the length of the surrender period). (**Qualified Yes**)

DEATH BENEFIT (Y/N)?

There is typically no death benefit unless you add a death benefit rider. Upon your death, your beneficiaries will receive what is left in terms of the value of the account. It is worth mentioning that some annuity companies do call this a death benefit. (**No**)

One of my clients, Beyoncé had $700,000 in her checking account. She did not trust the market. She had a good job and did not carry credit card debt. She had a mortgage and car payment to help her credit score, even though she really wanted to pay off that debt, too.

Moving $600,000 to a fixed annuity earning 3% guaranteed that Beyoncé would not lose any money. At 3%, her $600,000 would earn $18,000 a year (Figure 37). Her mortgage was $1,400 a month, or $16,800 a year. By moving the bulk of her money (changing where her money lived) to a fixed annuity, Beyoncé earned a guaranteed amount greater than the cost of her mortgage.

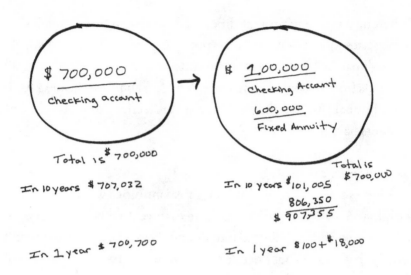

Figure 37: Holistic Financial Bubble—Fixed Annuity Example

Two good things happened here. One, she expanded the size of her financial bubble by $18,000 a year just by changing the account her money lived in. Further, compounded annually over 10 years she had significantly more money. Two, she created the ability to pay her mortgage if she wanted to. Additionally, she quickly realized that paying off her home would feel good emotionally, but once her money was sunk in her home, the only way to get the money out was to sell the house. She couldn't walk into the pantry and pull money out. However, creating an account (the fixed annuity earning a 3% rate of return) gave her the ability to pay her mortgage if she wanted to, and this satisfied her emotional need to be debt-free. Beyoncé had more freedom and control after choosing a fixed annuity because her money was working for her, was more liquid than it would be sitting in a property, and was not exposed to market risk. Looking at her money holistically helped her overcome some financial baggage about debt that was keeping her cash-poor and limiting her options.

Your table should be complete, and you can check yourself against Figure 38.

CHARAC-TERISTICS	ACCOUNT TYPES							
	SAVINGS	CD	ROTH IRA	TRAD. IRA	NON-QUAL.	WHOLE LIFE	TERM LIFE	ANNUITY
FEES*	Qualified No	No	Yes	Yes	Yes	Qualified No	No	No
INTEREST EARNED	Qualified Yes	Yes	Yes	Yes	Yes	Qualified Yes	No	Yes
TAXES	Yes	Yes	No	Yes	Yes	Qualified No	No	Yes
GUARANTEES	Yes	Yes	No	No	No	Yes	Yes	Yes
DISABILITY	No	No	No	No	No	No	No	No
LAWSUIT PROT.	No	No	Yes	Yes	No	Yes	N/A	Yes
CAN BORROW	N/A	N/A	Qualified Yes	Qualified Yes	N/A	Yes	No	Qualified Yes
DEATH BENEFIT	No	No	No	No	No	Yes	Yes	No

Figure 38: Comparisons of Basic Investment Types—Completed Table

I have put together a short case study at the end of this chapter that will help you see how this table can help you navigate money decisions—and how emotion can override logic.

TO WRAP UP

IN THIS CHAPTER, I'VE TALKED about several common investment options and how they embody positive investment qualities. You now know the characteristics of good investments and have started to decide what's important to you.

Before reading this chapter, you may have thought that having a Roth IRA meant you had to be in the market, even though you'd really prefer to shove money under your mattress or bury it in your backyard. Now you know it's possible to have guaranteed money in an annuity inside a Roth IRA. Are you very concerned about what kind of interest you may be able to earn? Are you very concerned about what kind of fees you may have to pay? Are you trying to figure out a way to pay the least possible amount in taxes? What kind of guarantees do you want? The good news is, this doesn't have to be all or nothing.

In fact, I recommend that you consider creating a balance between guaranteed options and growth options that have more associated risk. After you determine what problem you are trying to solve—how much is enough, and how much risk you can tolerate in your daily life—you will come back to this table and use it to create a course of action that carves a path for your success. The process of creating a financial plan will make more sense now that you have a basic understanding of these building blocks.

KEY TAKEAWAYS

- Investments are not good or bad. They do different things. When you understand the pros and cons, you will feel more secure in your plan.
- You must know what problem you are trying to solve first. Then you can select an investment tool that will help you resolve your issue. Cognitive dissonance happens when you have a tool that does not really fix your problem.
- There is no one-size-fits-all investment that will properly fill all the gaps in your retirement plan.
- Viewing your money inside of your financial bubble shows how all of your decisions align and how you can grow your bottom line.

TAKE ACTION NOW EXERCISE

IN FIGURE 39, CIRCLE THE types of accounts you have right now. Circle the characteristics they have that you really like. Make a note if a type of account that you do not currently have piqued your interest.

At the beginning of this chapter, you identified the kinds of accounts you currently have in your financial bubble. Now you can see if your accounts are solving your problems. Do you have any holes in your financial bubble? It's normal to focus on the "Get it" phase of your financial life cycle and not think about protecting your nest egg as you grow it. With the visual model of your financial bubble, you can now see that your decisions to grow and protect do not have to be "either-or" choices. You can pick some "yes, and" options.

	ACCOUNT TYPES							
CHARAC-TERISTICS	SAVINGS	CD	ROTH IRA	TRAD. IRA	NON-QUAL.	WHOLE LIFE	TERM LIFE	ANNUITY
FEES*	Qualified No	No	Yes	Yes	Yes	Qualified No	No	No
INTEREST EARNED	Qualified Yes	Yes	Yes	Yes	Yes	Qualified Yes	No	Yes
TAXES	Yes	Yes	No	Yes	Yes	Qualified No	No	Yes
GUARANTEES	Yes	Yes	No	No	No	Yes	Yes	Yes
DISABILITY	No	No	No	No	No	No	No	No
LAWSUIT PROT.	No	No	Yes	Yes	No	Yes	N/A	Yes
CAN BORROW	N/A	N/A	Qualified Yes	Qualified Yes	N/A	Yes	No	Qualified Yes
DEATH BENEFIT	No	No	No	No	No	Yes	Yes	No

Figure 39: Comparisons of Basic Investment Types—Completed Table

CASE STUDY: LOGIC VS. EMOTION

SALLY DESCRIBES HERSELF AS A very analytical engineer. She likes her spreadsheets. She likes it when numbers make sense.

Sally had $750,000 sitting in a savings account because she didn't trust the market, but because she is afraid to run out of money, she decided she wants to put money in the market after all. She heard that she should be able to earn a 10% return in the market, but was uninterested in any education. Her in-laws had market investments that covered their long-term care needs, and she wanted the same protection for her and her husband. She felt strongly that she and her husband did not need insurance and was uninterested in learning more about it.

Based on the table in Figure 39, what would you consider for Sally based on her brief bio? It's okay to have no idea. This case study shows the complexity of thinking that goes into selecting "equipment" or tools. Picking the right tools to solve your problem is further complicated when you aren't open-minded about all of the options available to serve you. Read on to see what Sally's solution becomes.

I will walk us through the table so you can see how to use it. You can fill in the table in Figure 40 as you read through this scenario.

CHARAC- TERISTICS	ACCOUNT TYPES								
	SAVINGS	CD	ROTH IRA	TRAD. IRA	401(K), 403(B), TSP, ETC.	NON- QUAL.	WHOLE LIFE	TERM LIFE	ANNUITY
FEES*									
INTEREST EARNED									
TAXES									
GUARANTEES									
DISABILITY									
LAWSUIT PROT.									
CAN BORROW									
DEATH BENEFIT									

Figure 40: Comparisons of Basic Investment Types—Fillable Table

Fees: Sally did not mention fees right away, so that does not help us narrow down our options.

Interest earned: She did mention that she wanted to earn 10%, so that rules out an annuity or whole life policy and drives us toward the market. Cross out savings, CD, whole life, and annuity on the table.

Taxes: She did not mention taxes directly, but they did come up later when we discussed active money management.

Guaranteed: Sally wanted something guaranteed based on her demonstrated fear of the market (she had her money in a savings account), but this was incompatible with her expectation that she should earn a 10% rate of return. She would not consider an insurance product. The challenge with the market is, the only guarantee is that it will go up and down. While you may see a past history of desired growth, that is not a crystal ball for the future.

IRA or non-qualified: Because the money was not in a Roth or traditional IRA, she needed to look at non-qualified money in the market. Cross out both IRA accounts. Non-qualified money has no tax advantages. The rules prohibit you from moving non-qualified money directly into an IRA in a lump sum. Non-qualified dollars can be invested in annuities, and those do grow tax-deferred, but she already ruled out insurance products.

Sally wanted her money somewhere it would grow at a guaranteed rate, and this does not exist.

Her mix of fear and personal mythology led her to keep $750,000 in a savings account. An annuity would provide her the guarantees of a savings account and allow her to earn better returns than she would with a savings account, but emotionally, annuities were off the table. A properly designed whole life policy would provide long-term and critical illness coverage, but emotionally, insurance was off the table. This left us with a non-qualified account in the market. Market recommendations based on historical performance data determine the amount of risk that would project the 10% growth she wanted. To hedge against market drops, I presented a plan for active money management with downside protection, meaning that the managers would try to move money to cash and cash equivalents when indicators predicted market drops. She agreed this seemed like her best option.

Sally didn't like the roller coaster quality that the market seems to have if you watch it on a daily basis, but she'd only allowed for a market solution. This is just one of the disconnects like those I discussed in Chapter 2. Because she was not open to hearing about different options that could prevent her from running out of money and help her achieve security with less risk, she signed up to live with a certain amount of stress in her life.

This goes back to one of the questions I've asked several times: "How much is enough?" After you've made your money, suffering through market uncertainty is unnecessary. Sally let her preconceived notions narrow her possibilities down to only one viable option: being in the market. Instead of starting with a better question, like, "What is it I really need?", she remained unable to overcome ingrained misconceptions. Trust has to be earned, and education is a great starting point. You can only help someone who is in a receptive headspace.

CHAPTER 7

WHERE YOUR MONEY LIVES

You can't go back and make a new start, but you can start right now and make a brand-new ending.

—James R. Sherman[57]

- Have you ever wondered if everyone else is organized and on track, but you're behind in your retirement planning and money management?
- Do you know your financial trigger words?
- Do you know how much is enough, or are you just trying to keep up with what you feel everyone else has?
- Did you know that money is more emotion than math? Are you aware that financial baggage exists?

YOU NEED TO KNOW WHERE your money lives in your brain. You are familiar with the concept of a junk drawer; there's one in every house. What I want you to understand is, there is also a financial junk drawer in your brain—and it is probably way overdue for a spring cleaning. You may have your money all over the place, and it could be very poorly organized. Even if you are one of those perfectly organized unicorns, you likely have at least one half-done spreadsheet. My books are filled with sticky notes. These are clues to where things are stored in my brain.

You have had good intentions at many points during your life. The older you get, the more good intentions you have. For most of us, life takes over and money management takes a backseat. When life is super busy, you focus on the short-range targets: paying your bills, taking care of the kids, keeping up with school, launching your business. Whatever your priority, it's keeping you busy. Organizing your money is usually not at the top of that list.

And the thing is, as you get older, life does move faster. How many times do you catch yourself thinking, "That was just the other day," but realize, "Nope, it was almost two years ago" when you go back and look? The stuff in your brain's financial junk drawer becomes intermingled with the items in your physical junk drawer: old bank statements, tax forms from various years, maybe a few power bills. You may have 401(k)s from previous jobs. You may have an IRA or two.

When I met with Miranda, it became clear that she didn't understand what an IRA was. Every year, the bank sent out mail asking if she would like to open an IRA, and no kidding, she had six IRAs with this bank and they were all savings accounts.

I asked her, "Why did you open a new IRA every year?"

She said, "Because the bank asked me."

It boggled my mind. It was the same bank, and they didn't look to see that she already had five other IRAs? She was paying separate fees for each account. All that money could have been in a single IRA, doing the same job for her, but instead it was in a mental and physical financial junk drawer. I'd like to think I'm much smarter than that, but this kind of thing happens. Have you ever signed up for a magazine subscription that's free for the first three months and then forgotten to cancel it? What about the collection of accounts through Amazon Prime, like BritBox and Acorn, that you also forget to cancel? The next thing you know, you're paying for many small subscriptions. The financial junk drawer just builds up, slowly and steadily.

We can all use a good spring cleaning every five to ten years, whether we need it or not. It's good to just take everything out, dump it on the front lawn, and pick through it. You figure out what you're going to keep, what you're going to throw away, and what you're going to reorganize.

We all account for money in very different ways, in our brains. I think it's fascinating how you can sit down with three different people to talk about money and they'll organize that money in three totally different ways. Some people will have a nice ledger or a spreadsheet. Some people prefer to use money management programs. Some people like to have separate bank accounts. There are so many different options and ways to deal with it. Some people like the plain old envelope method, where you just put your cash in an envelope and that's your ATM. And at the end of the day, there's no wrong way to organize your money. You do want to make sure that you know what you have. You don't want gaps. You work hard for your money, and you want your money to work smart for you.

The goal is to avoid having your money just sitting somewhere, like a bank account, when it could at least be protected and earning some interest or otherwise working for you. Organizing your money information is an important part of the holistic financial planning process because it creates visibility, and visibility will help you ensure that all of your money decisions are working together synergistically. Think about what happens if you're whitewater rafting and one or two people are paddling the wrong way. Best-case, you spin in circles. Worst-case, the raft flips over. This chapter highlights some common idiosyncrasies in personal systems for money management. Some are fine. You may want to consider how others impact your bottom line.

WHAT ARE THE ACCOUNTING SYSTEMS IN YOUR BRAIN?

YOU MAY BE THINKING, "I don't have accounting systems in my brain. I don't even like numbers." You don't have to say it out loud; just think about this idea of columns, accounts, and other money systems that live in your head. I'm going to introduce you to a couple of people who may sound more familiar than you care to admit right now. By the end of this chapter, you should be laughing—or at least feeling better, knowing you're not alone.

My friend Melissa is a numbers maniac. When I sat down with her and her husband to go through their finances, she didn't show me her spreadsheet at first. I wondered if something was up as we talked about some strategic ideas. I was getting affirmative nods from her husband while she just sat there with her eyebrows knitted together. It took me a little while to figure out that she was not necessarily confused; she disagreed.

Her husband, Phil, finally asked her to show me "the spreadsheet." She opened this massive document on her computer and I can honestly tell you, I still don't understand it today. I do understand that it revolved around a lesson firmly ingrained in her since childhood: "You never want to be in debt. Debt is bad. Get rid of debt at all costs."

Her complex spreadsheet dealt a lot with the new house they were building. Within five years of retirement, she and Phil had decided to sell their completely paid-off home and have a new, more expensive home built. Going into retirement with a new thirty-year mortgage is not something I would normally recommend, but it was something they really wanted. This new home was where they wanted to live, and a big part of how they wanted to enjoy retirement. We figured out how to make it work. They had to get a first and then a second mortgage for the new house. This is where Melissa's unique accounting and strong financial baggage from childhood kicked in.

Let me just throw out some facts from the spreadsheet. As in the example from Chapter 3, Melissa had $25,000 in a bank account earning about 0.1%, so she didn't have to pay an annual fee of seventy-five dollars. The couple had an amazingly low interest rate on the second mortgage, around 1.9%. They had the opportunity to overfund their whole life insurance (sometimes called a whole life savings plan, depending on how the insurance tool is being used in your plan) that had been paying typically more than 2% returns, grew tax-free, and was protected. Decisions were pretty clear to me, but Melissa had a different thing going on in her mental junk drawer that was overriding math.

She wanted to pay off the second mortgage—make double payments on this debt with the super low interest rate—rather than fund her whole life savings plan to grow her liquid asset, the cash value of her whole life savings plan. She just couldn't do what the holistic plan showed would be most beneficial.

Melissa said, "No, I've got to pay off that debt. I've got to pay off that second mortgage. I've got to get it paid off."

I looked at Phil and he said, "I'm so glad you are seeing these complex categories of money. If you can convince her another way may be good, I'm in. I wish you luck."

She couldn't argue with the math, but the math didn't sway her from her method. In addition to settling for a 0.1% return in order to avoid a seventy-five-dollar bank fee, Melissa also had a separate savings account to set aside money for her next car. She could have had her money growing in one consolidated account, earning higher interest, and kept track of how much was for the second mortgage, how much was for the new car, etc. She literally had individual locations for every category on her spreadsheet. I'm talking more than six. Building an asset of protection that earned 2-3%, her whole life savings plan, made better mathematic sense than paying off a second mortgage that only charged 1.9%. She acquiesced to funding the whole life savings plan, but it was so painful for her to have that debt hanging over her head that she confessed to pulling money from her travel category to get it paid off.

This was a purely emotional thing we went through. She had the numbers in her spreadsheet. She could see the math. But her emotional need to pay off debt hindered her ability to build assets that would create more actual freedom and security for her family.

We can have someone explain a better decision with numbers, but we feel better confirming our own beliefs. In Melissa's case, that was the overarching need to quickly pay down the mortgage. You just need to give yourself permission to do the best you can, rather than judging your decisions as good or bad. It's helpful when you are aware that there may be things you believe so deeply, you will not be dissuaded by facts. This is how the financial junk drawer in our brains works. It is filtered and organized by emotion.

Another client of mine, Sophie, is perfectly well off in retirement. Her late husband really took care of her. He was one of those few people left with a pension that extended past his demise to his wife. Sophie had his pension income in addition to Social Security. She receives more than $10,000 a month, which is very comfortable. Her house is paid off, and she and her husband had a very large 401(k) that we moved into a personal IRA.

Sophie had no income worries and ended up moving from a large estate on some land back home to a very ritzy part of town—the country club community. One of the hardest things in retirement, or just life in general, is that you can always compare yourself to others. Even though Sophie lived in this beautiful place with plenty of monthly income and two nice cars, she felt like she didn't have as much money as everybody else and was always worried about it. "Am I going to be okay?"

I reviewed her money situation with her a few times a year, when she called feeling panicky or lonely. We looked at how she spent her money and what she could afford to do. She would then breathe a sigh of relief. For her, money became about keeping up with the Joneses. "I don't have as much as I think they have."

The thing is, you never know about somebody else because we are all really good at presenting the face that we want the world to see. You don't know what's going on in their life. You don't know how much they're leveraged or mortgaged. Our brains can do unique accounting and create a sense of lack that may not be real, although the feelings are real. Keeping up with the Joneses is a very real mental stressor. I confess that I have my own moments of internal struggle with it, too. It is ideal to get to the place in your own head where you both have enough and know that you are enough.

WHAT IS MONEY, REALLY?

MONEY IS MORE EMOTION THAN math, and we all have financial baggage. This is so important, I could say it a hundred times. Money is really just a contrived way for us exchange value for services. Early societies used the barter system, but as the world got bigger and more complicated, the barter system didn't work for more complex trades involving multiple parties. Money became the tool we use to exchange value.

I have a personal example. When I was working with a fellow horse person, we discussed exchanging my riding lessons for her horse massages. But a problem arose because she thought her massages were worth more than my lessons. I thought the exchange of expertise was a fair hourly trade, but it was clear that this barter situation was just not going to work.

I said, "Well, why don't we go back to just paying each other? If I want a massage, I'll pay you for it and if you want a lesson, you can pay me for that." In this case, money allowed me to step back from an emotional confrontation about the value of our services. Money is just a conduit that allows us to trade. We are not on the gold standard anymore, so a dollar bill's value is relative—it's not pure math.

BUDGET IS A TRIGGER WORD

THE LANGUAGE OF MONEY IS so important. One of the main reasons for initial education with a new client is to level-set our language. Some words mean different things to different people. I need you to understand, for example, that the word "variable" means risk is a factor. Annuity contracts use the word "rider"—that means there will be a fee. Or, when you hear the question, "How much risk are you comfortable with?" the answer is more than just "conservative," "moderate," or "aggressive." The question really means, "How much money are you willing to lose?"

There are some words that convey very specific meanings. Then there are words that have different connotations and can spark real and sometimes unpleasant feelings. For some people, "insurance" is a trigger word. "Stock market" creates resistance in others. Identifying your unconscious objections is key to opening a dialog that helps us create something positive. It starts with ensuring that we have a common language with which to build a foundation of trust.

A word that is creating an unexpected change in the language I use in my business is "budget," also known as "the B word." You need to know where you're spending your money before you can make decisions. Are you spending money the way you want to spend it right now? You go through phases in life when you're not making as much money as you would like. We've all been there. In this space, it helps to live within your budget so you don't go into debt.

Kitiri was really struggling. We were talking about organizing her family's financial junk drawer and we began with the B word. When we started talking budget, Kitiri would have a meltdown and just check out of the conversation. Her body was at the table, but mentally, she was somewhere else. I was confused at first because she was good with numbers. She had a degree in math and had taught arithmetic, so I wondered why this disconnection happened.

I asked her, "Why is 'budget' a trigger word for you? You're way better with numbers than your husband."

We finally figured out that, when she was a kid, her mom would say, "Kids, we're going on a budget," after Kitiri's parents had a fight about money. In their home, this meant things like not having air conditioning, even though they lived in Mobile, Alabama. Her mom and dad would introduce austerity measures that didn't really save that much money, but did make life feel painful. For her, the word "budget" triggered a fear response: "Oh my goodness, this is really bad, life is going to suck, and no, we can't be on a budget."

After we figured out the problem, we were able to shift. "Oh, well, let's not call it a budget," I said. "Let's call it a spending plan." She was totally fine with a spending plan. This is the part about money that most books skip over, and I read a lot of books about money. If you want to be able to make some headway, you must understand your triggers. Otherwise, they will keep bothering you. You'll backslide and not even know why.

HOW MUCH FEELS LIKE ENOUGH?

ANOTHER TRUTH THAT LIVES INSIDE your brain is your personal comfort level of cash, the amount of money that makes you feel safe. How much is enough? How much *feels like* enough? This question has to be answered twice. I can talk with clients matter-of-factly about numbers all day long. Obviously, if you're spending $4,000 a month and you want to have a little cushion, you might need $5,000 a month. I can have that very formal talk with you about how much is enough. I can perch my reading glasses on the end of my nose and look at you over the rims, raising my eyebrows for emphasis. I can have that talk, but that's really not the conversation; the conversation is about how much feels like enough to you. You may not realize it, but you have a number that makes you feel okay.

One thing that really helps me feel better about life is carrying a hundred dollars in my wallet at all times. I also have a hundred dollars in my car for emergencies.

I used to be terrible about having cash. Stopping at an ATM is not part of my travel pattern or routine. I use credit cards, but there's nothing worse than that feeling when you get caught in a bind because your credit card expired, or they don't take American Express, or the card reader is out.

My husband, Kris, and I went out for breakfast during a much-needed getaway in Breckenridge, Colorado. The first place we selected had posted a sign that read: "Cash Only." I didn't have my wallet. I had twenty bucks and a credit card in my pocket, and you cannot even get coffee for twenty bucks in the middle of ski season.

We turned to leave and the manager said, "Stay, you can just send me a check later." Instead of feeling good that an allowance was being made for me, I had to leave quickly. I did not want to deal with the follow-up chores of having to write a check, look up the address, find a stamp— you see where my mind went. Experiences like this trigger feelings for me, so I have figured out for myself that just having emergency money all the time makes me feel better.

What about the emergency fund? One client I had struggled with maintaining an emergency fund. She made good money but could not seem to keep $3,000 in her savings account. If the money was there, she spent it. Here's what we figured out for her: Instead of having $3,000 in the bank, where it wasn't earning much interest anyway, she always has $3,000 at home, hidden away in her sock drawer. It makes her feel better.

Later, she told me about a trifecta of emergencies that all occurred at once. She needed to get her brakes replaced, the espresso machine quit (we're talking caffeine, here!), and the garbage disposal broke. Normally, she would have run up a credit card bill and carried the balance for a while. But this time, it wasn't a big deal because she had $3,000 cash right there in her sock drawer. She didn't have to experience even a moment of stress.

Our minds play these mental games whether we want to participate or not. So how much is enough? This is where it's nice to have your trusted money manager help you work through the numbers in a purely logical way. But it's also very important that you have the conversation about emotion because a plan is only good if you will execute it. You may figure out on paper that you only need $2,500, but you may realize, "I really feel better with $4,000." And that's okay. You don't have to justify it. Just know what your number is.

WE ALL HAVE FINANCIAL BAGGAGE

FINANCIAL BAGGAGE IS ANOTHER UNDER-ADDRESSED topic. From my point of view, you acquire financial baggage from your family growing up. Then there is the baggage derived from media and advertisements. More financial baggage comes from the uncertainty of the stock market. You are also bombarded with messages about how you should be able manage your money by yourself. This is so counterintuitive when you think about it. You play on sports teams in school. You work with teams in your professional life. Why on earth would you put your entire financial security into the hands of one amateur—you?

Most of us studied the Great Depression in school or heard about Black Monday, the stock market crash of 1987. There have been more recent market drops in the early 2000s as well. It's a little scary—you take on a lot of baggage related to things that you feel like you have to participate in but don't control or understand. You have baggage about taxes and changing rules and codes. How you retire today is a result of collective societal decisions, and that creates baggage. When you start looking at all that we drag around, you'll see—it's not about the math. Math will tell you that if you save $1,459.28 a month for thirty years and earn an interest rate of 4%, you will have $1 million to retire on. But life is not a straight line; it's not that simple. The math is a great starting point, but it only works if your assumptions match the numbers. Life is not math, which is why you have to understand the financial baggage you're dealing with in order to know where you want to go. Then math becomes a tool to help you get there.

Sometimes your past mistakes can paralyze you in such a way that you keep getting harmed by the same mistake, over and over. Have you heard of therapeutic shopping? I have a few family members, friends, and clients who suffer from this affliction. Do you? Perhaps you are not feeling good about yourself or are having a bad day. Now there's Amazon, the one-click nightmare for secret shoppers. Just as online poker games are irresistible for gamblers, Amazon has made retail therapy way too easy. Here's the problem: You have that minute when you shop and feel better, and then you slip into double stress because you've added to your debt again. This can be paralyzing. Find a place to break the cycle. We all have weaknesses like this; it's not always shopping, but odds are, it's something. You have to figure out what it is so you can do better. Confusing a pleasurable buying experience with money management happens all the time.

SHINE A LIGHT ON YOUR FEARS

WHEN KRIS AND I MOVED to Arkansas with the Air Force, we had three horses. We shopped for a property that was close enough to the base for emergency recalls and had a barn and pasture, and we agreed that we would just accept the house that came with the property that met these criteria. We found a place that was close and had an amazing barn—and it was going to cost $250,000! My mind raced. A quarter of a million dollars! The words struck fear into my heart. It was the first time I was even tangentially associated with the word "million." Our first home, in Texas, cost $142,000.

You don't realize the mental walls you have until you run into them. We had a patient realtor who stuck with us through the emotional roller coaster as we digested the fact that $250,000 *was* in our price range. The best way you can mitigate your fears is with education.

First of all, give yourself permission; you're going to have fears. If you told me you don't have any, I would say you're not telling the truth. Education is where you start to alleviate some fear because it is terrifying not to be in control. With money, people feel much more secure when they perceive that they're in the driver's seat. It's no fun to run every decision you make through your checkbook (and your gut). "Can I afford that?" It's a scary place to live.

PROVE IT TO YOURSELF WITH NUMBERS

GOOD, BAD, OR UGLY, IT's better to know the truth. Trevor quit his job to become an entrepreneur. He started a handyman service. His wife, Elle, kept her management job at the bank and was worried about their income situation. Trevor didn't create a business plan; he just focused on the individual jobs. When we sat down for an annual review, we found that while he was staying busy, his business was costing them money. He had joined some networking organizations with monthly fees and was paying for different marketing tools and website leads. He hadn't set up a separate business account and was using the family credit card for business expenses. It turned out that the marketing cost more than he was bringing in and, without a business plan, he didn't know when he would have enough clients to make money. He didn't want to go back to his office job and was afraid he would have to if he didn't show a profit. The stress was starting to spill over into their marriage. Tracking his business numbers and creating a plan with a timeline helped bring peace back to their home.

YOU ARE IN THE PERFECT SPOT TO IMPROVE

JULIE IS A SUCCESSFUL, SMART woman in her forties. She has a PhD in economics, is a homeowner, and has bearded dragons. She has a close-knit family and nephews she spends a lot of time with each year. Julie has never planned for her future.

Julie told me, "I know I'm in my forties, but I feel like I'm just getting to be a grown-up. I spent years working on my PhD and just surviving financially. Now that I have a job, I seem to be okay month to month, but I don't see how I have any extra money to start investing."

This made sense. Julie went from living with roommates as a starving student to owning a home, a new car, and a couple of bearded dragons. While she had a lot more money, she had expanded her life, too. This is a quandary. How do you plan for retirement and still feel like you're getting to live in the now?

YOU ALWAYS MAKE THE BEST DECISIONS

YOU HAVE ALWAYS MADE THE best decisions you knew how to make. Let's just be honest about that. You never intentionally sabotaged yourself. Got it.

I've been there. "Oh, I shouldn't buy that, but I just need it." Or, "I just want that cup of coffee at Starbucks. I know I was taking a caffeine time-out, but I'm just going to have it anyway."

Those decisions were the best you could make at the time. You may have been stressed. You had things going on in your life that overcame your ability to make the best numbers decisions. In each moment, your immediate circumstances impact your choices.

Maybe now that we've looked at how common it is to have your own personal brand of logic, you can see yourself through a lens of humor and kindness. Developing self-awareness is a process that can be a little painful, but pays dividends on the other side. Reading these stories, you are probably recognizing some of your own mental triggers. The solution to your money situation is almost always going to be an emotional one. Hopefully, you can see that trying to live austerely is like trying to go cold turkey when you diet or stop smoking cigarettes. Willpower can carry you for a time, but it alone rarely results in permanent, positive change. Positive shifts in how you live your life happen when you start identifying your stressors and creating space to make different choices.

TO WRAP UP

THIS CHAPTER IS PROBABLY THE most uncomfortable to encounter because financial baggage is, well, baggage. It can also be a relief to know you are not alone, and getting clear about what obstacles may be holding you back is wonderful. Because you now know that you have a mental financial junk drawer in addition to your physical junk drawer, you may see why money is even more challenging to manage inside of a relationship. Now you know.

KEY TAKEAWAYS

- First, recognize you that have a mental financial junk drawer. Second, realize that it needs to be organized.
- Be aware of how you mentally account for your money. Whether you are a numbers person or not, you have a system.
- Money is a tool to trade for experiences.
- "Budget" is a trigger word. "Spending plan" is better. Language is more important than you may realize as you start developing your financial freedom.
- Reflect on what is enough for you personally.

- Financial baggage and lack of self-awareness cause you to make the same mistakes, over and over.
- Money is more emotion than math.
- You can mitigate fear with education.
- Be kind to yourself.

TAKE ACTION NOW EXERCISE

CHECK ALL THAT THAT APPLY and feel free to add others:
I have these fears about money:

- ☐ I'm not going to have enough for retirement.
- ☐ Everyone I know is doing better than me.
- ☐ Other people know more about money than I do.
- ☐ I don't know who to trust.

I have these reasons for not saving more right now:

- ☐ I don't make enough money.
- ☐ I don't need to, my spouse/partner is our breadwinner.
- ☐ I'm good; I have a 401(k) at work.
- ☐ I'm swamped with student loans right now.
- ☐ I'll get to it after the kids are done with college.
- ☐ I'll get to it after my daughter's wedding.
- ☐ I don't have time to figure it out.

CASE STUDY: ACCOUNTING VS. EARNING

IS YOUR ORGANIZATIONAL STYLE WORKING against you?

Sheila is a spreadsheet master. She doesn't like surprises. She has a separate category for everything she can possibly spend money on in her financial world, from groceries to home insurance. She has a column in her worksheet that accounts for the taxes she will owe at the end of the year. This is a great idea because she knows she will not have to scramble at the end of the year, trying to figure out how to pay her tax bill. So far, so good. Can you guess where she keeps the actual money represented in this column in her spreadsheet?

If you guessed the bank, you are correct. What are the pros to having money in the bank? It's FDIC-insured, so it should never lose value. The Federal Deposit Insurance Corporation (FDIC) is an independent agency created by Congress to maintain stability and public confidence in the nation's financial system.[58] A bank account is readily accessible, so it's a liquid asset. What are the cons? Is it protected from a potential lawsuit judgment? No. Is it earning a good rate of return? No. Is it a tax-advantaged account? No.

The core message of this book is, changing where your money lives can change how your financial world grows. What if Sheila had a place where she could save her money for end-of-year taxes that would earn some interest, potentially be protected from lawsuits, grow tax-deferred, and still be liquid? Would it be a good use of her time to become familiar with how that could work? Do you think she might say, "That sounds too good to be true?" Do you think she might dismiss this option because it could move her out of her comfort zone or make her feel a loss of control? You will see that a repeating theme of these case studies is to highlight how you can get to "yes, and" (I say with a nod to improv comedy) instead of solving only one problem at a time.

CHAPTER 8

HOW TO SPEND YOUR NEST EGG

*Once you shift your order of priorities from
"having-doing-being"to "being-doing-having,"
your destiny will be in your hands.*

—*Sadhguru*[59]

- Are you ever afraid to let yourself dream about retirement?
- Do you know what a win looks like?
- Do you fear loss?
- Have you ever wondered why taxes are as important as the size of your nest egg?

IF YOU ARE ONE OF those people who likes to read the last page of a book first to see how it ends, this chapter is for you. As I mentioned in the introduction, I'm one of those people who looks at the last page of a magazine first. (There are many of us.) Have you noticed there's usually a fun article there now?

I've talked about a holistic approach to planning. Sometimes this can include working backwards to get the right solution. In my engineering classes, it wasn't always enough to have the right answer; we had to show our work, too. I got pretty good at being able to work backwards to get an answer. You saw the Financial Life Cycle chart (Figures 4 and 12) in Chapters 1 and 3. Now we're going to delve into why you have synergy looking at your life as an entire system instead of a series of unrelated decisions and actions.

A complete financial journey has three basic phases: accumulation, retirement, and a transfer of wealth—"Get it," "Got it," and "Give it" (Figure 41). Most marketing focuses on getting it. Buy these annuities, mutual funds, stocks, bonds, real estate, and so on, and your worries are over. Many advisors focus almost exclusively on the "Get it" aspect of financial health, building your savings. I find that most financial plans—if you have one—do not protect your nest egg as it grows. Many clients come to me earning in the high six figures, living large, with no safety net if the primary breadwinner gets sick or dies. You are good with this risk as long as life is good. It's too late once poor health or an accident happens.

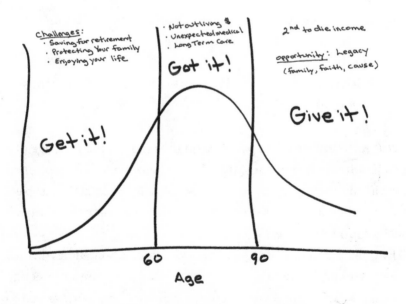

Figure 41: Financial Life Cycle Problems

I was a young lieutenant at Eglin Air Force Base in Florida for both Hurricane Erin and Hurricane Opal. I'd never lived on the coast before, so I asked my boss if I needed to evacuate. He said, "Do you feel scared?" Dumb question. I was twenty-three years old, still immortal. I replied, "No." I had no real-life experience to help me determine the risk I accepted by staying. The question tweaked my masculine energy, so there was no way I was leaving.

This is what you do during your "Get it" years. If you've never experienced an unexpected illness or death in your family or close circle of friends, you won't feel a need to protect your nest egg as it grows and may not incorporate a good strategy for defense in your plan to save for retirement (offense).

Holistic planning is all about making choices that set your money up to do more than one thing. For example, well-designed life insurance with disability coverage protects your young family. If you make it to retirement unscathed, this same policy shifts roles to protect your nest egg from a long-term care expense or other unplanned medical event in the "Got it" phase. Finally, this same policy will protect the second person to die in your relationship with a tax-free death benefit.

Pay attention here. What this means is, if you can spend and enjoy your savings, spend down closer to zero because the death benefit will support the living spouse. Some people choose to ignore the Rule of 100 and rely on keeping 100% of their money in the market, thus limiting their freedom. How do you spend your savings when you don't know if you'll need money for long-term care? What if you live an extra five or ten years? Do you see how you could force yourself into austerity if you fail to balance your risk between SMAs and GAs? All or nothing is a limiting choice.

Some marketing focuses on the "Got it" phase of retirement. Protect your assets with these annuities, estate plans, trusts, long-term care insurance, and so on. A few professionals focus on your transfer of wealth. Set up your estate plan, write a will, and identify beneficiaries in your insurance and retirement accounts. While my nice little graph makes it look like these phases are neat and linear, the planning process—done right—is more of an interconnected web that builds advantages in different places. This chapter explains how better planning now opens up more options later. Linear thinking does not allow you to reach your maximum financial potential.

A WIN

BARB SAID, "I CAN'T TAKE it with me."

We were in the middle of an annual review and these words struck fear into her husband, Gary. Barb is one of those loving people you meet who has a big heart and gives to everyone. I must admit, money seems to flow to her even when it doesn't seem possible.

Gary, on the other hand, has always been a hard worker, frugal, and a self-described realist. Opposites attract. I had helped them cocreate a retirement plan that worked for them, and at times it felt like I was brokering a United Nations peace treaty. Barb wanted to be and feel generous. Gary didn't want to run out of money.

Money is more emotion than math, and we had to bridge this divided worldview to make their money work. Because we used some of the strategic thinking from Chapter 4, they were set up to have a very comfortable income in retirement. Part of our review covered the various accounts they had that were earning different interest rates and exposed to different risks. The review showed their net worth to be a little more than $1 million, including their property. Barb had never made more than $100,000 in any given year and there were many years she had been a stay-at-home mom or earning in the $30,000-a-year range.

Her eyes twinkled at their net worth, and she almost trilled, "One million dollars."

The reason for Barb's generosity was twofold. She wanted to help her family, and she liked the strings that were attached to her gifts. Sheldon Cooper, a character on *The Big Bang Theory*, would say, "You haven't given me a gift, you've given me an obligation."[60] Barb gave her kids money. She paid for their college classes. She helped with their mortgages when they were behind on payments. She took them on vacation. Meanwhile, Gary watched their savings go down and down. Gary was at a loss. He wanted his family to live in joy and abundance but, as a realist, he didn't see how that was possible when they were hemorrhaging money.

I taught them a strategy to bridge this gap between intention and action. Retirement is a tricky thing. You can't take it with you, but you don't know how long you're going to live, so how can you spend down to the penny? You can use a conventional strategy of having your nest egg in the market, hopefully earning 7-10% while you withdraw 4% of the growth to live on. This works well if your account is big enough. This works well if the market is on an upswing. It gets dicey when the market drops, or a recession happens. This is where balance comes into play.

To solve the anxiety created by Barb's giving habit, we used a whole life savings plan that really took off once Barb and Gary wrapped their heads around how to use it. In Chapter 6, we talked about money having more than one job (based on the different characteristics of a good investment from Chapter 5). Barb and Gary both came from long-lived families and needed long-term care insurance. Barb's mother, Eve, had needed full-time nursing support and Barb and Gary had to pay for this out of pocket because no insurance was in place for Eve. They realized that a medical event could quickly drain retirement savings, and this was a problem.

On the other hand, what if you lived frugally and then ended up not needing the insurance? How much life would you miss out on? You can't take it with you. The whole life savings plan did multiple things for Barb and Gary. It had a death benefit to protect the surviving spouse or to be transferred to the children. It allowed for money to grow tax-deferred and be accessible. It also allowed for the conversion of the death benefit to longer-term care if needed; if long-term care was not needed, the cash was available. Flexibility. Keeping your money in your financial bubble to hedge against disaster while keeping the money available if problems do not arise is an advanced planning concept.

A good strategy can let you use a product to solve several problems at once, if you use it right. If your savings are large enough, you can let them keep working in the market and still ride out the ups and downs. A strategic approach becomes more crucial when you have finite resources.

Barb is now able to borrow money from her whole life savings plan to support her kids when needed. She can then repay herself at her own pace. Before, she would take money from her bank account, and it was gone. Now, when she borrows from the whole life savings plan to give money to the kids, she still has a death benefit in place—albeit a reduced amount—and when it is repaid, her full, tax-free death benefit is restored. Gary and Barb are good savers by nature. Gary's frugal nature also ensures that the whole life policy is replenished expediently. This strategy solved an emotional need and protected their retirement nest egg.

This success story of Barb and Gary didn't happen overnight. And there was an order of things. A whole life savings plan requires a medical exam, so not everyone can qualify for this strategy. Barb and Gary started their planning a few years before Barb retired, when Gary was still healthy enough to secure a good rating. Baked into this success were strategic thinking and decisions about Social Security, paying off the mortgage, and creating a balance of guaranteed and market investments (the Rule of 100). To have a truly holistic plan, you need to understand the tools identified in Chapters 5 and 6 and the concept of strategic thinking from Chapter 4. You need to become aware of your emotional baggage, as discussed in Chapter 7, and the myths you may buy into from Chapter 2. When it all comes together, you get to maximize your resources synergistically, with a much more sophisticated approach than the simple objective of making as much money as possible.

A LOSS

SPENDING YOUR NEST EGG IS different than growing it. This is an important concept, because most of your life is on the front end "Get it" phase of that bell curve, growing your accounts. Think about that golden egg you've seen in so many financial magazines and articles, sitting at the top of your bell curve. The egg is the target you plan to reach. When you retire, the time to crack open that nest egg arrives, and it can be nerve-wracking.

John and Abby approached me about planning for their upcoming retirement in a few years. They didn't have kids. Abby had worked in the past and had a few IRAs. They had no insurance. John planned to work for another three years. They had many questions, and many holes in their financial bubble. They didn't know how much was enough. They needed to move money from taxable to tax-free status without bumping up into the next tax bracket, if possible. They had no long-term care and John had already had a heart attack. They had no plan for Abby if John passed first. They were hyper-focused on growing John's 401(k). They still had 100% of their money in aggressive GAs even though, with John at sixty-four, it was time to consider some balance.

Because he had not been managing their money for years, John was really plugged into hoping his work account would be enough. He didn't know how much was enough for them because he was laser-focused on logging as much overtime as he could in his last few working years.

I talked about the goal of protecting themselves first and then creating a plan to spend their money so they could enjoy their retirement. Their strategy was different now that they had grown a big nest egg and were no longer forty years old but older than sixty. The concepts were clear to Abby right away. John took a little longer because he had to run every new concept through his preconceptions first and was uncomfortable when he found a disconnect.

We like it when our notions are affirmed, and it's challenging to find out that something you thought was true is not. John could not wrap his head around the smaller returns in a SMA that provided a guarantee to never lose value. And he could not reconcile paying fees for actively managed market accounts with downside protection to hedge against a large market drop like the one that occurred in 2008. Lifestyle and quality-of-life factors did not register for him. Many people struggle to prioritize peace of mind and even feelings in general as something of financial value because they don't grasp a holistic approach. They know the linear process of tackling one thing at a time.

This is why trust-building is so important. For the do-it-yourselfer, relying on other people is anathema and it can be hard to embrace a new concept or idea if you are not open to education. When your circle of trust is small, you limit your problem-solving capability. At the end of the day, it's your money and you make the decisions.

I value second opinions. In my Air Force role, I consult with my leadership team, even when—no, especially when—I think I know what I want to do. The extra input either affirms that I am making the right choice or introduces an alternative option I had not considered. When I was in pilot training, learning how to deal with emergency procedures in-flight, my instructor said step one was to "wind the clock." I'm dating myself here. Airplanes used to have analog clocks with a twisty knob; you wound the clock so it kept running. The point was that, in emergencies, the initial problem was not usually the cause of a crash. It was how the pilot and crew responded to the problem. If the plane was going to blow up, it probably already would have. The task was to figure out how to safely land as soon as was practical.

If you have a written, strategic plan for managing your money, it will include how you plan to react to market drops—your mental "wind the clock" space. It is a known fact that the market will drop from time to time. You are ahead of the game if you've already thought through how you will react if it does, how much of a drop you can tolerate, and the back-up plan you will have in place for sourcing your money. This is where trust comes in. Trusted advisors can help you think through options, and you can decide what feels best for you.

You see, financial planning does not stop when you retire or stop working. Spending your money is very different than growing it. Growing your savings doesn't really impact your life while you're in the "Get it" phase. You're working and adding money, so savings are just this thing off in the corner. But after you quit working, you don't have a regular income stream anymore. Maybe you have been lucky enough to develop some passive income sources, like rental properties, or maybe you've earned a pension, but much of your nest egg is going to be what you were able to save.

Time is still a factor. How long do you think you're going to live? Your personal family history is the best indicator. You may need to keep some of your money growing in the market. How much money do you need protected to cover your food, clothing, and shelter needs? Having all your money at risk when you are no longer working can be stressful. Who wants to wake up each morning in retirement, log onto the internet, and see how their 401(k) is doing—besides John? There is a very different plan for how you're going to spend your money than there is for how you're going to grow it.

I was unable to help John and Abby understand a holistic approach to their money. John was laser focused on fees and could not think strategically about the outcome. The adage "can't see the forest for the trees" really applied to him. He watched his accounts every morning and the number in his account ruled the quality of his day. If you recall, he had enough money he could have buried it in the backyard and just dug up a little each year and he would have been fine. You have to process your own financial baggage. No one can do that work for you.

I did show them the holes in their plan, especially how Abby was in danger of a severely reduced lifestyle after John passed. The bottom line was, they could have comfortably added protection to fill their holes, balanced their strategy in case of a big market drop, and had enough to live on quite nicely. This client story is a classic example of what happens when you cannot overcome your emotional baggage in order to enjoy your life in the present.

TAXABLE ➔ TAX-DEFERRED ➔ TAX-FREE

NOW I'M GOING TO TALK taxes. Wait, stay with me. This is important for you to know. These days, you create your own financial plan for retirement. But it was not always like this. It's really *crazy* how much legislation effects your bottom line.[61]

Pensions have been offered throughout history. Military men, from soldiers of Ancient Rome to soldiers of the American Revolution, were offered income for life—if they survived. Your retirement plan was to live through the battles.

Regular people—"civilians," as we in the military like to call you—started to see pensions in 1921. The Internal Revenue Act of 1921 gave companies tax breaks for creating retirements.[62] Tax breaks led to pensions. Because of them, you didn't focus on saving for retirement.

By the 1960s, almost half of the private sector work force had company retirements. My grandfather had an amazing plan, and my grandma continued to receive his monthly payments until she passed—almost *twenty years* after him! One reason we don't learn about money at home is that our parents didn't. There were pensions. Saving for retirement is a fairly recent thing!

Skip ahead to the late 1970s—early 1980s. Pensions started disappearing and 401(k)s arrived.[63] Why do companies prefer defined contribution plans over defined benefit plans?[64] Defined contribution plans are attractive to companies because they have tax benefits, provide a retirement benefit to employees, and pass all the risk and responsibility on to the employee. It was sold as, "Wouldn't you like the *opportunity* to be in charge of your own plan?" Here's the key point. A change in the tax code changed how you get to retire. Taxes are a primary driver in your success. Today, it's not what you make but what you get to keep that is important. Taxes drive how you spend your retirement.

Now that you know (in case you didn't know) how changes in the tax code have made you responsible for your retirement, what are you willing to do to help cocreate your financial plan for success? What I mean by this is, are you ready to become a partner in your retirement success?

Historically, with defined benefit plans, you could assume that you would receive both a fixed monthly benefit and Social Security in retirement. With defined contribution plans, companies do provide matching contributions in the "Get it" phase. The funds are normally in the market, and the value of your account fluctuates with market performance. Instead of receiving a guaranteed amount to live on, you have to decide who will manage your money in retirement. This means finding a trusted advisor. Or, if you do it yourself, you must decide where your money will be invested, how much risk you should have, and what constitutes a safe amount to start withdrawing from your account in retirement. I ask what you are willing to cocreate because you are now responsible for your retirement. You can find a trusted advisor to aid in the management process, but without pensions, it is no longer guaranteed that someone else will make sure you have enough money to support your lifestyle.

The tax code is more than 2,000 pages long.[65] There is some online discussion that it is more than 70,000 pages long because of additional material in the form of treasury regulations and other official guidance impacting tax considerations. The point is, it's complicated, and whoever knows the most rules wins. Therefore, it's important that you have a

CPA on your team along with your financial advisor. The tax code is written to benefit business owners. It can be advantageous to own some kind of business, even if you're working a W-2 job. If you can manage a rental property, sell Mary Kay, or do something else that qualifies as a business, there are rules in the tax code that you can take advantage of. It's legal and available for you. Paying your fair share of taxes is okay, but you want to make sure you're not paying more taxes than you need to. That starts with understanding what you can and can't do.

Grace and Karl have been outstanding savers. They have tucked away more than $1.5 million in their 401(k). They also have another $400,000 in an annuity. Grace has some small IRAs from early jobs she held. The couple is about five years out from retirement and ready to plan for it. Up to this point, they have just focused on stuffing money into their 401(k), which is managed by Karl's company, so they haven't really put any kind of plan into place. Their health is not great, so we were unable to look at a whole life savings strategy for their long-term care needs.

We focused on another big strategy: moving as much money as possible from taxable to tax-free accounts. Now that you understand the role legislation plays in how much of your money you can protect from taxes, you know that this can make a big difference. For example, if you have $100,000 in a traditional IRA and are in the 22% tax bracket, you will pay about $22,000 in taxes. It's kind of a bummer when you realize your $100,000 is really only $78,000 of spendable cash.

I explained to Grace and Karl that if they converted $1.5 million from a traditional 401(k) to a Roth IRA, they could expect to pay about $350,000 in taxes, depending on their tax bracket. (It typically takes about seven years after a conversion for an account to recover the dollars spent in taxes. As is true with most things, taking action today will allow more time for compounding growth to help you.) How are you feeling at this point? I can tell you that Karl was having sticker shock at the size of the tax bill. Grace's eyes had glazed over, and I'm pretty sure she was mentally running through her grocery shopping list since they were headed to the store after our meeting. The end goal was to set them up for a safer, more secure future, but these details were triggers that made them feel like a big chunk of their money was going to just leave their bubble.

We got over that hurdle but then ran into a wall. Nearly five years earlier, when Karl transitioned to a new job, he had converted his $400,000 401(k) to an annuity. Annuities are not good or bad, but they can be complicated because they are contracts. This particular annuity was set to start paying a monthly allotment when Karl turned sixty-five. The intention behind establishing this annuity was good. It had protected the lump sum and would provide a predictable income. The challenge was that the money was in a traditional account. Conversion to a Roth would require Grace and Karl to write a check for more than $100,000 because using the money from the account was no longer an option based on the contract.

Because Karl was still working, their tax bracket was higher than we were planning for in retirement. You're probably asking, "What's the big deal?" A big strategy for retirement is to get as many of your assets as possible into tax-free vehicles such as Roth IRAs, whole life insurance, and certain qualified bonds so that your tax bracket remains low. Their Social Security benefit combined with this traditional annuity income was going to keep them in almost a 20% tax bracket, even if we converted the rest of the account into a Roth.

This is why a successful retirement plan is holistic and is stronger when it includes the "Get it," "Got it," *and* the "Give it" phases. The advisor who put Grace and Karl's money into the annuity was focused on protecting the full value of the 401(k), but did not account for taxes in retirement. They are going to be okay, but it would have been possible for them to pay less in taxes if different decisions had been made earlier in their lives. Wrapping your arms around all of your money choices allows you to evaluate how one decision can impact your options.

The best time to start planning for retirement is when you're twenty. The second-best time is today. Starting early gives you more chances to get your money working for you so you can reach your number. There are three big problems you are solving in the "Get it" phase: how to save while you launch your career and maybe a family, how to enjoy your life along the way and not suffer through austerity, and how to protect your nest egg as you grow it in a way that makes sense.

In the "Give it" phase, you have one problem and a great opportunity. How do you ensure that your spouse, or the second to die in your relationship, is cared for? The reality is, the first person in your relationship to get sick and need care will suck dollars from your savings because we take care of each other. Without good planning, the second to die can face becoming destitute and relying on Medicaid. The opportunity with holistic planning is getting to choose your legacy. You can bequeath assets to your family, your church, a social cause of your choice, or some combination of these.

Depending on the mix of assets you have in your financial bubble when you reach the "Got it" phase, you create your spending plan—in other words, crack open your nest egg—with the intention of not outliving your money. Thinking about how much is enough, incorporating tax strategies, and balancing risk with GAs and SMAs will provide you with the most flexibility to enjoy retirement.

TO WRAP UP

You now know that looking at your life holistically—including the "Get it," "Got it," and "Give it" phases of wealth management—means tracking as many variables as possible. Because legislation and the tax code have such immediate impact on your savings, it is smart to try to have as much of your money in tax-free locations as possible. You will want to have a CPA working with your financial advisor—a tax expert to maximize choices—because tax laws can change subtly each year. Good communication is a key to a peaceful retirement. You will be amazed at how you and your spouse or partner may think differently about money, so the more open and honest you can be in communication, the fewer headaches you will have—at least after you've had the conversations and made agreements.

KEY TAKEAWAYS

- You must communicate with your spouse or partner about how you intend to spend your money in retirement. Differences in philosophy are magnified when you start withdrawing money from your retirement accounts.
- A good strategy keeps shifting your assets right: Taxable → Tax-deferred → Tax-free.
- You are now responsible for your own retirement. Pensions are all but gone.
- Holistic retirement planning includes all three of the "Get it," "Got it," and "Give it" phases. The sooner you start thinking about your entire picture, the more time you'll have to both enjoy your money and give more generously.

TAKE ACTION NOW CHECKLIST

ANSWER THE FOLLOWING QUESTIONS. IF you cannot, make a note and find some help.

- What tax bracket do you plan to be in during retirement?
- How much of your money (dollars or percentage) is growing tax-free right now?
- How do you plan to convert your current accounts to tax-free accounts?

CASE STUDY: LUMP SUM VS. MONTHLY INCOME

"I HAVE THE OPTION TO cash out my retirement or take a monthly income. What should I do?"

This situation is very common and pushes some emotional buttons. If you have worked your entire life, you are probably used to getting a monthly paycheck. For some of you, the idea of a regular monthly income can feel good, while the idea of having a large sum of money to parcel out yourself can feel overwhelming. It can also be scary to watch that sum get smaller and feel like you may run out.

You can move your spending power needle depending on your tax bracket. If you receive Social Security, you will have taxable income. Accepting the monthly payment option could potentially increase your taxable income. Will it be enough to move you to a higher tax bracket? You can check. You don't have to guess. Do you think taxes will go up or down in the future? You may be okay today, but things can change.

If you accept the lump sum, you may have the option to convert this into tax-free money. You may be able to control what tax bracket you are in. The concept is to try to convert as much of your money as possible into tax-free assets. There are several calculations you will need to run to determine if a scenario like this is possible for you. Here are a few questions you will want to answer before you make a choice:

- Is the monthly money for life or for a defined period of time?
- How long-lived is your family? In other words: How long do you think you will receive this monthly amount?
- How big is the lump sum? You will need to compare its value to the aggregated monthly value.
- How good is your health? If you cannot qualify for a whole life savings plan, you may have one less tax-advantaged vehicle option available.

- Do you have any other assets that may drive a tax bill?

Robert Kiyosaki, coauthor of *Rich Dad Poor Dad*, is known for saying, "It's not how much money you make, but how much money you keep…"[66] This is so very true when it comes to knowing how to protect and spend your nest egg.

CHAPTER 9

BUILD YOUR PLAN

A goal without a plan is just a wish.

—*Antoine de Saint-Exupéry*[67]

- Have you considered what a life well lived feels like to you? Is success more than a large home, nice car, and big bank account?
- Are you clear about how much risk you are comfortable with? Do you make risky money choices because you think you have to, or because you don't know another way?
- Do you have a written financial plan, or are you just hoping things work out?
- Have you identified how much is enough, or are you running on the indefinite treadmill of just needing more?
- What if you outlive your money?

HOW DO YOU GET STARTED? I've talked about a lot of the myths, and you've done a lot of the emotional work. I've also talked about numbers and how money grows in terms of time, rate of return, and investment amounts. Now you can say, "Okay, I got it. I have things to work on, but now I'm ready. How do I get started?" How do you eat an elephant?

One bite at a time. If you try to do everything at once, it's just going kick you right into analysis paralysis and you won't do anything. That's why it's important that you break down the planning and figure out how you're going start building your plan. I recommend that you take a quick look at the worksheet in the case study at the end of the chapter now so you can track your thoughts as you learn this planning process.

VISION: WHAT FEELS LIKE SUCCESS TO ME?

BUILD YOUR PLAN

3-PART FINANCIAL PLANNING FRAMEWORK

STEP 1: ESTABLISH BIG PICTURE VISION

STEP 2: STRATEGY AND RULE OF 100—WHERE ARE YOU IN YOUR FINANCIAL LIFE CYCLE?

STEP 3: TACTICAL EXECUTION

A. WHAT'S YOUR NUMBER? HOW MUCH IS ENOUGH?

B. ORGANIZE YOUR FINANCIAL JUNK DRAWER

C. FIND YOUR HOLES AND GAPS

You want to begin with baby steps, and there is an order to follow. First, figure out what feels like success for you right now. What does happiness mean for you? It's really hard to create any kind of plan when you don't know where you're going. It's like trying to shoot a target while blindfolded.

Your priorities will change as you move through life. When I was twenty, all I wanted to do was fly airplanes. At forty, I left military active duty before I was

216

eligible for retirement to become an entrepreneur. At fifty, I was still in the Air Force reserve and competing for my next promotion while running my business. Life is rarely a straight line. Set yourself up for financial success and create flexibility so you can adjust as life throws you curveballs.

To get started with Step 1, think about where you're trying to go, the big picture. Do you want to stay in your current job and retire at sixty-five with a pension? Do you want to be an entrepreneur with several businesses that will allow you to retire early, maybe at fifty? Do you want to get all your kids through college without loans? Or do you want to take amazing trips around the world? Give yourself permission to dream big, here, as if money were no object. It's important to have clarity in your own mind so you don't move in directions you will regret.

Every mission I flew in the Air Force had an end goal, a vision we focused on accomplishing. A successful flying career is one where your landings equal your takeoffs, and this begins with exhaustive flight planning. With each flight, my crew and I looked at the entire route we would be flying. We figured out how much extra gas we needed in case of an unexpected flight diversion due to weather. We calculated how heavy the plane would be to ensure that we could climb over any mountains in our path and that the runways we planned to land on were long enough. We established crew rest requirements to make sure everyone was performing at their best. We had checklists to make sure we didn't leave safety up to chance or memory. Our planning process was prescribed.

One afternoon, we landed at Bagram Air Base in Afghanistan and got a call on the radio to check in with base operations. I was notified that we had been re-tasked to fly a high-profile mission: We were to take a VIP all the way up the Persian Gulf to Bahrain (Figure

42). Bahrain was a great place to go at the time, so our crew was excited.

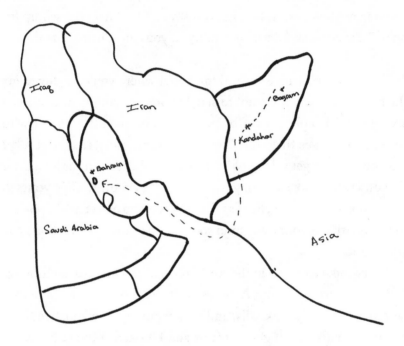

Figure 42: Middle East Map for Situational Awareness

If you've never been to Afghanistan in the summer, it is quite hot. It is also quite high in altitude. The air is thin, so it takes longer to gain enough airspeed to take off, requiring longer runways, and sometimes the C-130 could not climb over the mountains if the plane was too heavy. This was where the first shoe dropped. My engineer ran the numbers and determined that we needed to be very light to make it over the mountains (Figure 43). The good news was, we could stop in Kandahar and add more fuel for the trip to Bahrain.

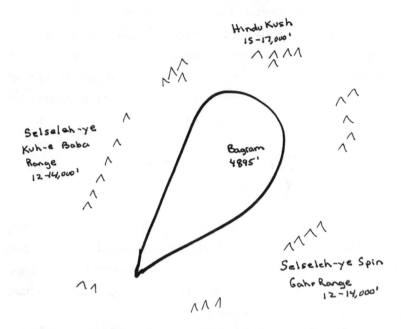

Figure 43: Mountains around Bagram Air Base

I reported our plan back to command post and was told it was unacceptable: We needed to take on enough fuel to fly to Bahrain because our VIP did not have time to sit on the hot tarmac while we refueled. I did agree that refueling was an inconvenient process. It would be hot, sticky, and add at least an hour and a half to the trip. I was asked to look at the numbers again and see if I could make the trip happen without the gas stop. We ran the numbers and determined that we could alter our route to fly through a saddle in the mountain pass. However, if we lost an engine for any reason, there was a stretch of about twenty miles where we would be unable to turn around and go back to Bagram or clear the remaining peaks.

It's important to get clear about what success is for you. Do you want to retire early? Do you want to be an entrepreneur and run your own business? Do you want to work for a large company until you feel you are able to retire? Do you want a family, or do you want to travel the world with your spouse? The big picture vision you choose sets the stage for the next two steps in your planning process. I was very clear that I wanted the number of my landings to equal the number of my takeoffs. This situation in Afghanistan drove some serious risk analysis as we strategized about the mission.

STRATEGY: WHAT RISK FEELS RIGHT FOR YOU?

STEP 2 IS ABOUT FIGURING out where you are in your financial life cycle. It's about time and what kind of risk feels acceptable. This depends on where you are in your life and who is dependent on you. Decisions that are acceptable when you are single may not feel right when you have family looking to you as a provider.

As an aircraft commander, I was not only responsible for accomplishing the mission, but also for the safety of my crew. I reported back to the controller that since this was not a life-or-death mission, I was unwilling to accept the potential risk even though, in my heart, I really wanted to go to Bahrain and thought we'd be fine. My boss at the time pointed out that the regulations had a "pilot discretion" clause that basically allowed me to make any decision I wanted. This piled on the stress. I wanted to go to Bahrain. I didn't want to be labeled a pilot who couldn't get the mission done. At that point, I developed my personal litmus test for accepting risk, and I carry this through to my financial recommendations.

Could I look the parents of my crew members in the eye, in the event of a fatal crash, and tell them that the mission had been necessary? If we had been carrying an aeromedical evacuation crew to an emergency or carrying a load of blood for wounded soldiers, I would have decided the risk was acceptable. To avoid the inconvenience of refueling—no way. We ran out of crew day and the mission went to another crew that evening. By the time the second C-130 lifted off, the temperature had cooled down twenty-three degrees, so the air was thicker and they were able to safely climb over the mountains.

You manage risk as you make choices about your money. You may go through periods when you are not making intentional choices. You may have your 401(k) on autopilot and not know if it's a Roth, if you have the full matching contribution, or if you are in aggressive or conservative funds. You may just be growing a large bank account.

What kind of lifestyle do you want? Do you want something that only works if everything in your life happens according to plan, no mountains in your flight path? Do you want to add some cushion to account for the unexpected, like adding extra fuel for your trip just in case? Do you think my high-profile passenger would have gotten onto my plane if I had agreed to fly the mission and said, "Welcome aboard, General Smith. We have an 85% chance of reaching our destination, as long as we don't lose an engine over the mountains!"

In the Monte Carlo simulations used to project market performance, 70-90% is good.[68] Do you want 100% of your nest egg exposed to market risk? Most people have their 401(k) entirely in the market while they are working and then just leave it there when they retire. The Rule of 100 suggests that you can have balance between risk and safety. It's your money, and you get to make these choices.

Risk you are willing to accept will inform the strategy you want to adopt as you grow your wealth. Where you are in your financial life cycle also matters. Are you twenty? Forty? Sixty? Are you working for somebody else or are you an entrepreneur?

You'll do very different things at different times in your life. In your twenties, unless you have inherited a nest egg, your financial journey will be focused on understanding money. In my twenties, I didn't have any money. I was just trying to pay all my bills and have a little money left over to enjoy life. This is also a time when you can be a little more aggressive because you will have time to recover from drops in the stock market. At this point, you are just getting started and seeing what is out there in the world. This is when you want to create foundational savings habits that will support you no matter where life takes you.

Transitioning into your thirties, you may have reached a place in life where you have a pretty good job. You're making some money, have purchased a home, and have some assets growing. You may also have started your family, in which case you've got a lot of responsibilities. You're making more money, but there are a lot more things competing for it (and your time). This is when you really want to start to understand how you are building your foundation for success. One major goal of retirement is to enjoy it, right? It's a balancing act; you want to enjoy life now, but you don't want to get to retirement and live like a college student, surviving on macaroni and cheese.

In your forties and fifties, you still have time to take advantage of compounding growth. This is when you do want to get clear on when you're planning to retire. Normal retirement age used to be sixty-five, but a lot of people now are trying to figure out how to retire early. There's been a big cultural shift since the 1950s and 1960s. Priorities are different. We have two-income households. A big priority for people is wanting to enjoy life. We work to live instead of living to work. This is where you want to figure out what retirement is going to look like for you and where you are with the Rule of 100.

Moving into your sixties, you shift toward protection. When you're younger, you have insurance to protect your dependents from an unexpected death and loss of income. In retirement, insurance becomes a tool to protect your income streams and the nest egg you've worked so hard to grow. You really don't want the market to have a drop where you could lose 40-50% of your money overnight because you actually have money now. A market drop that happens while you are in your twenties is not so painful because you don't have that much yet. In your sixties, you've actually started to build your nest egg, so this is where you start shifting some of your strategies from growth to protection. You are rapidly approaching the point where you will crack open that nest egg and start to live on some of the money.

Please know, these are broad examples. The takeaway is that your life is not a straight line. Time is a huge player in how you manage your money. There are no average people, so your plan will be tailored to you, but you can see now how your plan grows with you throughout your life.

TACTICAL EXECUTION: WHAT IS MY PLAN OF ACTION?

STEP 3 IS WHERE YOU figure out how you want to achieve your vision and the actions you will take to get there. Tactical execution is where you determine your number, as you did in Chapter 3. You establish where you are right now by organizing your financial junk drawer. It takes two points to make a line. After you know where you are now and have determined your number, you can figure out whether you're on track to get there. Part of this process is identifying any holes you have in your plan and determining how you can mitigate risk.

HOW MUCH IS ENOUGH (WHAT'S YOUR NUMBER)?

NOW THAT YOU HAVE DEFINED your vision and strategy, you can build on the work you did in Chapter 3. It is time to ask, "How much is enough?" Start with the amount you are living on right now. Are you comfortable? For example, if you're making $100,000 a year and are comfortable, this is a baseline for how much you will need in retirement. If you are in your growth phase because you've started a business or you are still in your twenties or thirties, you might feel you are not making enough money yet. In that case, you need to increase your number beyond what you are living on today.

Calculate two different target numbers. First, calculate what you need based on your current standard of living. You can refer back to Chapter 3. Then calculate your stretch goal, the "life would be awesome if I hit that target" number. With these target numbers, planning can begin.

There is no one-size-fits all number. You want to figure out *your* numbers. After your brain has established what you're aiming for, you can start to get there.

FINANCIAL JUNK DRAWER

THE NEXT STEP IS TO catalog your financial junk drawer. After you've thought about what your ideal future looks like, it's time to get clear on where you are now. What do you have going right now? This is going to vary from person to person and be very specific to you. Please do not compare yourself with others. It could be as simple as this—you have a checking account, a savings account, and massive student loans. Or your parents may have paid for your college education and you are now working and have a nice little 401(k) started. You could be sending your kid off to college and feel like your business is just now taking off and you are starting from scratch. If you've received an inheritance, you might have some protection. Maybe you own a rental property. Gather all the things in your financial junk drawer and put them together in one place.* You can also download the My Personal Plan Worksheet pdf as an organizational resource.† It's better to have a complete inventory of all the pieces you have to play with before you start building your plan, and you want to have an idea of where it is that you are trying to go.

---

* Download the Financial Junk Drawer Organizer at www.nolanfinancialpartners.com/tools.

† Download the My Personal Plan Worksheet at www.nolanfinancialpartners.com/tools.

TO WRAP UP

THIS CHAPTER BEGINS WITH TAKING baby steps so you can avoid becoming overwhelmed and letting your financial success slip to the bottom of your to-do list. In this chapter, you learned how the numbers are only as good as the assumptions you make. You know that life does not follow a neat XY graph. Part of your plan includes the strategy you want to follow to get to your target goal and have the nest egg you want. You also must decide the amount of risk you want to assume on your journey.

KEY TAKEAWAYS

- Define what success looks like for you. Is it retiring early? Is it continuing to work in a field you like? Is it traveling the world? You cannot cheat off your neighbor—this definition of success is personal and yours alone.
- Make time to organize your financial junk drawer. Before you can complete a puzzle, you need to know what pieces are missing.
- Your age determines how aggressive you need to be with your plan to retire well.
- "I want to save as much money as I can" is too vague to be an achievable goal.
- Decide how much risk you want in your portfolio. (Not making a conscious decision is also choosing.)

TAKE ACTION NOW CHECKLIST

1. What are you currently doing in preparation for your financial future?
2. What do you like most about your current financial position?

3. What do you *dislike* about your current financial position and would like to see enhanced or improved?

CASE STUDY: MY PERSONAL PLAN WORKSHEET

ADD IN YOUR PERSONAL INFORMATION after you've read this chapter. Completing the My Personal Plan Worksheet at the end of this chapter will ensure that you have organized your personal information and are ready to sit down with a professional planner. It will give you the knowledge to have transparent, honest conversations about where you are now, where you want to be in retirement, and how you want to get there successfully so you feel empowered instead of merely hopeful that you can trust your advisor. Get ready to achieve and retain the lifestyle you want.

Filling out the worksheet may feel overwhelming, so set aside time to take breaks when you start getting sloppy. This process is physically taxing because it involves digging up statements, resetting passwords on websites to get access to your data, and then entering the data into the worksheet.

This process will also be emotionally taxing because you will most likely become frustrated if you have not already started your retirement account. You may feel like your spouse or partner is spending too much money, or feel put-upon because you are stuck dealing with the bulk of the money stress in your home. I promise it will feel wonderful once you have this list done, though.

Here's a quick story. During basic training, our squadron would march over to the post office once a day to check the mail. It was fun to get a care package from Mom. I will always appreciate our flight commander because after we checked our post office boxes, he would line us up and say, "Okay, who got their 'Dear John' letters today?" Instead of letting one of us become depressed or feel isolated, he made it a shared joke and we were able to support each other. When you feel negative emotions rising up as you sort through your financial junk drawer, take a minute to smile because you're not alone—you're like the rest of us.

This worksheet includes visual aids to support different learning styles. Take note of your preferred ways to digest information. When you meet with a professional financial planner, you can let them know.

STEP 1: ESTABLISH BIG PICTURE Vision

Write a few lines or even draw a picture to capture your current vision of success.

STEP 2: STRATEGY—RULE OF 100

a. What is 100 minus your current age? 100 - _____ = _____

This is a starting point to decide how much of your money should be in GAs (exposed to risk) and how much should be SMAs (guaranteed). From here, you can decide what feels good for you and what is reasonable based on your responsibilities.

My preferred balance of safe and growth money is _____ % GA / _____% SMA.

b. Place an X on the graph in Figure 44 where you believe you are in your financial life cycle.

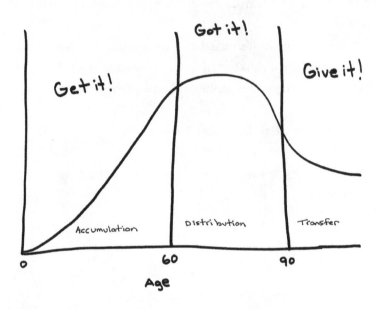

Figure 44: My Financial Life Cycle

STEP 3: TACTICAL EXECUTION

a. How much is enough? Write a sentence or two describing what "enough" feels like for you. You can also add a drawing, if that helps. It's important to write this down: Writing it down makes it real. Putting ideas on paper makes your planning process gain traction.

b. What's your number? Fill in your number on the graph (Figure 45). As we discussed in Chapter 3, here's a simple example: Assume you currently earn $100,000 a year and plan to retire at sixty-five and live for twenty more years. Multiply $100,000 times twenty, and your target number should be $2 million. You simply multiply the annual amount of money you want to live on by how long you plan to live.

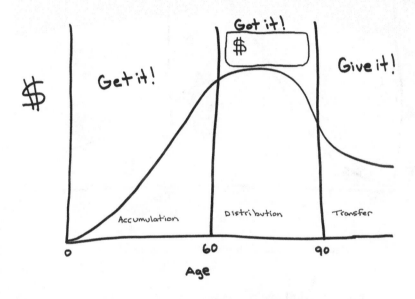

Figure 45: What's My Number?

c. Organize your financial junk drawer. Download the Financial Junk Drawer Organizer via the link at the bottom of page 224.

d. Find your holes and gaps. Review the phases of your financial life cycle and identify the potential holes in your plan. Think about your money as water that is filling a bucket. If there are holes in your bucket, you can keep adding more water (money), but it will just flow back out. A strong plan will ensure that your bucket is leakproof *and* focus on adding more water.

Place an X on the graph (Figure 46) in every phase where you may have a hole. Make note of the questions you want to discuss with your financial advisor.

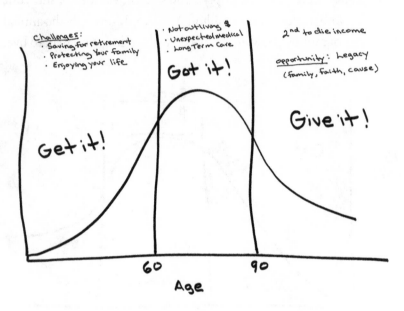

Figure 46: Potential Holes in My Financial Life Cycle

Get it: Do you have protection in case the primary earner in your life becomes disabled or dies? Do you have three to six months' worth of emergency funds in case you need to change jobs? Do you have medical care and savings to cover your deductibles? Is your money working for you in at least two or more ways? How are you balancing paying down debt (school loans, mortgages, etc.) with growing your retirement savings? Do you have enough growth in your investment strategy to help offset inflation?

Got it: Is there a chance that you may outlive your money? Do you have insurance to supplement Medicare? Do you have long-term care coverage in case you need it?

Give it: What happens to the second to die in your relationship: in other words, what income streams do they lose? Do you have long-term care coverage for the second to die if your savings are spent on the first person to become ill? Have you identified your legacy? What do you want to leave to your family, church, or charitable cause? Have you structured your legacy in the most tax-advantaged way?

CHAPTER 10

WEALTH IS A TEAM SPORT

*Great things in business are never done by one person,
they're done by a team of people.*

—Steve Jobs[69]

- Do you focus on value or zero in on eliminating all fees?
- Have you ever had the feeling that there is a better way to organize your budget?
- Have you ever made a money decision that you know in hindsight could have been better?
- Have you ever felt like you should be better off but are now too far behind?
- Have you even been afraid that you will be taken advantage of by a financial professional?
- Have you ever been afraid that everyone else "gets" money and you don't?
- Have you ever felt that you might fail at finances because you're old, divorced, lack knowledge, etc.? (Fill in the blank with your personal neurosis, wink wink.)
- What if your planning experience could be positive, light, and satisfying instead of stressful, heavy, and mystifying (or some other list of your choice)?

IF YOU WANT TO MAKE better choices, this chapter will help you begin walking that path.

Growing up, as the eldest child, I was in charge when my parents were out. With six of us, there was always a baby in diapers in the house. Mom and Dad both worked, so every kid had to pull their own weight. We used to scramble to have the floors swept, dishes done, and laundry folded before Mom got home from her twelve-hour emergency room shifts. At this point, I was more of a little dictator than a team player. I was a teenager, so what do you expect?

In high school, I played soccer and basketball and ran track. These three sports involve different kinds of teamwork. Basketball required the ability to read other players in order to pass the ball. You might think that both soccer and basketball involve dribbling, but a soccer field is much bigger than a basketball court. To play offense in soccer requires dribbling to be more than adequate, unlike defense, which is more about interception of the other players' momentum—teamwork that relies more on thinking and less on neuromuscular pathways that take years to develop. Running is very individual, so in track, I learned to attend to my mental health and that of my teammates. This is probably where I was first introduced to the idea of self-talk and that it could be either positive or negative. I was a champion at running myself down, I realized.

There are obvious analogies between sports teams and your wealth team. A sports team has an owner, and you are the owner of your financial world. A sports team has a coach calling the plays, and you will have a financial advisor on your team recommending investment strategies. A coach has different assistant coaches for different positions. Likewise, you will flourish when you have a complete financial team that includes a financial advisor, a CPA, and health insurance, disability insurance, home and car insurance, and umbrella insurance specialists (as needed). You may have a realtor if you include real estate in your portfolio. No one person can be the expert at everything, but a team working together can win the game. I find it odd that we collaborate in sports, at work, and to raise our families, and yet mass marketing drives us to try and go it alone with our money.

When you know which sport you are playing, you can pick the right equipment for your game. You wouldn't use a football to play soccer. Similarly, when you know what investment strategy you want to use to reach your retirement goals, you can select the right combination of investment tools—such as stocks, bonds, mutual funds, annuities, and insurance—to tactically execute your plan.

As an adult, I continue to grow my teambuilding skills so that I can lead effectively. In the military, we spend a lot of time deliberately developing communication and teambuilding skills because that is what it takes to accomplish a mission. In my finance business, I have developed a strong team of experts to address all the areas needed for my clients. I also invest in continuing education because the best way to lead and be part of a high-performing team is through continual self-improvement. It is possible to go it alone, but why would you want to carry the weight of your financial success by yourself when you don't have to? The reason most people don't work with a financial team comes down to trust. "What's this going to cost me, and what if I'm paying for something I should be doing myself, like a chump?" Trust begins with education and good communication. Taking your financial world to the next level of success also requires open-mindedness.

Use these three directives to successfully manage your finances:

1. Decide *how* you want your finances to be managed.
2. Apply concepts in this book to the realities of your life.
3. Understand that a team you lead is more powerful than you as an individual.

Wealth is a team sport. I'm talking about synergy: The whole is greater than the sum of its parts. I've been on many different kinds of teams in my life. After I started learning how to be a team player, I really found value in the team concept.

In this chapter, you'll learn how to be the owner of your own team and make sure you have the right coaches working for you.

FINANCIAL SELF-EFFICACY: BELIEVE IN YOURSELF AND DEVELOP TRUST

YOU WILL NOT REACH YOUR financial potential until you believe you can succeed. When you have confidence in yourself, you will be able to select experts to advise you. I am highlighting this because it is different from financial literacy. Knowing what you should do and being able to take action are two very different things.

During our discovery calls, I've started asking my new clients, "What are you willing to do to cocreate your vision of financial success?" Let me explain what I mean by this. A lot of emotion can be involved with money, and it is important to work together with a feeling of trust. I find that some people want to be completely disengaged from the process. They'll say, "Just tell me what to do." This is fine until it isn't. Financial advisors do not make you rich. The market does not make you rich. A good investment strategy, backed by a team of experts, will help you grow your financial world.

One client, Jill, was single and had a great corporate job. She had a 401(k), and we increased her contributions to take advantage of the matching contribution. This action did not address her overall financial life cycle success, but it did move us in the direction of adding value.

After discussing options, Jill elected to start a whole life savings plan to solve several issues and get her money working for her. She needed an emergency fund and a plan for long-term care. She wasn't keen to spend a lot of money on long-term care insurance. The whole life savings plan allowed her to save money in a tax-deferred vehicle and use the cash value at her discretion if she didn't need long-term care.

I explained that the cash value would start to grow because of dividends after about five years and that she could control this by how much she added to her policy.

At our next annual meeting, Jill was frustrated. "I thought you said this would make me money!"

We went back to the meeting notes and reviewed the policy. I reminded her that it could grow savings tax-deferred, but she had yet to add a single extra dollar to the account to spur the growth. Building wealth starts with a good savings habit and is boosted by saving money in tax-advantaged growth accounts. Jill was not being a team player; she was looking for me to magically make her money without doing her part of the agreed work.

When I ask the question, "What are you willing to do to cocreate your vision of financial success?" I also need to ask, "What problem are we trying to solve together when we plan for your dreams?"

I met Stewart and Felicity when they were newlyweds at fifty and fifty-five. Stewart had been a confirmed bachelor—I want you to picture this longish gray hair, a gray beard, and thick glasses, kind of a dot-com engineer type. Opposites attract. Felicity was put together—not a hair out of place, her makeup understated but never skipped over. A divorced mom of four kids, she was just finishing grad school.

"As soon as I defend my thesis, Stew's going to retire so we can move back to Arizona. Right, honey?"

Stewart sat back in a passive-aggressive posture, a smug look on his face, and shrugged.

I asked him about his investing experience.

"I got suckered into an 'amazing investment opportunity,' once," he said sarcastically. "I've stuck with my 401(k) ever since. My company stock did well!"

"When?!" Felicity said. "You lost money in 2001 and again in 2008—you've lost more than 75% of your net worth!"

He replied, "It will come back up. Everyone knows you have to be patient with the market."

"When?! When are we going to stop the bleeding? We want to retire."

We worked through some severe financial baggage and very different ideas of what retirement even looked like to determine how they could cocreate financial well-being.

Clients like this have driven me to research how I can help people help themselves. *Grit* by Angela Duckworth[70] is a current work on behavior. Duckworth's research has shown that a combination of passion and perseverance is demonstrated by high performers in nearly every domain. In articles about human behavior written by renowned psychologist Albert Bandura, I found the ten-dollar word: "self-efficacy." Self-efficacy is your belief in your own ability to accomplish a specific task or goal. What does this have to do with achieving a lifestyle you want in retirement?

Bandura identified key characteristics of people who have a strong sense of themselves. People with strong self-efficacy:

- *Learn from their mistakes.* Stewart didn't really learn from his bad investing experience. He just moved all his eggs to a different basket—from the broker to his 401(k).
- *Face challenges head-on.* Stewart was getting more and more uncomfortable with the path Felicity was driving down, but he didn't use his words to have the conversation.
- *Recover quickly from setbacks and disappointments.*[71] Stewart lost 75% of his nest egg and was in a new marriage, considering relocation, and stubbornly waiting to see if his stock would come back up. Not taking action is a choice.

Shlomo Benartzi is co-founder of the Behavioral Finance Forum. I highly recommend his TED talk "Saving for Tomorrow, Tomorrow," which shows that just knowing about money doesn't guarantee financial well-being.[72] Stewart thought that by staying away from the one broker he'd had a bad experience with, he had removed risk and solved his retirement problems. If knowledge and action are stovepiped, you will have a lot of gaps in your financial strategy. You need a better play.

What does this have to do with achieving the lifestyle you want in retirement or plugging the holes in your retirement plan?

Bandura did not leave us hanging. There are four major ways to cultivate self-efficacy. You can do this by:

1. Experiencing success
2. Choosing good role models
3. Responding to encouragement
4. Managing emotional responses[73]

Applying these actions will help lead you toward financial well-being and success.

1. Experiencing Success

You build confidence when you perform a task successfully. I like to think of saving for retirement as a muscle you build with practice. One fun way I like to do this with my clients is by setting up a travel account with the sole purpose of collecting savings for an amazing vacation. You can get bogged down when approaching saving as a practice of self-denial. I like to create an experience where planning helps you find the balance between growth and living your life!

2. Choosing Good Role Models

What are your family and friends doing? I'd like to share a story from my family's holiday Zoom call. As I shared earlier, when I started my business, one of my mantras was, "If I do nothing more than help my family, the effort of starting this business will be a win." I grew up in a family that worked paycheck to paycheck. My siblings and I always knew when it was time to pay bills because of the tension in the house. We were taught that you don't talk about politics, religion, or money in polite company, so I had a financial literacy gap.

During our call, my little brother asked me if he should open up a simplified employee pension (SEP) for his business or push more money into his endowment contract. Before I could answer, one of my other brothers (there are four of them) jumped in. No stress, no weird feelings—just good advice going back and forth. This kind of confidence is created through education. Financial conversations don't have to be stressful or leave anyone feeling behind. I was able to be a role model, not by directing or telling them what to do (this engages the contrarian in most of us) but by openly sharing what I was doing, including my failures and successes.

3. Responding to Encouragement

It's so important to recognize the small wins on the path to building your number. Are you a glass half-empty or half-full kind of person? During annual reviews with my clients, I like to see what worked over the course of the year. And if some investment plans have fallen short, I discuss what happened and make a new plan. I find that this positive approach allows my clients to keep progressing toward achieving and retaining the lifestyle they want. When you feel good about your money, you will continue to make choices and take actions that will cause more small wins. These actions can be as simple as automating a draft from your checking account to your savings account each pay period or ensuring that your 401(k) takes advantage of your company's matching.

4. Managing Emotional Responses

I've talked about how money is more emotion than math. I can tell you that open communication is key to helping couples reach financial freedom. Guess what—most couples have different opinions about money, particularly when it comes to risk.

During initial educational meetings, I make sure that each person has their own "notetaker." When I was teaching biology to freshman cadets, I found they did not always know how to take quality notes. Another professor shared her idea of creating a handout called a "notetaker" that had fill-in-the-blank spaces or guiding questions to help student focus on key concepts. This allowed our students to listen but be able to pick out important facts without getting lost in the information download from the lecture. I find this tool useful and fun for my financial meetings, too, because it's so easy for one spouse to dominate the conversation. A great plan really comes together when each person's feelings about the process and the way ahead are out in the open. For a plan to truly succeed, everyone involved needs to have a voice.

Think about how you feel about money and really notice it in your body. Do you feel a pressure in your chest, butterflies in your stomach, or even a tightness in your throat? In Carolyn Myss's book, *Anatomy of the Spirit,* she discusses how we feel physical discomfort in our bodies when we think or talk about topics related to money and power. Awareness of your own physical cues when talking about money can help you understand which topic needs to be clarified. You'll know you are clear when your body agrees and feels calm, as after a deep exhalation.[74]

Understanding is a part of empowerment, which leads to joy. Financial well-being and achieving the lifestyle you want in retirement are possible when your knowledge meets with action to execute your plan.

You cannot succeed until you believe that you can succeed. You've heard about financial literacy. It's a good starting spot. Financial self-efficacy is where knowledge meets action. You can have a lot of information and knowledge about investing, how money grows, and different financial tools to use. You might even be able to teach a class on investing. But even if you're the smartest person in the room, it won't matter until you take action. Financial self-efficacy matters because money is more emotion than math.[75] You may have financial knowledge, but until you uncover your financial and emotional baggage—the things lurking in your subconscious that may block you from being successful—you may struggle to act.

BUILDING TRUST

NOW THAT I'VE TALKED ABOUT finding your footing when it comes to taking care of yourself, it's time to talk about trusting others and how to do it. My friend Jeffrey Shaw, author and business coach, told me in an interview, "I believe the best way to get to know someone is to know what they value, what they support, and what they prioritize."

In Chapters 2 and 7, I talked about emotional baggage from your family, from advertising, from the stock market and taxes. Finding team members you trust can be hard, especially if you have previous bad experiences. Now, I want to talk about the connection between science, emotional baggage, and money and how they relate to trust. Going deep can give you insights that will help level up your approach to your finances.

I found this cool case study on the neurobiology of trust. I say "cool" because the experiment used biology to test an economic theory. The experiment set up a situation where the participants could make more money if they collaborated. They were not allowed to talk to each other, so they had to go out on a limb, extend some trust, and risk being burned. The experiment found that the people who led with trust had measurably higher levels of oxytocin, a neurotransmitter, in their blood samples.[76] Oxytocin has been called "the love hormone" because it is associated with childbirth, breastfeeding, empathy, and trust.[77] Research continues on this question, but I like when I find social observations being tested scientifically to see if behavior can be quantified.

I can speak from experience that trust is an essential ingredient for building an actionable financial plan. One of the best financial mentors I ever had explained that the initial meeting with a new client is really a two-way interview. He assured me that one element that must exist is the ability to trust. I'm not talking about a slick car salesman "trust me," but rather the ability to build a relationship. Money is as personal as you can get, and trust makes for a strong relationship—leading to more productive discussion and decision-making. Critical thinking is essential, and so is asking questions. People who are overly skeptical, however, who lack the ability to trust, do not seem to do as well as they could financially.

One thing I noticed early on is that wealthy people work with trusted advisors in most areas of their lives. For them, working with a team of experts is as normal as breathing. Less successful people, I find, are either do-it-yourselfers (often from necessity) or people who just are not making any decisions. When you find an expert you trust, who can show you how, for example, changing where your money lives can change how your financial world grows (without really changing your lifestyle), you can breathe a sigh of relief.

SELECTING YOUR TEAM

WHEN YOU BELIEVE IN YOURSELF, you'll have the confidence to select your financial team members. Have you ever noticed how nice it is to work with self-confident people? It is hard to move around other people's insecurities all the time. When I was first starting my business, I had to clear out a lot of emotional baggage I was carrying around. I was plugged into the idea that I wouldn't be able to start my own financial advisory business because I had been flying airplanes, not sitting in a cubicle working in a finance company.

It took a lot of intentional self-growth on my part to be able to share my unique, strategic-planning approach to financial well-being. My time flying and teaching biology did add the value of my real-life experience using systems thinking. Tracking a drop of fuel through the airplane fuel system or a bit of food through the digestive system helped to instill my holistic thinking because everything is connected. Building on this, I met an amazing financial coach, and she did two things.

One, she asked me, "How are you making yourself small to validate other people's realities?"

Two, she told me this story: When she was working at a very large finance firm in New York City, firm management did an experiment with a group of new hires. They told one of them, Eric, that he had been selected to work in the high-net-worth client program. This meant that any clients that came his way with less than $10 million to invest would have to be handed off to one of his colleagues. After six months, Eric had three times the amount of assets under management than the others who were hired on with him. The thing was, there was no high-net-worth client program. Eric just performed to the expectations he was given. No one can give you confidence. You must decide to have it yourself.

In America, we're taught about the spirit of the West, rugged individualism, and that we should do everything for ourselves. You can feel pride about doing things yourself, but I can tell you, it isn't what wealthy people do. Wealthy people work with mastermind teams and experts.

You are an expert in what you do. Whether you are a doctor, a farrier, a writer, or a plumber, you spent time learning and becoming good at your craft. It's very unrealistic to expect that you will also have the time to learn everything you need to know about your finances. For a very small number of people, personal finance is a hobby. They love it, and that works for them. But what I tend to find is that people think they should be able to do it by themselves. They fully intend to find time to figure it out for themselves. All the advertising tells them they should be able to do it themselves. But they end up not actually doing it.

Here's the key. When you start thinking of yourself as the owner of your team, you can pull together experts to advise you. At the end of the day, though, it's your decision. You make the final calls; you just don't need to make choices alone, in a vacuum. The fact is, you already have a lot of people on your financial team. People take care of your mortgage, your car insurance, your disability insurance, and your umbrella insurance. You should have life insurance, and someone takes care of that, too. Your CPA helps you prepare your taxes. You may be working with a broker if you're in the market. Odds are, you've worked with a realtor before either buying or renting a place to live. You relate to a lot of different financial experts out there that can help impact how you make decisions. I invite you to consider that you are in a higher state of maturity and confidence when you're able to put together and manage your financial team. It is much more impressive than trying to be the know-it-all do-it-yourselfer.

HOW DO ADVISORS GET PAID?

"BUT WHAT IS THIS GOING to cost me?" There should be complete transparency in how your advisor is paid. Transparency builds trust. This is absolutely true. You know the saying, "follow the money." It's always important to know how someone is getting paid because it will always be part of their motivation. Now, ideally, you will work with a professional who takes what's good for you into account. In the financial world, we have something called a fiduciary standard.[78] That means that the advisor is required to do what is best for you. Coming from my military background, I was surprised to learn there's also a suitability standard,[79] which just means that the advisor has to do something that is good for you. In theory, a fiduciary is held to a higher standard. But it's even better for you to work with somebody who has a high ethical standard because that's just the kind of person they are.

There are three basic ways that most advisors get paid. Now, investments can get very complex, and I'm not going to get into all the different possibilities. I want to go over these three basic ways so that you understand the kind of questions you should ask when interviewing an advisor to be part of your team.

The first way applies to money that's in the market. Typically, advisors get paid by a percentage of assets under management. This is generally 1-2% and, ideally, you should be getting a better value in terms of performance than you would if you just had your money in an index fund. When you pay for active management, you generally pay for downside protection. Money in the market is straightforward.

The second way advisors get paid is for any kind of insurance product, such as life insurance or annuities. These fees are managed and established by states and are commission-based. As the customer, you don't necessarily get a better deal by trying to do it yourself. You may find a company yourself, versus working with an advisor, but because the commissions are built into the product, you won't see a difference in price. If you don't have an advisor, the insurance company will just keep that money. In the case of insurance, there is no advantage to trying to do it yourself versus working with someone who can help you make good decisions.

The third way advisors can get paid, especially registered investment advisors, is by charging a flat or hourly fee. Some people prefer to have help putting a plan together and then want to manage it by themselves. They elect to pay an hourly fee for planning services.

So again, advisors are paid in three basic ways—via a percentage of assets under management, commissions on commission-based products, and hourly fees. If you get into the market and do it yourself, there will still be charges. Disclosure of fees is required, but like everything else in life, it can take some work to find the data. An example is the 12b-1 fees[80] that are built into the mutual fund expense ratio,[81] which will not stand out to you as fees unless you read the stacks of disclosures you will receive.

I met with a prospective client once who was not very interested in having a financial advisor and was just part of the conversation because his wife wanted a plan. As I always do, I went through how I get paid.

Two days later, I received an email from this man explaining that he was staying with his old company's 401(k) manager because they were a nonprofit company. He had pasted a passage from their website into his note. He was convinced that their nonprofit status meant he was not being charged for the investments he had with them, but this was not the case. Presentation of disclosures can be very misleading.

Please do not think you are getting a service for free. Does anything in life work like that? Fees are built into the process. Another good example of this is when it comes to store credit cards. It is always best to have a simple Visa or MasterCard instead of a Gap or Target card. There may be hidden fees built into these store-specific accounts that you don't see because you're excited about getting 10% off today.

GameStop was in the news in January 2021, and even late-night comedy hosts tried to explain what happened because of the David and Goliath-like nature of the situation.[82] I want to key in on the point that there are multiple competing low- or no-cost trading platforms available.[83] I've overheard young investors talk about different apps offering free trading, but this is not quite accurate. For example, it has been common for years for brokers to charge fees for trades. New platforms are now available that do not charge transaction fees. But you know they are making money somehow, right? Cost-saving can come from little to no customer service, charging for services like wire transfers, or offering upgrade options. Fees aren't good or bad in themselves. Understand how you're being charged. The bad thing is paying a fee that you're getting no value for.

One thing I've learned as I've gotten older is, I'm a pretty smart person. If I am purchasing a service and the person explaining it to me is making me feel stupid, the provider is not the right fit.

As a young lieutenant, I was giving a two-star general a tour around our deployment processing facility.

I asked him, "How do you know I'm not just telling you a bunch of BS?"

He laughed and said, "If you can break down what you do and explain it to me so that I understand it—explain it to me like you're explaining it to your grandmother—I know you know your job. If you can't bring it down to my level, I know that you don't know your job very well."

This is a very important point, and you could apply to transparency with advisors.

IT'S NOT ALL ABOUT YOU

FINANCIAL PLANNING IS NOT ALWAYS something you can do for yourself. There are a lot of factors involved beyond math. As a financial advisor, I can tell you that financial planning involves conversations about the dark things, such as what happens if you get killed in a car wreck. What happens if you *and* your spouse get in a wreck? Who's going to take care of your kids?

A big part of financial planning is figuring out answers to the what-ifs. Planning is to make sure that you and your family will be okay. When you're single, especially when you're young, it's a little easier to think, "I'm fine. I'll be okay. If something happens, I'll figure it out." And of course you will, one way or another. But I can tell you that, as you get older, there will come a point when you need help. If you don't have a family or a strong network, you need to know who will take care of you as you age. There are things you can plan to help yourself, especially when you start early.

I came across a quote once that really stuck with me. I don't know who said it, and I'm paraphrasing, but essentially it was, "Successful people do hard things that make life easy. Unsuccessful people do easy things that make life hard." Holistic financial planning is doing strategic, big-picture thinking up front to save you angst in times of chaos.

NO ONE CAN KNOW EVERYTHING

As I've progressed in my military career, one of the lessons I've had to learn is that as a colonel or general, your span of responsibility is larger than you can manage alone. You succeed at this level if you develop the ability to delegate and still have accountability. You really can't micromanage at this point.

I think this is where a lot of people struggle with their finances, too. If you don't know how to delegate to a team of experts and feel comfortable being helped, you get trapped trying to do everything yourself or, worse, just not doing anything. The challenge is, if you're not educated, it's hard to know if someone *is* helping you. This is why, when you're putting together your financial team, you want your CPA, financial advisor, insurance specialists, and all these folks to be able to explain their recommendations in a way that that makes sense to you. You want to be able to say, "Yeah, that solves my problem." With some education, you are empowered to ask questions (and ask fast talkers to slow down). If the person you're working with is unable to answer your questions, you probably don't have the right fit.

Money can be complicated, but it can also be broken down simply enough for you to understand what you really need to grasp. You can try to do it all yourself, but there will probably be gaps. You know what you know—you just don't know what you don't know. And that's why you have a team of experts to help you. They can see the gaps because they do this every day. At the end of the day, you still get to make the decision. It is nice to have backup in the form of a team that can present you with a few courses of action to pick from and explain the pros and cons of each.

After you've approved your plan, you'll want to delegate its execution to your team of experts. That is exactly what I did with my business model. Early on, I worked for advisors who tried to do it all. Move money in the market. Meet with clients. What I soon learned is, it is not possible to do it all well. These advisors tended to have one or two strategies that they applied to all of their clients in a one-size-fits-all approach. There was no personal touch.

Some clients want safe money investments. Some want aggressive market growth. Some want balances and downside protection. Most need some tax-free growth accounts. Rather than limit my services to what a single person can manage, I approached my boutique business like a CEO or military general and built a team of experts so I can tailor solutions to each individual I serve. My primary focus is integrating your entire financial bubble to maximize your financial potential. One of my mentors told me early on, "You don't have to be the smartest person in the room. It's more important to surround yourself with the smartest people, and together you will accomplish great things."

MANAGING YOUR TEAM

IF YOU DELEGATE WITH INTENTION, you *are* taking control and making a good decision. While it can be a point of pride for some people to manage their own money, it's really entry-level work. In the military, we would say it's lieutenant or captain work. A young officer wants to prove themselves, know that they're good at the mission. As they move up in rank, they start leading and are not the doers anymore. I would have you consider that you are in fact the senior ranking officer of your life and you would be well served to delegate your money management to a professional rather than adding "lieutenant work" to your to-do list.

You don't need to be the doer in your financial world. Unless personal finance is your passion hobby, you don't want to spend your time that way. You can have people for that. Your job is just to make sure things are getting done. And that's where you want to get to with your financial team. You don't have time to do everything yourself, but you can make time for your quarterly updates and in-depth annual reviews.

You want to be able to set the vision for your financial success and say, for example, "I want _____ money by the time I'm _____ age, and here's how I want to be able to spend it." You want to be able to say, "I want this much money absolutely protected, 100%," or, "I'm comfortable with _____ risk so this money can be in the market." It's a shift in mindset to realize that by bringing together experts to work for you, you are taking responsibility, every bit as much as if you were trying to do it yourself.

You will do annual check-ins to make sure your plan is still on track. This is when you can approve some adjustments, if needed, to make sure you are on track to reach your final number. This annual review is critically important and a meeting you cannot become complacent about. Every year, you need to look at where you are on your march toward your number. Life is going to keep throwing unexpected curveballs, and you'll probably need to make some adjustments each year. Some years you will be ahead, and that's awesome.

Some years, you'll get behind and need to make those adjustments. You may need to change some of the investment tools you are using. You may want to take on more risk, or reduce your risk. It's all about making intentional decisions so that you have the right balance. Financial planning isn't something you do once and never look at again. It is a living process. The thing is, it's a lot easier to make adjustments from a known position (in other words, a plan). It is much more complicated when you don't know where you are in the world. If that is the case, how do you know if you're close to getting where you want to go? It's hard even when the challenge is good. Trying to figure out your plan when you get an unexpected influx of cash, an inheritance, or a great new job is overwhelming—you will be amazed by how many friends come out of the woodwork. It's much better to figure out what to do with money before it comes to you.

It's an interesting question, how to get started when you are young and have no initial lump sum. My first investment foray at twenty-three was to put a hundred dollars a month into a mutual fund. I was introduced to dollar-cost averaging. The idea was that each month I'd buy, and when the market was down, I'd buy more. I didn't gain much traction because the frontloaded fees ate up a large amount of my small monthly investment.

Another thought would be to invest in something guaranteed that doesn't charge fees but has a time requirement. This can allow a new investor to safely build an account for long-term growth without losing any money and then, when a large enough sum is accumulated, venture into the market. This approach has an emotional appeal because it brings some predicted success. A financial advisor can run numbers to see which strategy may be best for you.

Now that you have begun thinking about how you manage your money, you will discover that people approach money in different ways. People can be left- or right-brain dominant. You will also realize that there are some defined theories about investing. When you are aware of the power of self-knowledge, you will experience how to expand your own financial world.

TO WRAP UP

You now know that it is okay to build a team to help you with your money. There are no gold stars for doing it all by yourself. Transparency and trust go together. Financial self-efficacy means you are able to combine your knowledge with action to see movement toward your retirement goals.

KEY TAKEAWAYS

- Financial success happens when you believe in yourself and take action.
- You must build trusting relationships in order to joyfully grow your wealth.
- Fees should be transparent: Ask what value you receive for a fee you pay.

TAKE ACTION NOW EXERCISE

To REVIEW, THERE ARE FOUR major ways to build self-efficacy:

1. Experiencing success: What is one way that reading this book has inspired you to take control of your financial space?
2. Choosing good role models: Who is your trusted personal agent when it comes to your money?
3. Responding to encouragement: What is one thing that reading this book has inspired you to recognize you have done already?
4. Managing emotional responses: What is one thing that reading this book has made you realize about how you think about money?

CASE STUDY: MUTUAL FUNDS VS. ANNUITIES

"How DO I KNOW WHO's telling me the truth? I'm so confused. I've been shopping around, and all the advice seems to be at odds. I just want to find someone I can trust and put this task to bed. I have my family and my work—I don't want to become a financial expert, too!"

Company A says, "Only mutual funds."

Company B says, "Only annuities."

First, here are the financial considerations.

Figure 47 shows how a $600,000 investment would grow over a twenty-five-year period in the market. It grows to $12.89 million.

YEAR	BALANCE AT BEGINNING OF YEAR	RATE OF RETURN	BALANCE AT END OF YEAR
1	$600,000	-14.67%	$511,980
2	$511,980	-26.31%	$377,280
3	$377,280	37.13%	$517,380
4	$517,380	23.82%	$640,620
5	$640,620	-7.19%	$594,540
6	$594,540	6.52%	$633,300
7	$633,300	18.45%	$750,120
8	$750,120	32.45%	$993,540
9	$993,540	-4.88%	$945,060
10	$945,060	21.50%	$1,148,280
11	$1,148,280	22.46%	$1,406,160
12	$1,406,160	6.22%	$1,493,640
13	$1,493,640	31.64%	$1,966,200
14	$1,966,200	18.62%	$2,332,320
15	$2,332,320	5.18%	$2,453,160
16	$2,453,160	16.61%	$2,860,620
17	$2,860,620	31.69%	$3,767,100
18	$3,767,100	-3.10%	$3,650,340
19	$3,650,340	30.47%	$4,762,620
20	$4,762,620	7.62%	$5,125,500

21	$5,125,500	10.08%	$5,642,160
22	$5,642,160	1.32%	$5,716,680
23	$5,716,680	37.58%	$7,864,980
24	$7,864,980	22.96%	$9,670,740
25	$9,670,740	33.36%	$12,896,899

Figure 47: $600,000 over 25 Years

Figure 48 shows how a $600,000 investment would grow in a guaranteed account earning 4% over a twenty-five-year period. It grows to $1.59 million.

YEAR	BALANCE AT BEGINNING OF YEAR	RATE OF RETURN	BALANCE AT END OF YEAR
1	$600,000	4.00%	$624,000
2	$624,000	4.00%	$648,960
3	$648,960	4.00%	$674,918
4	$674,918	4.00%	$701,915
5	$701,915	4.00%	$729,992
6	$729,992	4.00%	$759,191
7	$759,191	4.00%	$789,559
8	$789,559	4.00%	$821,141
9	$821,141	4.00%	$853,987
10	$853,987	4.00%	$888,147
11	$888,147	4.00%	$923,672
12	$923,672	4.00%	$960,619
13	$960,619	4.00%	$999,044
14	$999,044	4.00%	$1,039,006
15	$1,039,006	4.00%	$1,080,566
16	$1,080,566	4.00%	$1,123,789

17	$1,123,789	4.00%	$1,168,740
18	$1,168,740	4.00%	$1,215,490
19	$1,215,490	4.00%	$1,264,110
20	$1,264,110	4.00%	$1,314,674
21	$1,314,674	4.00%	$1,367,261
22	$1,367,261	4.00%	$1,421,951
23	$1,421,951	4.00%	$1,478,829
24	$1,478,829	4.00%	$1,537,982
25	$1,537,982	4.00%	$1,599,502

Figure 48: $600,000 over 25 Years at 4%

Here is the context you need to make an informed decision. Imagine you are sixty-five and planning to retire in the next few years. This is your entire nest egg. Would you be comfortable with the market drops in years one and two as shown in Figure 47? Yes or no? Your account dropped from $600,000 to $377,000 in the beginning-of-year balance. Because of market volatility, demonstrated in this table, a conservative advisor may recommend you consider putting your money into an annuity because you are guaranteed not to lose any of your account value. You may or may not agree now that you are so much more educated, but this advice is not unreasonable.

Now imagine you are forty-five and plan to work for at least another twenty years. If you look at the same years in Figure 47—years one and two—you see the same big drop. But what is different in this scenario? Will you be pulling money out of this account? Not for nearly twenty years. At this stage in your life, you can accept more market risk because time is on your side. In this case, if an advisor recommends you put all your money in an annuity, you may want to get a second opinion because historically, the market will outperform a fixed return account. You might be a super risk-averse person, and if so, the advisor's recommendation could appeal to you emotionally. However, if you don't participate in the market when you are young, you miss out on some potentially significant growth in your account. This is where you want to get very clear on your strategy. Be sure to discuss the Rule of 100.

How does the person you are getting advice from get paid? This is a question you should have complete transparency about. Do they only manage money in the market? If so, they will consider market options. They will not be paid if you decide to put your money into an annuity. This does not necessarily drive their recommendation, but it is a consideration. The reverse is also true. Does the person you are talking with only sell insurance products? Then they will not be paid if you decide you want your money in the market. Again, professionals should be, well, professional. But if you feel like there is any fast talking or you don't understand the "why" behind the recommendation, you can always get a second opinion. This becomes a matter of trust. I believe that after you understand the characteristics of a good investment, how different investment tools work, and your personal strategy, you will be able to select a course of action that makes sense for you.

CHAPTER 11

PUTTING IT ALL TOGETHER

You are what you do, not what you say you'll do.

—*Carl Gustav Jung*[84]

- Have you ever felt overwhelmed by life and that not everything can be a priority?
- Do you feel like you have a lot of information and need to see how the 3-Step Financial Plan Framework works in action?
- Have you ever wondered, "How can I invest when I have so much debt?"

I'VE SHARED A LOT OF information with you so far. It's been eye-opening for me, too, to review how much information must be processed and how many little decision points there are when it comes to managing your money.

There is the emotional baggage, the marketing you are fed each day from various sources, and the aversion to numbers—now we reach dreaded procrastination, the enemy of financial self-efficacy. Your financial literacy is so much higher; now you just need to start doing things to take care of yourself. In Chapter 9, I talked about baby steps to get you in the right place mentally. I showed you how to look at where you are in your process, figure out how much is enough, and determine whether you are on track to get there.

To model for you how to put all your information together, I am going to introduce you to Jenny and Laura. I believe their story will help you see how to apply all this information you have learned so you can plug the holes in your retirement plan and cocreate a financial team to boost your personal success. Please add a zero to or subtract a zero from their income of $200,000 to make the example more applicable to your reality. You can skip down to the key takeaways if the numbers become overwhelming, but I invite you to take this chapter slowly and let some of this reality wash over you. The good news is, the financial puzzle is more solvable than you might think, especially when you build a team of experts to help you.

MEET JENNY AND LAURA

WHEN JENNY LEFT CORPORATE AMERICA and Laura quit teaching, I got a call.

"We're going back to school, and we need to do something with our 401(k) and 403(b)."

I said, "I can help you with your retirement accounts. Are you interested in examining your whole financial picture?"

"We don't have any money to invest right now, so, no thanks."

A few years later, life had not gotten simpler for them. Their first child had come along. They were carrying big school debt. Laura had started a law program because she liked the idea of being able to help people through tough situations. Jenny was becoming a programmer, so she had loans as well. They were okay while in school, living off their loans, but it got tough when they were new college graduates looking for jobs and had this huge debt hanging over their heads. I got another call.

They explained, "We were not ready to take action before because we were just focusing on school and didn't feel like we could invest while we were getting our degrees. It's just not done that way. We were investing in ourselves. Now we feel like we are in a bigger hole than before we went to school. What can be done now?"

I asked again if they were ready to look at their financial world holistically. Using the medical analogy I learned from my mom, a doctor of osteopathic medicine (DO), I shared that my financial philosophy is more like that of a DO, who looks at whole-person healing, than that of a traditional MD, who generally focuses on treating specific conditions with medications. When I managed only their retirement accounts a few years earlier, I had treated a symptom, but had not really healed their overall financial picture. Life had pushed Jenny and Laura to an uncomfortable place, so they were in a more open-minded space and ready to try something new.

We started with a conversation. I asked if they had heard the adage that you should save at least 15% of your annual gross income. I explained to them that I like using a percentage because it will grow, expand, or contract with whatever amount of money you have. And if you think about it, 15% of one dollar is just fifteen cents. It's doable. I unpacked where it comes from. With the three of us sitting around my computer, I googled "Why save 15%?" and came up with 699,000,000 results in less than a second. Although there are a lot of opinions about *why* this specific amount matters, there is a strong agreement that it is a good savings target. We did the math to show why it was the right number.

I asked, "How much are you making right now?"

They said, "Between the two of us, $200,000."

Laura said, "I see the number we need to save and it's overwhelming. We're struggling to pay off our student debt and you're showing us we need to save almost a million dollars! Fifteen percent of our income didn't sound so bad but $30,000 and over the next thirty years feels like an unscalable mountain right now How is that even possible?"

"Okay," I said, "Take a deep breath and let it out slowly. I needed you to have sticker shock right now."

I went on to explain that if you only saved 10% of your income and arrived at age sixty-five with $619,384 (Figure 49), you would have about $31,000 a year to live on in retirement (dividing $619,384 by twenty). Please note that this is the most conservative scenario because I did not include any investment return. A comprehensive financial planning process would include assumptions about investment returns based on your individual risk tolerances, goals, and such.

Comparison of Growth for 20 years @ 4% interest

Percent of 200K Income	Dollar Amount	20-yr Growth
10%	$ 20,000	$ 619,384
15%	$ 30,000	$ 929,076
30%	$ 40,000	$ 1,238,768

Figure 49: Comparison of Growth

"You are living on $200,000 a year now. Do you feel like $31,000 will be enough to live on when you are retired? We will plan to have some of your bigger expenses managed by retirement, like student debt and mortgage, but right now I want you to understand the problem we are trying to solve together."

Jenny and Laura still looked overwhelmed, but they were beginning to see the problem I was trying to help them solve. When they came to me, they didn't know which questions to ask. Please forgive my digression with a horse training analogy, but I think horses are some of the most honest creatures. John Lyons wrote a book about horse training that said horses go through two phases. In the first phase, they don't understand. In the second phase, they understand but don't want to do the work.[85] Jenny and Laura were past the first stage because we'd covered what they should be doing. Now we were moving on to proving it with the math, and this is the part that can make your brain hurt.

"Now that we have a target of 15%, we will start where you are right now. You are making $200,000, yes?" They both nodded. "So, 15% of that is $30,000. If you divide that by twelve you get $2,500 per month. That is the amount of money you should 'pay yourself first' with today. This table (Figure 50) shows what you have available to live on if you are serious about your financial future and paying yourself like you do your taxes. If you get a W-2 paycheck, you are familiar with the fact that the government takes taxes out before you get paid. I'm suggesting you pay yourself 15% in the same way before you even consider spending it."

I showed Jenny and Laura a quick breakdown of what it looks like to "pay yourself" first.

Figure 50 shows Jenny and Laura each making $8,300 a month. If they set aside 15% of their $200,000, that would be $2,500, and taxes are $4,000. This leaves $10,166 available to spend each month.

NOTE: This is about 55% of their monthly gross income. People get into trouble when they look at their total income, in this case $16,600, and spend it in their heads before paying themselves first.

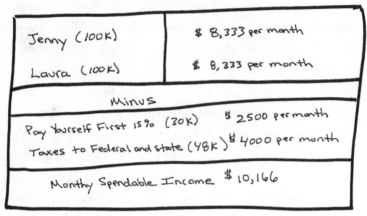

Figure 50: Spending Plan Gross Income

ORGANIZING THE FINANCIAL JUNK DRAWER

I TOLD JENNY AND LAURA, "Before you start making any changes, it needs to be clear what you are already doing right now."

I gave them homework to complete a spending plan so we could talk with real numbers instead of just concepts.*

At the next meeting, Jenny and Laura came back with their spending plan (Figure 51).

SPENDING PLAN: LAURA AND JENNY'S CURRENT PROJECTED MONTHLY EXPENSES	
Shelter	$2,000

---

* In my Money Moves Master Class, I discuss how you get started approaching your finances in a holistic way. In my DreamLife Planning Suite, you will be able to work through your own scenario so you know your exact numbers. If you'd like access to the class and the spending plan spreadsheet, visit www.nolanfinancialpartners.com/tools.

Transportation	$866
Food	$1,800
Laura Student Loan ($145,000 @ 6% interest)	$872
Jenny Student Loan ($71,000 @ 6 % interest)	$425
Laura Retirement Account ($36,000)	$0
Jenny Retirement Account ($25,000)	$83 (1% matching)
Life Insurance	$0
Savings (Emergency Fund) ($1,200)	$100
Total	**$6,146**

Figure 51: Spending Plan Expenses

We created a spending plan to first see what was working before we start changing anything. This is highly simplified and you can get more comprehensive. Jenny and Laura had retirement plans from their previous jobs, but they had not been contributing to them while they were in school. Jenny was a computer programmer and worked for a company that offered a 4% matching contribution. Laura opened her own law practice and still needed to start her own retirement plan. I noted that they only had $1,200 in savings.

We reviewed the rest of the spending plan, verified that they were in the black, and looked to see if there was a gap between income and expenses (Figure 52). At this point they had $4,020 to play with over and above expenses. Good news—they were living within their means. I encouraged them to go ahead and feel good for a minute.

How Are They Doing?

Monthly Spendable Income	$ 10,166
Total Monthly Expenses	$ 6,146
Discretionary Money	$ 4020

Figure 52: How Are They Doing?

If you subtract total monthly expenses from their spendable income ($10,166 - $6,146) you get their discretionary money: $4,020. The 15% goal is $2,500 ($200,000 x 0.15 = $30,000; $30,000 / 12 = $2,500 per month, ideally). They are already saving $183 per month (adding $83 to Jenny's retirement and $100 to savings), so $2,317 will round out the goal of $2,500.

APPLYING FINANCIAL CONCEPTS

NOW THAT WE KNEW THEY had enough money left each month to invest, where were they supposed to put it? As a team leader who had been down this path before, I proposed we look at their emergency fund, retirement savings, and insurance needs first. This would ensure that their allocations were working for them. Then we would look at their debt payoff plan and "enjoying life today" plan and discuss how to allocate their discretionary money.

I reminded Jenny and Laura, "You have $1,200 in savings right now. Do you remember how much an emergency fund should be?"

"Three to six months of our income or expenses?" they replied.

"Yep. So that's going to be $50,000 to $100,000." I asked what the alternative solution was if they didn't have an emergency fund.

They thought about it for a minute. "Our credit cards."

I asked, "How do you feel about credit card debt? Are you okay with it and feel like it's something everyone deals with? Or do you want your card paid off every month no matter what?"

Jenny replied, "We should always pay it off at the end of the month."

Laura countered, "We need to be reasonable; we work so we can have a life, right?"

I chuckled. "Now we're getting into the mix. It's an extra challenge when couples really start talking about how they manage money in their heads. We will need to come to agreement on how you two will manage your money by the end of our process together." I pointed out that they had been putting a hundred dollars a month toward their savings/emergency fund and asked how much they wanted to increase this amount.

Laura suggested, "Why don't we increase it to $800 a month? That will get us to our goal of three months' emergency savings in five years." Jenny frowned a bit because she wanted to get to their goal right away, but said the jump to $800 a month felt big so she agreed for now.

Turning to retirement accounts, Jenny told us she was eligible to have up to a 4% matching contribution at work, meaning that she could increase her $83 dollars a month to $332 dollars a month and have her employer match that amount dollar for dollar. With employer matching, her account would grow $664 dollars per month.

"This is as close to free money as you will find," I told her. "But don't worry about putting in more than that. There is no good reason to overfund your employee retirement account unless you don't have another investment you control available." (This gets into a conversation about fees that is good to have with one of your advisors.)

Laura didn't have any employees yet, so we needed to discuss whether she wanted a SIMPLE IRA or a SEP at this point.

Before we went down that road, though, I told Laura and Jenny, "This is a conversation we should bring your CPA in on to ensure we capture the best tax savings, too. After all, it takes a team."

To be somewhat balanced with Jenny's account, Laura suggested setting up her account at an initial $500 a month.

After we squared away the retirement accounts focused on accumulation, it was time to get into plugging some of the retirement holes.

"So far, we've looked at the 'Get it' phase of your financial bell curve (Figure 53), but what if something happens to one of you?" I asked.

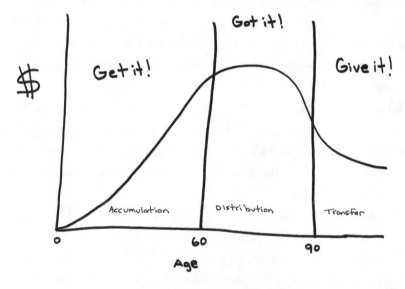

Figure 53: Financial Life Cycle

"What do you mean?" they said.

"What if one of you cannot keep working? How do you plan to protect the family and the plan you have in place?"

A little glumly, Jenny said, "I guess you're talking about insurance."

"Yep."

"How much should we have?"

"What problems do you want to solve?"

"What do you mean?"

"I mean, can you solve the immediate need if one of you cannot work right now? This can be as simple as buying some term insurance."

Jenny said, "I don't like the idea of putting money into something and getting no return on my investment."

Then Laura jumped in, saying, "Yes, but what about the idea of buying term and investing the rest?"

STRATEGIC THINKING

"Now you're starting to get into some advanced strategic thinking," I said. "Here are some options that you have to pick from. A healthy forty-year-old woman could expect to pay twenty to thirty dollars a month for a term policy."

In Chapter 5, I explained that a term policy is not really an investment in and of itself because it doesn't have any characteristics of a good investment. However, it serves the critical purpose of protecting your family and all your other investments. A convertible term policy would run about forty-five to sixty-five dollars and require a clean medical exam. In Chapter 6, I explained that whole life insurance *does* have many characteristics of a good investment. This investment choice gets into advanced strategic thinking and knowing how you want to put your money to work. Deciding to use whole life is a consideration if you want to plan for both now and the future. I explained to Laura and Jenny that if they were both able to keep working, they would still need to solve the problem of protecting their nest egg and potential long-term care needs.

Jenny asked, "I've heard some people like whole life insurance. But, like Laura said, some people really advocate for the idea of buying term and investing the rest."

"I like the way you're thinking this through," I said. "We'll have to sit down with the financial calculator so I can show you the differences."

Buying term and investing the rest can work depending on the assumptions you make, but a whole life savings plan can solve future tax problems and gets into strategies about putting your money to work for you now. Looking at the numbers side by side is the ultimate proof of concept, assuming you make apples-to-apples comparisons.

Jenny said, "I'd like to learn more about how our money can work for us."

"To keep our planning moving today," I said, "why don't we apply for some convertible term and see how your medical exams pan out. If you qualify as standard or better, you have the option open once you've gotten more education about whole life. In the meantime, you've plugged a hole that currently exists in your plan."

Assuming they each got a policy for fifty dollars a month, they would still have $768 to pay themselves first.

Laura said, "Can I increase the amount I'm contributing to my retirement account?"

"You can, and this is where we will want to involve your CPA. If we set up your account as a traditional account, you can deduct this expense from your taxes."

"We said our emergency fund needs to be between $50,000 and $100,000, right?"

"Yes."

"I don't want $100,000 sitting in a bank account, not earning much interest. How is my money working for me in that kind of account?"

"You have hit on a key takeaway. You need your emergency fund to be liquid, but it does not all need to be in a bank account. What's catching your eye in the 'Characteristics of a Good Investment' table?"

Laura chimed in, "The table says that you *might* be able to borrow money from your IRAs, but you *can* borrow money from your whole life insurance. Does that mean we could double up, and a whole life policy could serve as our death benefit protection and a place to grow our savings in a tax-deferred account?"

"Now you're starting to catch on to the notion of putting your money to work for you. When you are still in the 'Get it' phase of your bell curve on the way to retirement, you gain traction by changing where your money lives to change how your financial world grows."

Jenny recapped, "So we could set up a whole life savings policy now that allows us to reach our goal of $100,000 of emergency money that we can access, but will earn dividends that add to the cash value of the policy? And this account value will continue to grow our entire lives? If, God willing, we don't need the death benefit, this money will be available in the future to use for unplanned medical expenses, even long-term care?"

"You got it."

Laura interjected, "Why would we even want any money in the market?"

"The market is a good tool for growth when you're young and working. There are no guarantees in the market, but historical data shows a larger return on investment over a twenty-year period. The market is a tool you adjust for as you get older. It's a question of balancing risk, potential return, and what lets you sleep well at night.

"The pros of a whole life savings plan in your forties are, you will lock in a lower permanent insurance rate. You will grow cash value tax-deferred but have access to borrow and repay the money as it grows. You have a death benefit if something happens to you. You can set it up to self-complete if you become disabled. It will be available for future long-term care needs. You are also building your emergency fund in such a way that your money is working for you.

"The pros of investing more money into your retirement accounts in the market at forty is, you have easily another twenty years of growth time and should be able to earn a good rate of return. The money will grow either tax-free or tax-deferred depending on how you set up the account. The end goal is to have as much money in a tax-free status as possible when you enter retirement and are spending your money."

"Ladies, the bottom line here is that you want to be saving at least 15% of your income to pay yourself first. You know there are different kinds of accounts available to you. Be intentional and take action and you will be much better off than you are right now."

Of course, I pointed out to them, it almost goes without saying that 15% is the minimum recommended to save for retirement. They could always do more and put themselves in a better position for retirement when their spending plan allowed.

Next, we talked about their debt payoff plan. I was preparing for this to be a more contentious discussion because it's common to have a strong emotional need to want to pay off debt.

Jenny shared, "I don't think we should invest anything extra until we have all our debt paid off."

Laura said, "We have to be able to live, but the loans do kinda worry me in the back of my mind, like an irritating earworm."

Considering both valid points, I reminded them that they are in control, and it's their money, so here is what they need to understand: If they waited to pay off all their debt before starting to invest in their future in a sequential way, they would be working a long time. You may remember Figure 10 in Chapter 3, which compared time, money, and rate of return. Time is your best friend when it comes to growing money. Check out the case study at the end of this chapter to see what you would do. Would you pay off student loans more quickly or invest for your future?

The thing I believed was important to include in their spending plan was their entertainment money. Planning for retirement is essential—and they also get to live *today*. In Jenny and Laura's spending plan, Figure 52, they had $4,020 dollars of discretionary income to allocate. Most people enjoy having more choices and being in control when it comes to their money. I expected them to allocate some of this money to either paying down their loans or setting up an alternate account that would allow them to pay off the loans if they decided to do so.

I also expected them to take a significant amount of this discretionary money and think about what they valued. For example, did they want to collect stuff or experiences? Did they want to spend time with their family eating out or traveling? There are no wrong answers here. As long as they were intentional with their money, they would not make a bad choice. Regrets usually come from money that is unaccounted for. Just imagine having a twenty-dollar bill in your wallet for weeks. Once you break it, it's gone.

"Ladies, we covered a lot today. How are you feeling?" I asked.

Jenny said, "I see why it's easy to just do nothing and stay focused on the distractions of daily life."

"No kidding. My brain is full, but we have our numbers written down so we can take some time to go over the plan," Laura said.

Jenny pulled out some notes. "I read about the impact of inflation, taxes, and market risk on money. But after our meeting today, I think being a good saver is the secret."

I said, "Jenny, you're spot-on. Success begins with saving 15% of your income. You have a lot of options, and writing your plan down helps you take small doable steps in the right direction."

Jenny and Laura were typical overachievers. After they began managing their money, they became great savers. When a house on their block came up for sale, Jenny had the down payment saved for an investment loan. They went from being buried in debt to owning assets in just ten years because of their diligent saving habits. This is amazing. Not everyone starts from zero like Jenny and Laura, but a lot of us do. I remember hearing Mitt Romney, on the campaign trail in 2012, asking why people didn't just borrow money from their dads to buy their first house. He wasn't trying to be elitist; he just didn't have the experience of building assets from scratch. The first-time homebuyer loan is a safety net that helps a lot of people get started on a better financial path.

It takes money to make money. It takes understanding how money works to leverage what's available to you so you can get to the next level. While you may not start out with cash money, if you understand how the game works, you can start making decisions that will help you get there.

Jenny and Laura were able to use their whole life savings account to help them save money more efficiently, leveraging their money like a bank to pay student debt. Meanwhile, their IRAs were left alone to grow in the market and take advantage of compounding interest over time. How many people do you know who've cashed out their IRAs or 401(k)s at different stressful times in their lives? It's all about creating options for yourself so you can manage your money, not have your money manage you.

TO WRAP UP

IN SUMMARY, THIS CHAPTER PUTS a fine point on how you get to a secure retirement. If you do nothing else, organize your spending plan to see what you are already doing. The textbook answer is, you want to save at least 15% of what you earn. You may notice that this will not be enough to replicate your current income 100%, but it is a reasonable starting point. It's an extra challenge because you have to do some math to prevent double accounting in your head: There is the money you make and then how much of that money is spendable money today. If you make $100,000, you need to pay yourself first using 15% as a reasonable starting number. You also want to subtract your recurring expenses first so you make plans based on the actual dollars you have available to spend. Although you know you pay taxes, you may not be used to thinking about the difference between what you make and what actually is deposited in your account. If you get a W-2 paycheck, you will see the amounts pulled out for FICA and Social Security. The government is taking the amount they require. Do the same for yourself. Set aside 15% of each paycheck to pay yourself first and mentally prepare yourself: This money is for your future, not spendable today. This is the gold standard because you will be taking good care of yourself each month right off the bat. It is hard for most people to mentally set aside what could be accessible money. Some urgent need is always popping up, and you can always make a strong case that you need that money, just this one time. And so it will go every month, unless you choose differently.

Employer matching is a must. This is as close to free money as you can get. You also need to ask if you can set up your account as a Roth. Many companies will now allow at least a portion of your monthly contributions to go to a Roth IRA.

Set up an emergency fund contribution to work on autopilot. Just have your checking account forward money into your savings each month. When your savings is at your desired level, move the extra dollars into one of your other accounts that will earn more interest and work harder for you while you sleep.

KEY TAKEAWAYS

- Invest at least 15% of your income right now.
- Set up an automatic funding process for your emergency fund until you have saved three to six months' worth of your annual income.
- Employer matching is as close to free money as you will get.
- Find additional investment routes to get to 15%.
- Investing becomes more advanced when you look at the number you want to achieve and the age at which you start working toward that number.
- Include enjoying your life in your spending plan.
- Good savings habits grow retirement money.

TAKE ACTION NOW EXERCISE

1. How much do you make right now?
2. How much should you be investing at a minimum (multiply your pre-tax income times 0.15)?
3. How much money is in your emergency savings account?

CASE STUDY: DEBT VS. INVESTING

HERE IS THE PROBLEM THIS case study addresses: I have $6,000 a year ($500 per month) available in my budget. Should I make an extra payment on my student loans or invest this $6,000 somewhere else?

This case study looks at paying down installment credit with amortized debt, as you would typically see with student or home loans. An amortized loan is a type of loan that requires the borrower to make scheduled, periodic payments that are applied to both the principal and interest. An amortized loan payment first pays off the interest expense for the period; any remaining amount is put toward reducing the principal amount. As the interest portion of the payments for an amortization loan decreases, the principal portion increases.[86] In simple terms, at the beginning of this kind of loan, you pay mostly interest. Toward the end of the loan, say, year twenty of a thirty-year note, you are paying mostly principal.

Please note that revolving credit, typically seen with credit cards, is a different kind of debt and requires different consideration. I know that each time I break these concepts down to simplify, I offer a disclaimer. This is why you may see a lot of "it depends" answers to financial questions. Therefore, I keep emphasizing that you first need to be clear on the problem you're trying to solve. Get ready to see money in a different way than you (probably) ever have before with this case study.

To those of you who like to have a clean slate (in other words, all debt cleared as soon as possible), stick with me here. Paying off debt is a good character trait and I'm going to show you a win-win scenario that is more advanced than the simple black and white answer you may expect. You will like the outcome if you can wrap your head around it, I promise.

ASSUMPTIONS:

Given student loan note: If you have a $100,000 student loan at 4% interest, it will take you thirty years to pay it off at approximately $500 per month (4%, $100,000 note, thirty years—paid off).

OPTIONS:

Option 1—Alternate investment: If you invest $6,000 a year into an investment earning 4%, after thirty years you will have $349,970 in your account (4%, $6,000/year, thirty years—$349,970).

Option 2—Extra payment on student loan: If you double your monthly payment on this student loan, you will pay off the note off in eleven years.

To present this comparison in a more visual way hitting more learning styles, Figure 54 shows that if you pay an additional $6,000 a year on the student loan, you will reduce the note from thirty to eleven years. Sounds pretty good.

If you invest in an alternate account, you will have $349,970 in thirty years.

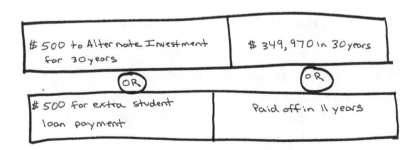

Figure 54: Debt vs. Investing

Would you rather make an extra payment on your student loan debt and pay it off in eleven instead of thirty years? Yes or no (circle one)?

Here we go. If you answered, yes, I'd like to pay off my note sooner, prepare to expand your mind. It's all about asking more and better questions. What if this can be a "yes, and" question instead of an "either-or" question (Figure 55)? Here's what should pop into your mind now: "Paying off my note early sounds good, but how much money do I have in my alternate investment account at eleven years and how much is my student loan debt at eleven years?"

Alternate investment at eleven years: At eleven years, your alternate investment will have grown to approximately $84,000.

Student loan at eleven years: At eleven years, with your payment of approximately $500 a month, your loan will be down to less than $76,000.

Alternate Investment at 11 years	$ 84,000
Student Loan Paydown at 11 years	$ 76,000

Figure 55: Debt vs. Investing at 11 Years

In this scenario, at the eleven-year point, do you have the ability to pay off your student loan if you choose to do so? Yes or no (circle one)? How much money do you have left in your alternate investment?

Here is the problem this case study is addressing: "I have $6,000 a year ($500 per month) available in my budget. Should I make an extra payment on my student loans or invest this $6,000 somewhere else?"

You can see here that if you invest the extra $500, you retain control. You have the ability to pay off the student loan at the eleven-year point, just as you would by making extra payments. However, you also have an extra $8,000 in your account. You can serve your emotional need to pay down debt and grow your assets at the same time. If any unexpected emergencies arise during this time period, you will have created an account of available, liquid money to draw from so you will not have to use credit cards and create more debt. Often, if you understand the numbers, you do not have to make either-or decisions. You can find the right strategy to help you achieve your goals of less debt and more assets.

This case study answers the questions:

"What's my number?" In this case, clearing $100,000 debt.

"Am I on track to get there?" Yes, and you actually can choose from more than one track to get there.

"Am I paying too much in taxes?" This question will be further addressed by the alternative investment vehicle you choose to use. This refers back to Chapter 6 and understanding how to put your money to work.

CHAPTER 12

YOU CAN HAVE YOUR DREAM

Go confidently in the direction of your dreams.
Live the life you have imagined.

—Henry David Thoreau[87]

"THAT'S YOU, RIGHT THERE," MY navigator said as we walked back to our trailer after having lunch on our day off. We were at Al Udeid Air Base in Qatar, a hot, flat landscape with rock and sand in every direction.

I looked where he was pointing. There was a woman in a flight suit throwing dusty, army-green canvas mobility bags off a truck; a new aircrew was arriving. She was red-faced and sweaty, with the disheveled hair that refuses to stay neatly tucked into a bun after traveling eighteen hours or so. It hit me hard. "That's how he sees me? On this pre-planned life path, deploying to the Middle East over and over until I'm old enough to retire?" I thought, "I'm still young, and while I'm grateful for this role as aircrew, it cannot define me."

This was a limbic brain experience in which I became acutely aware of a disconnect between how people saw me and my potential and how I saw myself. The amygdala, part of the limbic system, is involved in our experience of emotion and in tying emotional meaning to our memories.[88] How could I change the trajectory of my life so I could have more control over my lifestyle and experiences? I started thinking that more money might be key to having more control.

What do you believe is within the realm of the possible? The show *Black-ish* tackles tough topics that apply to a lot of Americans today. In the episode "Inheritance," the main character, Dre, talks about how most people of color don't have assets to hand down to their children, aside from life insurance payouts.[89] This caught my attention as true and also true for many people of all ethnicities who deal with situational poverty.

My friend Monique shared her story with me. Her mom, Fran, and dad divorced when she was three. Child support was nonexistent, so Fran raised Monique and went to school at the same time. As you can imagine, there was little left over after bills were paid and groceries were on the table. Fran was not raised poor; she grew up in a nice middle-class neighborhood. She was educated and had a doctorate. However, her married life didn't work out as planned, and Monique's views about money were strongly shaped by this experience.

My parents chose to live below the poverty line when they moved to The Farm and started a family instead of finishing college. I was also raised poor. Although this was a voluntary decision on my parents' part, it still took many years for them to start earning living wages again. Two of the best tools available today to start creating generational wealth are real estate and whole life insurance. This is not magic. This is the tax code. I cannot fix how you arrived where you are, but I challenge you to start thinking bigger today.

Wealth and inheritance are not only about money. They are also about knowledge. If you can set your kids up for success financially, that is wonderful. If you can ensure that your kids know how to manage the money you leave them, you are getting somewhere. If you can instill a good work ethic, so your kids allow their inheritance to work for them side by side while they are creating their lives, you can keep this ball rolling in a good way. It takes money to make money. If your kids understand a concept of wealth preservation that allows them to enjoy life because they can make good decisions, that's great.

In his book *The Buddha and the Badass*, Vishen Lakhiani says that "the greatest gift you can give someone is to invite them to share in a dream."[90] My dream is to inspire and motivate people who believe what I believe—that success is possible.

The first time I sat down with Beryl and Nick, I got a sense of what was important to them. They were nearing retirement and wanted a plan in place. They had gone through a big course correction when the company they'd worked with for almost twenty years filed for bankruptcy. It was painful, because all their retirement was in company stock, so they went from having a few million in their account to a significantly smaller settlement. They had two kids in high school and were in the process of building a new home. I asked for their thoughts about weddings, college, and insurance.

Having been quiet up to this point, Beryl cleared her throat. "The kids are on their own. They're going to have to get scholarships. You can see what happened."

I said, "I see what happened to your retirement account. I also see that you're taking on a new thirty-year mortgage as you head into retirement. Talk to me about that."

Beryl said, "It's always been our dream to build our own house. This house is paid off."

I said, "You're going to be paying on this note until you're eighty-five. What happens if one of you cannot keep working? You don't have an account to pay it off."

Nick jumped in. "That's why we're talking to you."

I finished gathering the resources they had to work with and laid out a way ahead at our next meeting.

"You have about ten to fifteen more years to work, so you will need to get serious about saving. If you qualify for life insurance, that tool will be able to help plug some of your big retirement holes. We can make sure your death benefit is large enough to pay off your mortgage, and we can design a policy with long-term care riders. If you need it, you have it, and if you don't need it, your kids will receive an inheritance. I'm going to recommend that you take advantage of market growth for the next ten years while you are still working."

I was surprised that when I delivered their final plan, Beryl smiled and said, "We're going to be able to leave something for the kids?"

"Yep."

"I thought I'd just have to keep trying to make extra payments on the mortgage so we could pay it off before we retire. Now we are going to be able to set aside something for the kids."

I see a Beryl and Nick situation quite often. People come to me thinking they're locked in to their financial destiny. They think they are doing well if they can make sure they don't run out of money and that transferring any wealth to their kids is something rich people like the Kennedys do. It's exciting when people realize that they may not be facing an either-or decision matrix.

I want to share an example of good to great. Ralph owns a family bank. He is a conservative guy and, as a banker, made his money over the years on smart, low-risk deals. He held a lot of real estate because he liked tangible assets. He had saved up almost $9 million and was planning to leave half to his kids and half to St. Jude's Hospital for personal reasons. That's a nice inheritance and gift. But when I showed him the options available to make his money tax-free, more protected, and still accessible, it got very exciting. Ralph was able to turn his $9 million into almost $20 million without having to accept market risk. Changing where his money lived grew his financial world so he could leave a legacy both for his family and for charity!

These two scenarios may read differently, but the common ground is parents who want to set their kids up for success. Everyone is going to have different resources available to do this, but my goal is that you don't sell yourself short before you know what is within the realm of possible.

You've worked your way through a lot of dense material. I'm hoping you can see more nuances in money now. Instead of seeing money as something you either have or don't have, can you see how it is like the Word program on your computer? You may be able to open it up and type a memo, but if you know how to use the advanced tools, you can prepare an entire manuscript for publication. Before you read this book, you may have thought that stuffing as much money as you could into your retirement account was the best thing you could do. Now you know that there are more complexities to consider—like your tax strategy, how your age can impact how you invest in the market, and how a cash-value whole life insurance policy can put your money to work solving many different problems. You now know that planning is more of an interconnected web than a straight line.

Decisions you make in your "Get it" phase of wealth-building can impact how you are able to spend your money in retirement and even pass on your assets to heirs. How will you use this knowledge? I hope you will ask better questions. The good news is, you don't have to go it alone. Unless money is truly your hobby and you will donate the hours of research necessary to take care of yourself properly, please give yourself permission to build an amazing team of experts to support you in your process.

Close your eyes, take a deep breath, and then exhale slowly. Notice if you feel tight or constricted in your throat, chest, or belly. Now, just imagine. Remember a time you felt happy, peaceful, comfortable. How did your gut feel? Your heart? Your throat? Again, close your eyes, take a deep breath, and feel those pleasant sensations in your body. When your money decisions align to produce a sense of independence, freedom, and security, when your moments of action create spaces of stillness and comfort in your own skin, you have arrived in a good place.

Now is the time. Don't let the world define you. Dare to dream, achieve, and retain the lifestyle you want. What's in that bubble above your head? You've read how Laura and Jenny, Joe, Melissa, and all the others shifted their financial worlds with newfound knowledge and the support of a team. My family and my clients have expanded their financial bubbles and enjoy feeling more in control of their lives. When you take care of yourself, you are better able to help others. Imagine how your circle of family and friends will benefit when you stop keeping yourself small to validate other people's realities. Take your first step today and enter your bold new world. You now have the tools for success. What do you want your legacy to be?

IN GRATITUDE

IN MY GRATITUDE JOURNAL, ONE line I write is, "I am now attracting clients who want my support and prosper with my guidance." Fairly recently, I learned that what transforms affirmations from "I'm good enough, I'm smart enough and doggone it, people like me"[91] to something more tangible is the feeling attached to the words. Effective affirmations are more than the pages of knowledge I memorized and regurgitated in basic training. Abundance is more than just money, and in writing this book, I've tried to help you crack the code on cocreating financial success in your life in concert with your dreams and goals.

The old saying goes that when you are ready, your teacher arrives, and I had an amazing team of teachers enter my life to bring this book together. Or maybe six degrees of separation came into play. My brother, Michael, introduced me to his friend Kim after we had a conversation about my journey to become a professional speaker. Kim introduced me to Amy and Michael Port of Heroic Public Speaking (HPS). Learning the craft behind a well-executed keynote talk, I connected with AJ Harper and Top Three Book Workshop. AJ and Laura and the amazing Top Three community supported me in ways I didn't even know were available (which is also one goal of this book—to let you know that the realm of possible is greater than you might imagine when it comes to wrapping your hands around your money). I was a little chagrined at first to learn that there are not just editors but developmental editors, copy editors (Zoë Bird), proofreaders (Linda Morris), and typesetters

(Choi Messer) involved in a producing a good book. (And, by the way, a publisher does not market your book.) Top Three introduced me to Amber Vilhauer and her team at NGNG, and that led to a new website and more personal development on how I communicate my intentions. Amber helped me find my first virtual assistant, Taylor, who helped make the workload behind writing and publishing a book doable. The line I will cherish from these women is, "I got you."

Top Three also connected me with an artist to design my book cover. Listen to this! A woman from New York whom I met online introduced me to Choi Messer. Choi turned out to be an Air Force Academy graduate and biology major, just like me. In addition to being a talented artist, Choi is patient. In the Air Force, we are taught not to criticize without having a solution or two to offer. Cover design is a process of another person trying to create a picture that I didn't know I had in my head. I believe I said no seven times—and then Choi created *my* cover.

Speaking of patience, one thing I learned in this process is, you have your timeline and the universe conspires to adjust it. I got to test another of my gratitude journal affirmations, that things work out for the highest good of all, involved many times. And, I can honestly say that the hiccups and delays gave me more time for ideas to gel and improved the way I communicate.

An invaluable part of the process was hearing from my group of volunteer advanced readers. They selflessly gave of their time to help me identify what stories and examples worked in the book. My developmental editor, AJ Harper, said she could always tell the feedback from my military readers because they always had suggestions to go along with the passages they felt needed work. I think one of my favorite negotiations (and I use that word intentionally) was with my longtime mentor, retired Major General Mark Volcheff. He agreed to provide input if I agreed it was okay for him to go well beyond what I asked for in terms of feedback. I replied I would expect nothing less from aircrew (referring to our mutual C-130 background) and the book did a serious up-level as a result.

Thank you to Dr. Jeanne Wahl, Dr. Leon Barringer, Col, USAF (ret), Mara Yale, Dr. Damon Brown, Crystal Ross, Jeff Armentrout, Col, USAF (ret), Cyndi Thomason, Mary Tess Rooney, Dr. Samantha Weeks, Col, USAF (ret), Carole Mahoney, Jordan Murphy, Col, USAF, Tony Shore, Jeff Armentrout, Jim Devere, Col, USAF (ret), Heidi Hernandez, Lt Col, USAF (ret), Laura Frombach, Dr. Gena Cox, Mark Volcheff, Maj Gen, USAF (ret) and a few more...

Special thanks go to my husband, Kris, as our partnership is bigger than marriage or business. Emotional support alone is a full-time commitment.

There were many more people who were instrumental in supportive roles, and I wish to thank all of my family and friends who contributed simply because they are part of my life. This book really is the sum of my life experiences as much as it is about money, so thank you to everyone else who has shared parts of my life, too.

GLOSSARY OF KEY TERMS

actual rate of return. A formula that reflects the actual gain or loss of an investment over a certain period of time compared to the initial investment's cost. This is the preferred way to measure actual returns on investments because it isn't based on an average percentage, but rather on the actual investment return compared to the original cost.

alternative investments. A financial asset that does not fall into one of the conventional stocks, bonds, mutual funds, ETFs, or cash categories. Examples include private equity, venture capital, hedge funds, real estate, art and antiques, and commodities.

amortization. The gradual repayment of a debt over a period of time, such as monthly payments on a mortgage loan.

asset cash flow. The aggregate total of all cash flows used to determine the net amount of cash being spun off by or used in the operations of a business.

asset class. A group of investments that exhibit similar characteristics and are subject to the same laws, regulations, and market forces.

average rate of return. A formula that reflects the percentage rate of return on an investment or asset compared to the initial cost of the investment. Be careful: This average can be misleading and doesn't necessarily reflect the actual rate of return.

beneficiaries. Any person or entity who gains an advantage and/or profits from something. In the financial world, a beneficiary typically refers to someone eligible to receive distributions from a trust, will, or life insurance policy.

bridge loan. Short-term financing used until a person or company secures permanent financing or removes an existing obligation. Bridge loans are short-term, typically up to one year.

cash flow. The amount of income earned from investments and other assets.

cash-on-cash return. A rate of return often used in real estate transactions and other income producing assets that calculates the cash income earned on the cash invested in that asset. Cash-on-cash return measures the annual return the investor made on the asset in relation to the amount of cash invested. It is considered one of the most important real estate return-on-investment calculations.

direct recognition. A company in which the earnings rate on cash value is affected both positively and negatively when the cash value is used as collateral. In a non-direct recognition company, the earnings rates on loaned cash value are totally unaffected by loans against cash value.

diversification. A risk management strategy that mixes a wide variety of investments within a portfolio. A diversified portfolio contains a mix of distinct asset types and investment vehicles in order to limit exposure to any single asset or risk. The rationale behind it is that a portfolio constructed of a mix of assets will, on average, yield higher long-term returns and lower the risk of any individual holding or security. See "Rule of 100."

due diligence. An investigation, audit, or review performed to confirm the facts of a matter under consideration. In the financial world, due diligence requires an examination of financial records before entering into a proposed transaction with another party.

fiduciary. A person or organization that acts on behalf of another person or persons, putting their client's interests ahead of their own, with a duty to preserve good faith and trust. Being a fiduciary requires being bound both legally and ethically to act in others' best interests. It also involves trust, especially with regard to the relationship between a trustee and a beneficiary, and always having the beneficiary's best interests at heart.

financial life cycle. The phases of financial freedom you move through and how they align with your age. To achieve and retain the lifestyle you want, it is necessary to know where you are now and where you want to go in order to create a plan for success.

holistic financial plan. An approach to money that looks at the aggregate total of all financial decisions you make, including what you pay to the government (taxes) and financial institutions (banks, insurance companies, 401(k) managers, etc.) and your personal lifestyle choices. Most financial decisions are stovepiped, meaning that they are considered in isolation and without regard for alignment in the big picture.

illiquid investment. An investment that cannot readily return your cash. Access to your money usually involves paying a fee or penalty or perhaps selling at a loss. Examples include real estate, CDs, IRAs, and annuities.

lost opportunity cost. The benefit foregone by choosing another course of action, also known as opportunity cost. Chapter 1, Figure 5 provides an example of opportunity cost.

liquid investment. Accounts where your money is readily accessible. The best example is a checking or savings account.

non-direct recognition. A strategy used by insurance companies in which the earnings rate on cash value is unaffected by any loans against the cash value. Unlike direct recognition, there is no cost with a lower dividend when a loan is taken out against the policy.

passive income. Income received from investments and other assets that requires little to no effort to earn and maintain.

points. Also known as discount points, these are fees paid directly to the lender at closing, often in exchange for a reduced interest rate.

Roth IRA. Retirement account as defined by the IRS where taxes are paid upon funding and can be drawn out after the age of 59.5 tax-free.

Rule of 100. This is a concept used to determine the ideal balance of risk in a retirement plan. The formula is 100 minus your age to determine how much money should be at risk versus guaranteed. This also sparks conversations to determine much liquidity is needed and around specifics such as longevity in a particular family.

surrender fee. A penalty charged to an investor for early cancellation or withdrawal of funds from an insurance or annuity contract.

sweat equity. A person or company's contribution toward a business venture or other project that is generally not monetary and, in most cases, comes in the form of physical labor, mental effort, and time. Commonly found in real estate and the construction industry as well as in the corporate world, especially for startups.

traditional IRA. Retirement account as defined by the IRS, where taxes are deferred until withdrawn. Ordinary income tax rates apply.

volatility. A statistical measure of the dispersion of returns for a given security or market index. In most cases, the higher the volatility, the riskier the security. Volatility is often measured as either the standard deviation or variance between returns from that same security or market index.

whole life insurance. Coverage for the life of the insured. In addition to paying a death benefit, whole life insurance also contains a savings component in which the cash value may accumulate. These policies are also known as "permanent" or "traditional" life insurance. Whole life insurance policies are one type of permanent life insurance. Universal life, indexed universal life, and variable universal life are others.

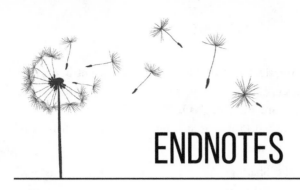

ENDNOTES

[1] Dr. Muhammad Yunus, Nobel Lecture. The Nobel Foundation, 2006. NobelPrize.org. https://www.nobelprize.org/prizes/peace/2006/yunus/lecture/, accessed January 16, 2022.

[2] Christine Lagarde, "Empowerment Through Financial Inclusion," Address to the International Forum for Financial Inclusion. Mexico, June 26, 2014.

[3] Jim Windolf, "Sex, Drugs, and Soybeans," VanityFair.com, April 5, 2007. https://www.vanityfair.com/news/2007/05/thefarm200705, accessed January 16, 2022.

[4] American Commune, directed by Nadine Mundo and Rena Mundo Croshere (Mundo Films, 2013). Available on Netflix.

[5] Anonymous (Albert Einstein quote). The Ultimate Quotable Einstein, ed. Alice Calaprice, section: "Misattributed to Einstein," p. 474 (Princeton, New Jersey: Princeton University Press, 2010).

[6] Carl Jung, Psychology of the Unconscious: A study of the transformations and symbolisms of the libido, a contribution to the history of the evolution of thought, trans. Beatrice M. Hinkle (London: Kegan Paul Trench Trubner, 1916).

[7] Nelson D. Schwartz and Michael Corkery, "When Sears Flourished, So Did Workers. At Amazon, It's More Complicated." NYTimes.com, October 23, 2018. https://www.nytimes.com/2018/10/23/business/economy/amazon-workers-sears-bankruptcy-filing.html, accessed January 16, 2022.

[8] "Choosing a Retirement Plan: Profit-Sharing Plan," IRS.gov, November 8, 2021, https://www.irs.gov/retirement-plans/choosing-a-retirement-plan-profit-sharing-plan, accessed January 16, 2022.

9 Joseph Blasi tells the American history of shares in his recent book, The Citizen's Share (New Haven, CT: Yale University Press, 2015), written with Richard P. Freeman of Harvard and Douglas L. Kruse of Rutgers. Blasi is the J. Robert Beyster Distinguished Professor at Rutgers University's School of Management and Labor Relations.

10 Joseph R. Blasi, "Profit Sharing: An American Presidential History," HuffPost.com, August 28, 2016, https://www.huffpost.com/entry/profit-sharing-an-america_b_8056668, accessed January 16, 2022.

11 Buckminster Fuller quote. Everything I Know lecture series, January 1975, The Buckminster Fuller Institute, BFI.org, https://www.bfi.org/about-fuller/resources/everything-i-know, accessed January 16, 2022.

12 "Disruptive Innovation," Clayton Christensen Institute, ChristensenInstitute.org, 2022, https://www.christenseninstitute.org/disruptive-innovations/, accessed January 16, 2022.

13 Tara Nolan, Out of the Saddle: 9 Steps to Improve Your Horseback Riding (Peyton, Colorado: DARC Press, Inc., (2011).

14 Vishen Lakhiani, The Buddha and the Badass: The Secret Art of Succeeding at Work (New York, NY: Penguin-Random House, 2020).

15 Friedrich Nietzsche, Twilight of the Idols (1888).

16 Dr. Saul McLeod, "Maslow's Hierarchy of Needs," SimplyPsychology.org, December 29, 2020, https://www.simplypsychology.org/maslow.html, accessed January 16, 2022.

17 Daniel Kurt, "Stock Allocation Rules," Investopedia.com, December 31, 2021, https://www.investopedia.com/articles/investing/062714/100-minus-your-age-outdated.asp, accessed January 16, 2022.

18 "What is the difference between a DO and an MD?" MedicalNewsToday.com, last medically reviewed February 19, 2020, https://www.medicalnewstoday.com/articles/do-vs-md, accessed January 16, 2022.

19 Brené Brown, Daring Greatly: How the Courage to Be Vulnerable Transforms the Way We Live, Love, Parent, and Lead (London, England: Penguin Publishing Group, 2015).

20 Brené Brown, Rising Strong (New York, NY: Random House Publishing Group, 2017).

21 Paolo Crivelli, Aristotle on Truth (Cambridge, England: Cambridge University Press, 2004).

22 Oscar Gelderblom, Abe de Jong, and Joost Jonker, "The Formative Years of the Modern Corporation: The Dutch East India Company VOC, 1602–1623," Cambridge University Press, Cambridge.org, November 15, 2013, https://www.cambridge.org/core/journals/journal-of-economic-history/article/abs/formative-years-of-the-modern-corporation-the-dutch-east-india-company-voc-16021623/E16FF67D27465278E442A974954741BB, accessed January 16, 2022.

23 Dana Griffin, "Economic Systems of Mercantilists," SmallBusiness.Chron.com, https://smallbusiness.chron.com/economic-system-mercantilists-3903.html, accessed January 16, 2022.

24 Macrotrends website: https://macrotrends.net, accessed January 16, 2022.

25 J. David Stein, "Podcast Episode 298: The Stock Market Is Not the Economy," MoneyForTheRestOfUs.com, May 19, 2021, https://moneyfortherestofus.com/?s=THe+stock+market+is+not+the+economy, accessed January 16, 2022.

26 Definition of "stock exchange." Lexico.com, https://www.lexico.com/en/definition/stock_exchange, accessed January 16, 2022.

27 Definition of "economy." Lexico.com, https://www.lexico.com/en/definition/economy, accessed January 16, 2022.

28 "S&P 500 Historical Annual Returns," Macrotrends.net, January 14, 2022, https://www.macrotrends.net/2526/sp-500-historical-annual-returns, accessed January 16, 2022.

29 "S&P 500 Historical Annual Returns," https://www.macrotrends.net/2526/sp-500-historical-annual-returns, accessed January 16, 2022.

30 "Social Security History," SSA.gov, https://www.ssa.gov/history/50ed.html, accessed January 16, 2022.

31 "Legislative History," SSA.gov, https://www.ssa.gov/history/35actinx.html, accessed January 16, 2022.

32 Social Security and Medicare Boards of Trustees, "Status of the Social Security and Medicare Programs—A Summary of the 2021 Annual Reports,"

SSA.gov, https://www.ssa.gov/OACT/TRSUM/index.html, accessed January 16, 2022.

[33] John A. Svahn and Mary Ross, "Social Security Amendments of 1983: Legislative History and Summary of Provisions," Social Security Bulletin, July 1983/Vol. 46, No. 7, SSA.gov, https://www.ssa.gov/policy/docs/ssb/v46n7/v46n7p3.pdf, accessed January 16, 2022.

*See also: "Legislative History—Summary of P.L. 98-21 (H.R. 1900), Social Security Amendments of 1983, Signed on April 20, 1983," November 26, 1984, SSA.gov, https://www.ssa.gov/history/1983amend.html, accessed January 16, 2022.

[34] Larry DeWitt, "Agency History—Research Notes and Special Studies by the Historian's Office—Research Note #12: Taxation of Social Security Benefits," February, 2001, SSA.gov, https://www.ssa.gov/history/taxationofbenefits.html, accessed January 16, 2022.

[35] "The 2019 Annual Report of the Board of Trustees of the Federal Old-Age and Survivors Insurance and Federal Disability Insurance Trust Funds," SSA.gov, https://www.ssa.gov/oact/TR/2019/index.html, accessed January 16, 2022.

[36] Simon Sinek, David Mead, and Peter Docker, Find Your Why: A Practical Guide for Discovering Purpose for You and Your Team (New York, NY: Portfolio/Penguin, 2017).

[37] John Steinbeck, The Grapes of Wrath (New York, NY: The Viking Press, 1939).

[38] You can visit https://www.macrotrends.net for more detailed data on historical market ups and downs.

[39] Brown, Daring Greatly

[40] Tombstone, directed by George P. Cosmatos and Kevin Jarre (1983, Buena Vista Pictures); Wyatt Earp, directed by Lawrence Kasdan (1994, Warner Bros.).

[41] Top Gun, directed by Tony Scott (1986, Paramount Pictures).

[42] Saturday Night Live, Season 46, Episode 18, "Elon Musk Monologue," May 8, 2021, NBC, https://www.youtube.com/watch?v=fCF8I_X1qKI, accessed January 16, 2022.

[43] Amy McCullough Hudson, "Erasing Artificial Barriers," AirForceMag.com, November 1, 2020, https://www.airforcemag.com/article/erasing-artificial-barriers/, accessed January 16, 2022.

[44] Phil M. Jones, Talk at Heroic Public Speaking, 2021. See Phil M. Jones's website: https://www.philmjones.com (accessed January 16, 2022).

[45] Definition of "cognitive dissonance." Lexico.com, https://www.lexico.com/en/definition/cognitive_dissonance, accessed January 16, 2022.

[46] William P. Bengen, "Determining Withdrawal Rates Using Historical Data" (PDF), Journal of Financial Planning: 14–24, October, 1994.

[47] Benjamin Franklin, The Way to Wealth (1758).

[48] "H.R. 2--Employee Retirement Income Security Act," Congress.gov, https://www.congress.gov/bill/93rd-congress/house-bill/2, accessed January 16, 2022.

[49] Peer Fiss, "A Short History of Golden Parachutes," Harvard Business Review, HBR.org, October 3, 2016, https://hbr.org/2016/10/a-short-history-of-golden-parachutes, accessed January 16, 2022.

[50] "Taxpayer Relief Act of 1997," Congress.gov, https://www.congress.gov/105/plaws/publ34/PLAW-105publ34.pdf, accessed January 16, 2022.

[51] Benjamin Graham, The Intelligent Investor (New York, NY: HarperBusiness, 2003).

[52] Nolan Financial Radio, Radio.FinanciallyTuned.com, https://radio.financiallytuned.com/ -nolan, accessed January 16, 2022.

[53] "Deposit Insurance," FDIC.gov, https://www.fdic.gov/resources/deposit-insurance/, accessed January 16, 2022.

[54] Libby Wells, "Historical CD interest rates: 1984-2021," BankRate.com, January 8, 2021, https://www.bankrate.com/banking/cds/historical-cd-interest-rates/, accessed January 16, 2022.

[55] "Deposit Insurance," FDIC.gov, https://www.fdic.gov/resources/deposit-insurance/, accessed January 16, 2022.

[56] "Warren Buffett, Secretary Debbie Bosanek Discuss Tax Rate Inequality in Interview," ABC News, January 26, 2012, YouTube.com, https://www.youtube.com/watch?v=zB1FXvYvcaI, accessed January 16, 2022.

[57] James R. Sherman, Rejection (Keene, NH: Pathway Books, 1982).

[58] FDIC: Federal Deposit Insurance Corporation: https://www.fdic.gov/, accessed January 16, 2022.

[59] Sadhguru, Twitter post, June 7, 2016, 8:45PM, https://twitter.com/SadhguruJV, accessed January 16, 2022.

[60] The Big Bang Theory, Season 2, Episode 11, "The Bath Item Gift Hypothesis," directed by Mark Cendrowski and written by Bill Prady, Richard Rosenstock, Tim Doyle, and Stephen Engel, aired December 15, 2008 on CBS.

[61] Emily Brandon, "The History of Your Social Security Payments," U.S. News and World Report, Money.USNews.com, March 4, 2019: https://money.usnews.com/money/retirement/social-security/articles/the-history-of-your-social-security-payments, accessed January 16, 2022.

[62] "Revenue Act of 1921," Wikipedia.org, December 12, 2019, https://en.wikipedia.org/wiki/Revenue_Act_of_1921, accessed January 16, 2022.

[63] Congressional Research Service, "Worker Participation in Employer-Sponsored Pensions: Data in Brief," Sgp.fas.org, November 23, 2021, https://fas.org/sgp/crs/misc/R43439.pdf, accessed January 16, 2022.

[64] Sebastian Devlin-Foltz, Alice M. Henriques, and John Sabelhaus, "The Evolution of Retirement Wealth," Finance and Economics Discussion Series 2015-009. Washington: Board of Governors of the Federal Reserve System, http://dx.doi.org/10.17016/FEDS.2015.009, accessed January 16, 2022.

[65] Tax code: USCode.House.Gov, https://uscode.house.gov/view.xhtml?path=/prelim@title26/subtitleA&edition=prelim, accessed January 16, 2022.

See also, Internal Revenue Service website: https://www.irs.gov, accessed January 16, 2022.

See also, "Tax Code, Regulations, and Official Guidance," IRS.gov, https://www.irs.gov/privacy-disclosure/tax-code-regulations-and-official-guidance, accessed January 16, 2022.

[66] Robert Kiyosaki and Sharon Lechter, Rich Dad Poor Dad (Brentwood, TN: Warner Books, 2000).

[67] Antoine de Saint-Exupéry. The Little Prince (New York, NY: Reynal & Hitchcock, 1943).

[68] Chris Cordaro, "Goldilocks and the 'Just Right' Probability of Retirement-Planning Success," RegentAtlantic.com, August 25, 2016, **https://regentatlantic.com/blog/goldilocks-just-right-probability-retirement-planning-success**/, accessed January 16, 2022.

Chapter 10

[69] Walter Isaacson, *Steve Jobs* (London, England: Abacus, 2015).

[70] Duckworth, A. (2016). *Grit*: The power of passion and perseverance. Scribner/Simon & Schuster.

[71] Albert Bandura, "Self-efficacy: Toward a unifying theory of behavioral change," *Psychological Review,* 84(2), 191-215, 1977, https://doi.org/10.1037/0033-295X.84.2.191, accessed January 16, 2022.

*See also: Albert Bandura, *Social Foundations of Thought and Action: A Social Cognitive Theory* (Englewood Cliffs, NJ: Prentice-Hall, Inc., 1985).

*See also: Albert Bandura, *Self-Efficacy: The Exercise of Control* (New York, NY: Worth Publishers, 1997).

[72] Shlomo Benartzi, "Saving for Tomorrow, Tomorrow," Filmed in New York City, NY, November 15, 2011, TEDSalon video, 17:29, https://www.ted.com/talks/shlomo_benartzi_saving_for_tomorrow_tomorrow?language=en, accessed January 16, 2022.

[73] Bandura, *Self-Efficacy*

[74] Caroline Myss, *Anatomy of the Spirit: The Seven Stages of Power and Healing* (New York, NY: Harmony Books, 1996).

[75] Jianping Hu, Lei Quan, Yanwei Wu, Jia Zhu, Mingliang Deng, Song Tang, and Wei Zhang, "Financial Self-Efficacy and General Life Satisfaction: The Sequential Mediating Role of High Standards Tendency and Investment Satisfaction," *Frontiers in Psychology,* March 17, 2021, https://www.frontiersin.org/articles/10.3389/fpsyg.2021.545508/full, accessed January 16, 2022.

[76] Paul J. Zak, "The Neurobiology of Trust," ScientificAmerican.com, June, 2008, https://www.scientificamerican.com/article/the-neurobiology-of-trust/, accessed January 16, 2022.

[77] Inga D. Neumann, "Oxytocin: The Neuropeptide of Love Reveals Some of Its Secrets," Elsevier, Volume 5, Issue 4, April 4, 2007, pages 231-233, ScienceDirect.com, https://www.sciencedirect.com/science/article/pii/S1550413107000691, accessed January 16, 2022.

[78] U.S. Securities and Exchange Commission, "General Information on the Regulation of Investment Advisers," SEC.gov, March 11, 2011, https://www.sec.gov/divisions/investment/iaregulation/memoia.htm, accessed January 16, 2022.

[79] Financial Industry Regulatory Authority. "2111. Suitability," FINRA.org, June 30, 2020, https://www.finra.org/rules-guidance/rulebooks/finra-rules/2111, accessed January 16, 2022.

[80] **Danielle Klimashousky,** "What Are 12b-1 Fees?" SmartAsset.com, July 17, 2019, **https://smartasset.com/financial-advisor/what-are-12b1-fees**, accessed January 16, 2022.

[81] **U.S. Securities and Exchange Commission,** "Mutual Funds and Exchange-Traded Funds (ETFs) – A Guide for Investors," SEC.gov, January 26, 2017, **https://www.sec.gov/reportspubs/investor-publications/investorpubsinwsmfhtm.html#Fees**, accessed January 16, 2022.

[82] Alexander Jones, "GameStop: What Happened, and What It Means," InternationalBanker.com, March 29, 2021, https://internationalbanker.com/brokerage/gamestop-what-happened-and-what-it-means/, accessed January 16, 2022.

[83] Jing Jun Ma, "How to buy GameStop stock," Finder.com, January 7, 2022, https://www.finder.com/buy-gamestop-corp-stock#compare, accessed January 16, 2022.

*See also: "Hidden Fees at Robinhood in 2022," TopRatedFirms.com, 2022, https://topratedfirms.com/account-charges/hidden/robinhood-hidden-fees.aspx, accessed January 16, 2022.

Chapter 11

[84] Carl G. Jung, H. Read, M. Fordham, and G. Adler, *The Collected Works of C.G. Jung* (New York, NY: Pantheon Books, 1953).

[85] John Lyons and Maureen Gallatin, *Communicating with Cues: The Rider's Guide to Training and Problem Solving* (Norwalk, CT: Belvoir Publications, 1998).

86 Julia Kagan, "Amortized Loan," Investopedia.com, April 14, 2021, https://www.investopedia.com/terms/a/amortized_loan.asp, accessed January 16, 2022.

Chapter 12

87 Henry David Thoreau, *Walden* (Boston, MA: Ticknor and Fields, 1854).

88 "The Limbic System and Other Brain Areas," LumenLearning.com, https://courses.lumenlearning.com/wmopen-psychology/chapter/reading-the-limbic-system-and-other-brain-areas/, accessed January 16, 2022.

89 *Black-ish*, Season 4, Episode 11, "Inheritance," directed by Millicent Shelton and written by Stacy Traub, aired January 9, 2018 on ABC.

90 Lakhiani, *The Buddha and the Badass*

91 Al Franken, *I'm Good Enough, I'm Smart Enough, and Doggone It, People Like Me!: Daily Affirmations by Stuart Smalley* (New York, NY: Dell, 1992).

ABOUT THE AUTHOR

TARA NOLAN IS THE FOUNDER and CEO of Nolan Financial Partners, a holistic financial planning company that supports women entrepreneurs and professionals in achieving and retaining the lifestyles they want. She combines her knowledge of finance, background in strategic military planning, and focus on personal development to create transformational financial plans. Tara believes that financial uncertainty is one underlying cause of the fear and tribalism in our world today. She works to expand awareness among individuals and small business owners and bring a feeling of financial empowerment back into the collective psyche. www.nolanfinancialpartners.com

CPSIA information can be obtained
at www.ICGtesting.com
Printed in the USA
BVHW061127210322
632004BV00004B/67

9 780984 541409